VICTORS' JUSTICE

VERSO

VICTORS' JUSTICE
From Nuremberg to Baghdad

DANILO ZOLO

TRANSLATED BY M. W. WEIR

V
VERSO
London • New York

First English edition published by Verso 2009
Copyright © Danilo Zolo 2009
Translation © M. W. Weir
First published as *La giustizia dei vincitori. Da Norimberga a Baghdad*
Copyright © Edizioni Laterza 2006

1 3 5 7 9 10 8 6 4 2

Verso
UK: 6 Meard Street, London W1F 0EG
US: 20 Jay Street, Suite 1010, Brooklyn, NY 11201
www.versobooks.com

Verso is the imprint of New Left Books

ISBN-13: 978-1-84467-317-9

British Library Cataloguing in Publication Data
A catalogue record for this book is available from the British Library

Library of Congress Cataloging-in-Publication Data
A catalog record for this book is available from the Library of Congress

Typeset by Hewer Text UK Ltd, Edinburgh
Printed in the US by Maple Vail

CONTENTS

ACKNOWLEDGEMENTS

There have been numerous scholars who, while not necessarily sharing my assessments, have been generous with their criticism and suggestions for improving this book. In particular I wish to thank the friends with whom I have enjoyed an intense exchange of ideas for years: Luca Baccelli, Richard Bellamy, Nicolò Bellanca, Franco Cassano, Alessandro Colombo, Pietro Costa, Luigi Ferrajoli, Gustavo Gozzi, Giovanni Mari, Tecla Mazzarese, Pier Paolo Portinaro, Geminello Preterossi, Giuseppe Tosi and Emilio Santoro. Various younger researchers with specific domains of competence have made valuable contributions, and I wish to place on record at least those of Filippo del Lucchese, Giulio Itzcovich, Juan Manuel Otero, Stefano Pietropaoli, Lucia Re and Filippo Ruschi. I also want to thank the members of the editorial board of the online *Jura Gentium* journal for their generous, day-to-day collaboration, and first and foremost the webmaster, Francesco Vertova.

A particular vote of thanks goes to Antonio Cassese, without whose affectionate theoretical and political diffidence this text of mine would be much more vulnerable. And finally I am grateful to Geminello Preterossi, who once again had no hesitation in recommending one of my productions to my Italian publisher Laterza.

It is with heartfelt regret that I dedicate this book to the memory of Andrea Orsi Battaglini.

INTRODUCTION

Until the end of the Second World War, international law contemplated political, economic or territorial sanctions for countries which violated its norms, but there was no provision for punishing individuals. In fact, important multilateral treaties specifically excluded individuals from being subjects in international law, and thus liable to penal sanctions. However, from the early decades of the twentieth century onwards, the idea began to take hold in the West, under the influence of North American culture, that a war of aggression should be considered an international crime, and that penal justice should be introduced into the international legal system in order to punish those responsible for wars of aggression on a par with any other war crime.

The first sign of this radical change in the legal approach to war was the incrimination, at the end of the First World War, of Kaiser Wilhelm II of Hohenzollern. The victorious nations accused him of committing a 'supreme offence against international morality and the sanctity of treaties' and asked for him to be handed over for trial as a war criminal by a court made up of judges they were to nominate. The trial did not take place, but what had been attempted unsuccessfully with respect to the old German emperor was put into practice some twenty years later by the powers which emerged victorious from the Second World War. At Nuremberg and Tokyo, international criminal tribunals were organized to try the defeated enemy. Twenty-two Nazi leaders and twenty-eight high-ranking members of the Japanese administration and army were arraigned. At the conclusion of the two trials, exemplary punishments were handed down, including seventeen death sentences which were carried out immediately. Altogether, some 500 German citizens were executed at the end of subsequent trials organized by the Americans, the British and the French in Nuremberg and other cities in Germany, while we know very little about the many trials held by the Soviets in their occupied territories.

In the meantime, the victors in the Second World War—essentially the United States, Great Britain and the Soviet Union—met at Dumbarton Oaks, near Washington, and drew up the Charter of the United Nations. In practice, the Charter was then imposed on the fifty countries that were invited to San Francisco in 1945. Under its terms, aggressive war is considered a crime and the Security Council is charged with using force to prevent or punish it. But, thanks to the power of veto they accorded themselves, the victorious nations are able to make free use of military force: in the post-war years both the United States and the Soviet Union did so systematically without facing any consequences. Each of the super-powers embarked on lengthy wars of aggression—the United States in Vietnam, the Soviet Union in Afghanistan—or in single interventions, the former in Guatemala, Lebanon, Cuba, Santo Domingo, Grenada, Libya and Panama between 1954 and 1986, and the latter in Eastern Europe in 1956 and 1968.

After the long parenthesis of the Cold War, the experience of 'victors' justice' has been renewed: in the early 1990s it targeted the political and military leadership of the Yugoslav Federal Republic, and notably its president Slobodan Milošević. Demonized as being responsible for the wars in the Balkans and as the instigator of grave violations of human rights, including 'ethnic cleansing' in Bosnia-Herzegovina and Kosovo, Milošević was allegedly handed over by the Yugoslav government to the International Criminal Tribunal for the former Yugoslavia. In reality, the government yielded to economic blackmail by the United States and pressure from NATO, and in a surprise action the former president was captured and transferred to the Hague, the seat of the Tribunal. A few years later, in Iraq, victors' justice was applied to the political and military exponents of the Ba'ath party, principally the president of the Republic, Saddam Hussein, who was also accused of grave violations of human rights. The head of state was captured and imprisoned in a secret location by US troops, and tried in Baghdad by a Special Tribunal, pressed for and set up by the United States while Iraq was under its military occupation. Both Milošević and Hussein were imprisoned and brought to trial at the instigation of the United States and Great Britain following the victorious conclusion of two wars of aggression: one 'humanitarian', in the name of the international safeguarding of human rights, launched in 1999 by NATO against the Yugoslav Federal Republic, and one 'preventive', against Iraq, begun in 2003 and still tragically in progress. If he had not died unexpectedly in March 2006, Slobodan Milošević would have been sentenced to life imprisonment, since the statute of that Tribunal does not contemplate the death sentence, while the dictator Saddam Hussein was hanged. This was a case of retributive, exemplary, sacrificial justice in the best tradition of the 'Nuremberg model'.

On the other hand, nothing has befallen the criminals responsible for the atomic massacres at Hiroshima and Nagasaki in August 1945, or for the saturation bombing which, with the war already won by the Western allies, killed hundreds of thousands of civilians in various German and Japanese cities. Nothing has happened to the political and military leadership of NATO, responsible for the 'humanitarian' war of aggression against the Yugoslav Republic, which surely ranks as a 'supreme' international crime. The NATO leadership was also guilty of committing grave war crimes during the seventy-eight days of uninterrupted bombing raids on Serbia, Vojvodina and Kosovo in 1999. Complaints against NATO were duly lodged with the Hague Tribunal, but were dismissed by the Chief Prosecutor's Office, headed by Carla del Ponte. She showed no compunction about placing international justice—and human rights—at the service of the victorious Western powers which supported and financed the Tribunal (and still do).

In 1991 these same Western powers, with the backing of the Security Council, organized one of the most massive military expeditions in human history against Iraq, which was guilty of the illegal invasion of Kuwait. Over half a million US military personnel were mobilized and joined by troops from numerous other countries. During the forty-two days of bombing raids, the quantity of explosives used was greater than that employed by the Allied Forces during the whole of the Second World War. At least 100,000 Iraqis lost their lives in the fighting, and hundreds of thousands more civilians perished as a result of the harsh economic and territorial sanctions applied subsequently with the approval of the United Nations.

Nothing like the aforementioned cases of 'international justice' were pursued after the aggression against and invasion of Iraq by the United States and Great Britain in 2003. And we can be quite sure that the political and military leadership responsible for the massacres of thousands of troops and innocent civilians, perpetrated first in Afghanistan and then in Iraq by Anglo-American forces, will go unpunished. This includes the slaughter of civilians in the Iraqi city of Fallujah carried out in November 2004, which saw the use of napalm and white phosphorus. And the same goes for the crimes committed by Israeli troops during decades of military occupation of Palestine, and indeed for the ethnocide currently being carried out in Chechnya.

Thus it seems reasonable to denounce, as I have tried to do in the following chapters, the 'dual-standard system' of international justice. There is a justice tailored to the major powers and their political and military authorities, who enjoy total impunity for war crimes—and above all for the wars of aggression undertaken in recent years, disguised as humanitarian wars in defence of human rights or preventive wars against 'global terrorism'. From 1946 to the present, not a single trial has been held, at either the national or international level, for crimes of aggression. And then there is the victors' justice applied to vanquished, weak and oppressed peoples, with the collusion of international institutions, the acquiescence of the majority of academic jurists, the complicity of the mass media and the opportunistic support of a growing number of self-proclaimed 'non-governmental organizations', which in reality are at the service of their governments' interests.

Neither the universalistic institutions created in the first half of the twentieth century at the behest of the victors in the two world wars, nor international criminal jurisdiction, have to date shown themselves worthy of their task. No one expects the United Nations, or the international criminal courts, to ensure a stable and universal world peace, for this is a Kantian utopia devoid of theoretical and political interest. But they have both proved incapable even of restraining the major powers in their determination to dispose of the overwhelming military strength they possess. This is the case, above all, for the United States of America, which now seems set on fulfilling the role of an imperial power *legibus solutus* ('beyond the law'), placing itself above international law generally, and the law of war in particular.

THE CRIMINALIZATION OF WAR

The juridical negation of war

In some celebrated pages of *Der Nomos der Erde*, Carl Schmitt argued that the conclusion of the First World War coincided with the end of the centrality of Europe and the passing of the *jus publicum Europaeum*. This marked the end of an international order conceived of in spatial terms—as established at Westphalia—which, in the celebrated formula of Emmerich de Vattel, sought to *mettre la guerre en forme*.[1] It was replaced at Geneva in the second decade of the twentieth century by the League of Nations, a universalistic and 'de-spatialized' institution which came into being at the instigation of the United States and was dominated by the cosmopolitan credo of Woodrow Wilson. Its declared aim was to ensure a lasting peace throughout the world, and not only in Europe. In Schmitt's view, international law as formulated at the Geneva conference table no longer served to 'ritualize' warfare between the states of Europe so as to limit and moderate it and prevent the sort of 'war of annihilation' experienced in the wars of religion. Instead, the League of Nations set out to 'be simultaneously a European order and a universal and global order'. At Geneva, in the name of the universalistic dogma, 'there was much talk about the proscription and abolition of war, but none about a spatial bracketing of war'.[2]

---

1. See E. de Vattel, *Le Droit des Gens, ou Principes de la Loi Naturelle, appliqués à la conduite et aux affaires des Nations et des Souverains*, London, 1758—second edn, Washington: Carnegie Institution, 1916, vol. III, cap. XII, §190: 'La guerre en forme doit être regardée quant aux effets comme juste de part et d'autre'.

2. See C. Schmitt, *Der Nomos der Erde im Völkerrecht des Jus Publicum*

The League of Nations, according to Schmitt, was doomed to failure because the new institution was an attempt to abolish war simply by declaring it illegal. In reality, he maintained, 'any abolition of war without true bracketing resulted only in new, perhaps even worse types of wars, such as reversions to civil war and other types of wars of annihilation'.[3] In common with universalistic pacifism, the grandiose design of making 'aggressive war' an international crime was bound to fail, for it was viewed not only as a crime to be imputed to the nations at war, but also as involving the penal responsibility of individual persons. In Schmitt's opinion, the criminalization of wars of aggression is a return to the notion of *bellum justum* and the whole medieval issue of *justa causa belli* which had been elaborated by Francisco de Vitoria to justify the conquest of the New World by the Catholic powers.[4] It was no coincidence, he adds, if authors such as the Belgian Ernest Nys and, in particular, the American internationalist James Brown Scott had gone out of their way to revive the doctrines of Vitoria in the first decades of the twentieth century.[5]

Europaeum, Berlin: Duncker und Humblot, 1974, English translation: *The Nomos of the Earth in the International Law of the Jus Publicum Europaeum*, New York: Telos Press Publishing, 2006, pp. 243, 246.

3. See Schmitt, *Nomos of the Earth*, p. 246:

At this point, two facts should be remembered: first, international law sought to prevent wars of annihilation, i.e., to the extent that war is inevitable, to bracket it; and second, any abolition of war without true bracketing resulted only in new, perhaps even worse types of wars, such as reversions to civil war and other types of wars of annihilation' ('Es muß hier wiederholt an zwei Wahrheiten erinnert werden: erstens, daß das Völkerrecht die Aufgabe hat, den Vernichtungskrieg zu verhindern, also den Krieg, soweit er unvermeidlich ist, zu umhegen, und zweitens, daß eine Abschaffung des Krieges ohne echte Hegung nur neue, wahrscheinlich schlimmere Arten des Krieges, Rückfälle in den Bürgerkrieg und andere Arten des Vernichtungskrieges zur Folge hat', Schmitt, *Der Nomos der Erde*, p. 219).

4. As Schmitt noted, 'President Wilson believed in the doctrine of just war', C. Schmitt, *Nomos of the Earth*, p. 268.

5. See Schmitt, *Nomos of the Earth*, pp. 117–19. In reality Nys, unlike Scott and Joseph Kohler (for the latter, see J. Kohler, *Grundlagen des Völkerrechts*, Stuttgart, 1918), had considerable reservations about the theses of Vitoria, whom he saw as merely a precursor of Grotius (see E. Nys, *Les origines du droit international*, Paris: Thorin, 1894).

This neo-scholastic philosophy lay behind the Western internationalist doctrine which, in the first decades of the twentieth century, sought to rid itself of the legal notion of *justus hostis* intrinsic to the *jus publicum Europaeum*. What was being rejected was the Westphalian principle of the legality of war between states, conducted by sovereign authorities which could lay claim to equal rights, including the right to use force to assert the interests of the state. This was replaced by an ethico-political evaluation of the 'causes of war', which gave a negative connotation to the notion of 'aggression' (*le crime de l'attaque*), even though in the Judeo-Christian tradition, and in particular in medieval Catholic theology, this notion had no such negative overtones. The medieval doctrine of the *bellum justum* made explicit provision for the possibility of a 'just aggression'. In much the same way as the Jewish doctrine of the *milchemet mitzvà* ('obligatory holy war'), the theory of a just war considered wars of aggression to be morally acceptable—*bellum justum offensivum*—if waged by Christian rulers against any rulers and peoples who refused to recognize the authority of the Church. Turks, Arabs and Jews were thus automatically deemed to be *hostes perpetui*.

According to the new doctrine, Schmitt maintained, the aggressor was no longer a *justus hostis* but a 'criminal' in the full penal sense of the term; an 'outlaw', indeed, on a par with a pirate, with no claim to rights of any kind, just like the infidels under the doctrine of the *bellum justum*. Thus the procedural guarantees that European international law had come up with for the 'state of war', in an attempt to contain the most devastating and sanguinary consequences of armed conflicts, were lost to view. Instead, alongside the medieval model of a 'discriminatory war', 'confessional civil war' as waged between religious factions in the sixteenth and seventeenth centuries made its reappearance.[6] As Schmitt laments, this involved the destruction of a 'marvellous product of human reason' which had only been achieved by dint of 'laborious legal work' and thanks to which there had been no war of large-scale annihilation on European soil for more than two centuries.[7]

---

6. Schmitt, *Nomos of the Earth*, pp. 119–25, 150–1.
7. Ibid., p. 151.

Such a reconstruction of the history of modern international law begs some important questions. In particular, one must doubt whether the *jus publicum Europaeum* really introduced any significant elements capable of attenuating violent warfare during the two centuries in which it was in force, in spite of the attempt, dating from the treaty of Münster in 1648, to set up a system of collective security designed to stop individual states from having recourse to the use of force.[8] One only has to think of the Napoleonic wars, which hardly receive a mention in *Der Nomos der Erde*, or the military expansionism of the European colonialists, principally the British Empire. Schmitt treats the colonial wars as an adiaphorous phenomenon with respect to the European scenario, since he believes that the juridical ritualization of European warfare required a spatial delimitation which, by its very nature, excluded the limiting of colonial conflicts. And we could add that the First World War, with its eighteen million victims—ten million of them civilians—and over twenty million wounded, was itself an irrefutable indictment of European international law, which patently failed to contain the devastating effects of new weapons and military strategies.

Nonetheless, there is some corroboration for Schmitt's thesis in the conviction that gradually gained ground in the first decades of the twentieth century that new international institutions were called for: the Westphalian system of sovereign states had led to a situation of anarchy that the treaties and multilateral diplomacy of the 'Concert of Europe' had been unable to redress. This involved moving beyond the *jus publicum Europaeum* and its excessive pluralism and particularism. It also required a drastic revision of the notion of the sovereignty of nation-states, making way for the construction of institutions which were 'supranational' and not simply inter-state. This point is forcefully made by the foremost European jurist of the twentieth century, Hans Kelsen, in his essay *Das Problem der Souveränität*, and again in his celebrated manifesto for 'legal pacifism', *Peace through Law*, which takes its cue from Christian Wolff and Kant.[9] It became necessary

---

8. As is well known, this attempt came to nothing. See A. Cassese, *International Law*, second edn, Oxford: Oxford University Press, 2005, pp. 22–5.

9. See H. Kelsen, *Das Problem der Souveränität und die Theorie des Völkerrechts. Beitrag zu einer Reinen Rechtslehre*, Tübingen: Mohr, 1920; H.

to dispense with not only the traditional normative and institutional structures pertaining to states, but also the hidebound European strategies of the balance of power, with their attendant diplomatic formalities such as the protocol of 'declaring war'.[10] A stable, universal peace could only be achieved by means of a global legal system able to transcend the particularism of state sovereignty and vest the legitimate use of force in a supranational authority—a 'universal state'— unfettered by the domestic jurisdiction of the individual states. It was also essential to affirm the ethical and political primacy of the inter- national legal system as *civitas maxima*, recognizing all members of the human community as its subjects.[11]

In the framework of these very general premises, it may be instructive to consider to what extent—in the context of the legal prohibition of war that asserted itself in the course of the twentieth century at the instigation of the victors of the two world wars—the identification of 'aggressive war' as an international crime produced the results its advocates had claimed for it. An analogous question can be raised concerning international criminal justice. But we might also ask whether, on the contrary, these institutions did not in fact bring nearer the apocalyptic vision Carl Schmitt evokes repeatedly in *Der Nomos der Erde*: a comprehensive discriminatory war—or 'global civil war' (*ein globaler Weltbürgerkrieg*)[12]—no longer subject to the

Kelsen, *Peace through Law*, Chapel Hill: University of North Carolina Press, 1944 (second edn: New York, Garland Publishing, 1973).

10.   Article 1 of the Convention on the opening of hostilities, adopted by the Peace Conference of the Hague in 1899, obliged the state which first had recourse to warfare to communicate to the enemy state a formal 'declaration of war', or an ultimatum setting out the conditions that it had to meet in order to avoid war. If the attacking state commenced military operations without respecting this obligation it was guilty of an international crime, but this would not prevent the initiation of a 'state of war' between the two parties and the consequent application of the law of warfare, including the regime of neutrality for non-combatant third parties.

11.   See H. Kelsen, *Das Problem der Souveränität*, pp. 314–7. For a critique of Kelsen's 'judicial globalism', see my *I signori della pace*, Roma: Carocci Editore, 1998, pp. 21–48.

12.   In *Der Nomos der Erde* the term *Weltbürgerkrieg* appears only once, on p. 271 in the German edition already cited. Previously, in the article 'Strukturwandel des Internationalen Rechts', 1943 (now in C. Schmitt, *Frieden oder Pazifismus? Arbeiten zum Völkerrecht und zur internationalen Politik 1924–78*, Berlin: Duncker & Humblot, 2005) Schmitt argued that the discriminatory war being conducted by

legal limitations of the 'old inter-state war', and hence sanguinary and destructive in the highest degree.

According to this prophecy, the doctrine of universalism, more ethical than juridical, preached by the Western internationalists— primarily the United States—gave rise to international institutions which were incoherent in normative terms and politically ineffective. It was the failure or impotence of these institutions which ended up by legitimizing the global use of force in the name of civilization, or humanity, against enemies branded as the new barbarians or infidels.[13] In the light of an abstract, moralistic notion of world order, modern warfare turned, under the impulse of American imperialism, into 'global war' *legibus solutus* ('beyond the law'). Having suffered military defeat, the enemies of humanity were to be indicted as barbarian aggressors and subjected to exemplary punishments, sanctioning their moral worthlessness and exclusion from the civil world, putting them beyond the pale of any peace treaty or amnesty, and even denying them any right to humane compassion. In a word, they became 'bandits' to be exterminated in the name of the victors' justice.[14]

---

the imperial expansionism of the United States was transforming traditional inter-state warfare into *totalen und globalen Welt-Bürgerkrieg*. In his preface to the Italian edition of essays, *Le categorie del 'politico'* (Bologna: il Mulino, 1972, p. 25) Schmitt returns to this topic:

Today humanity is seen as a unitary society which is largely already living in peace ... instead of global politics there is a call for a global police force. It seems to me that today's world and modern humanity are quite far from political unity. A police force is not something apolitical. Global politics is a very intensive politics, the outcome of a will for pan-interventionism; it is only one particular type of politics, and by no means the most attractive: in fact it is the politics of global civil war [*Weltbürgerkriegspolitik*].

13.   As Schmitt says,

The discriminatory concept of the enemy as a criminal and the attendant implication of *justa causa* run parallel to the intensification of the means of destruction and the disorientation of theaters of war. Intensification of the technical means of destruction opens the abyss of an equally destructive legal and moral discrimination (*Nomos of the Earth*, p. 321).

14.   Schmitt, *Nomos of the Earth*, pp. 320–2.

The failure of universalist institutions and the normalization of war

There is nothing to be gained by presenting a brief, highly charged denunciation of how juridical–institutional universalism came to grief in the twentieth century. It would be all too easy to cite empirical evidence for the way military violence triumphed in the Second World War just as it had in the First, and how, in spite of the United Nations, one armed conflict after another broke out in the 1950s, '60s and '70s. One need look no further than the attack on Vietnam launched by the United States, and the Soviet Union's offensive against Afghanistan. Or again, the 'new wars' launched at the turn of the new millennium: from the Gulf War in 1991 to the two 'humanitarian wars' in the Balkans, the aggression against Afghanistan by the United States following the terrorist attack of 11 September 2001, and the 'pre-emptive war' launched by the United States and Britain against Iraq in 2003.

In the course of these conflicts, hundreds of thousands of innocent people have lost their lives, been mutilated or wounded, or had their families and property destroyed. Hundreds of thousands more civilians have died from hunger or disease on account of the embargoes imposed by the West—above all the one on Iraq following the war in 1991. In contrast, the military losses sustained by the Western forces have been very limited, and in some cases nil. To the scourge of war we have to add the ongoing ethnocide of the Palestinian people, the continuous violence being inflicted on the Chechens, Kurds and Tibetans, and lastly the atrocities of international terrorism. The escalation of hate, grief, destruction and death has had its counterpart in the inertia or sheer impotence of the international institutions which are supposed to safeguard peace.

One might say that war has been totally 'normalized', both in practice and, all the more, in the way it is being explicitly endorsed by the leading Western powers. The 'industry of collective death' has never been so flourishing, in spite of the generous but ineffective campaigning of the pacifist movements. The production and commerce of arms, including nuclear weapons, is no longer under the control of the so-called 'international community'. Indeed, the use of arms depends on the decision to kill, which the major powers take in the light of their own strategic interests. A collective death sentence is pronounced, with total impunity, against people (in their hundreds, even thousands) who are neither guilty of any crime nor morally reprehensible in any way whatsoever. War has come to be seen as the supreme expression of scientific and technological progress, unstoppable and invincible. It has become an 'intelligent', 'surgical' activity, technologically sterilized and sublimated, in which death, the mutilation of bodies, the devastation of everyday life, and terror are the familiar ingredients of a ritual spectacle which fails to provoke any emotional reaction. Collective killing, whether in the name of public authority or in the service of private interests, has once again become a prized and noble undertaking, affording financial reward, social standing and public acclaim.

In spite of all this, I do not believe any decisive arguments can be inferred—in the normative and institutional domain—from the simple fact that violent warfare was never stopped during the twentieth century and that, on the contrary, it actually erupted in forms of exceptional virulence in the last years of the century, following the collapse of the Soviet empire and the end of the juxtaposition of the two superpowers. If this were not the case, it would be all too easy to share Schmitt's pessimism and regard his critique of Anglo-American institutional universalism as an acute and far-sighted diagnosis. But the fact that violence and bloodshed remain at the centre of human history can hardly come as a surprise to any realistic spectator of international relations. And besides, Schmitt's own criticism of the discriminatory ruthlessness of the United States' warmongering cannot be ingenuously accepted as deriving from limpid pacifist and anti-imperialist motivations.[15]

Today 'pre-emptive' global war, as theorized and practised by the United States and its closest Western allies, seems to be part and parcel of the development of globalization processes that are increasingly dividing the world between the rich and powerful, on the one hand, and the poor and weak on the other, while so-called 'global terrorism' has become the no-less-sanguinary-and-nihilistic

---

15. For a dramatic documentation of the relations of Carl Schmitt with the National Socialist regime in the years 1933–36, see C. Schmitt, *Antworten in Nürnberg*, ed. H. Quaritsch, Berlin: Dunker & Humblot, 2000.

counterpart of the neo-colonial conflict which sets the West against the countries that resist its claim to planetary hegemony.[16] In these circumstances, it is not easy to imagine a reform of international institutions such that they could condition the hegemonic strategies of the major powers—the United States in particular—by disciplining and limiting the use of international force. The recent failure of the (highly prudent) project of reform of the United Nations proposed by Kofi Annan and his High-Level Panel is just one more confirmation of the stalemate.[17] The only function which international institutions seem able to carry out today—and this may be precisely why they are kept in being—is that of adapting to the status quo and legitimizing it. Confronted by a concentration of power which increasingly takes on the form of a neo-imperial world constitution, the international institutions are once again revealing their inability to stand up to the powers that be. As Alessandro Colombo has written, in a historical condition like that of the present, in which the distribution of power and wealth is as unequal as it could possibly be, even the fundamental principles which have regulated international society for centuries—state sovereignty, the legal equality of states, non-interference in internal jurisdiction, the regulation of warfare—tend to become the instruments of the strongest.[18]

Leaving this turbulent and alarming scenario to one side, and remaining as far as possible in the normative and institutional domain, I intend to explore one key question: whether the definition of a 'war of aggression' as an international crime, and the recourse to international criminal jurisdiction in order to repress crimes against peace and other grave international crimes, has given rise to a unitary and coherent legal system. I shall ask whether the criminalization of war has produced a normative system designed to submit the use of force to general rules and established procedures:

---

16. See my *Globalization: An Overview*, Colchester: ECPR, 2007, in particular chapter 7, pp. 62-74.

17. See the text of the document produced by the High-Level Panel in *Jura Gentium Journal*, at <www.juragentium. unifi.it>.

18. See A. Colombo, 'La società anarchica tra continuità e crisi. La scuola inglese e le istituzioni internazionali', *Rassegna Italiana di Sociologia* 44 (2), 2003, pp. 237–55.

a system, that is, with the potential not to guarantee a stable and universal peace—a Kantian ideal which really has very little political or theoretical interest—but to limit the most destructive effects of violent warfare on persons, property and the natural environment. In other words, I wish to ascertain whether the universalist institutions created by the powers that emerged victorious from the two world wars have achieved the objectives which, as was generally maintained in the first decades of the twentieth century, had not been secured under the 'anarchic' Westphalian system by means of the allegedly sterile formalisms of the *jus publicum Europaeum*.

War as a state crime

The use of military force by individual states was not ruled out by the Covenant of the League of Nations, as it was to be twenty-five years on by the Charter of the United Nations. In founding the League, the victors of the First World War—Britain, France, Italy, Japan and the United States, the latter energetically represented by President Woodrow Wilson[19]—were intent on controlling the use of force by subjecting it to precise procedural conditions. Articles 10–17 of the Covenant prescribed a sort of cooling-off phase lasting three months, after which it was legitimate, on certain conditions, for a state to have recourse to arms.[20] In this case, its act of war was in practice recognized, if not as actually just, at least as legally justified: one of the conditions for legitimacy was prior reference of the controversy to the League's Council or the Standing Court of International Justice, or else to a tribunal of arbitration.

Obviously, the resolutions passed by the League's organs had to be acted on by all the contenders, but there was no provision for direct intervention against any country which, by irregular conduct, precipitated a war of aggression. The Assembly and the Council—the latter with the five founding nations as permanent

---

19. As is well known, the United States, after setting up the League of Nations at the behest of Wilson, did not join it on account of the opposition of Congress in Washington.

20. See the text of the Covenant in an appendix to F.S. Northedge, *The League of Nations: Its Life and Times 1920–1946*, New York: Holmes & Meier, 1986, pp. 317–27.

members[21]—were empowered to advise member states as to the sanctions to be adopted against the aggressor, and indicate measures to be taken to assist the state which was victim to the aggression. However, neither of the two organs had the power to send in troops or organize a collective military reaction.[22] Moreover, as everybody knows, both the Assembly and the Council had to reach unanimous decisions, with the understanding that states directly involved in a particular controversy were obliged to abstain from casting a vote.[23] Thus each state possessed the power of veto.

The core of 'permanent members', and in particular the powers such as France and Britain which had won the war, exercised a decisive influence on the League's decisions, and it never managed to operate as a proper collective organ, whether in the Assembly or in the Council. A series of violations of the international order and authentic wars of aggression thus came to be tacitly tolerated: from the Italian occupation of Corfù to the Japanese invasion of Manchuria and China—as well as the continuous violations by Germany of the Treaty of Versailles, culminating in the invasion of Poland in 1939. As for the sanctions agreed against Italy for her invasion of another League member, Ethiopia, they were deliberately left unenforced.[24] And finally, the expulsion of the Soviet Union for

21.   Originally there were four non-permanent members, but the number grew to as many as eleven, so that from 1922 a large majority of the Council was made up of non-permanent members. In its heyday the League of Nations numbered about sixty member-states.

22.   Article 10 of the Covenant reads:

The Members of the League undertake to respect and preserve as against external aggression the territorial integrity and existing political independence of all Members of the League. In case of any such aggression or in case of any threat or danger of such aggression the Council shall advise upon the means by which this obligation shall be fulfilled.

23.   In reality Article 15, section 10 of the League of Nations Covenant introduced a second exception to the requisite of unanimity: when the controversy was referred to the Council's Assembly. In this case only a majority of the members of the Assembly was required, as long as this majority included the representatives of the states that were also members of the Council.

24.   On this topic see Q. Wright, 'The Test of Aggression in the Italo-Ethiopian War', *American Journal of International Law* 30 (1), 1936, pp. 45–56.

its attack on Finland had absolutely no consequence. By December 1939, the Second World War was under way and the League of Nations was already practically dead and buried.

The League of Nations was thus a dramatic failure as the first attempt to set up a universal institution under a steering group of the major powers, with the aim of contrasting 'wars of aggression' on the basis of what was in any case an extremely prudent restriction of states' national sovereignty. Just as the Holy Alliance of a century before had failed to usher in political and normative compromise between the particularisms of national sovereignties, so too did the universalism of a cosmopolitan project (championed by Wilson), and the ambition of guaranteeing world peace by recourse to the collective action of nations on a purely voluntary basis.

When the Covenant was approved in Geneva, the formal equality of states on the grounds of equal sovereignty was still too strong a principle for there to be an explicit legal prohibition of war. But the idea of an ethical and legal condemnation of wars of aggression took hold in the heart of Europe thanks to the strong pressure of the internationalist culture that thrived on the other side of the Atlantic. On the initiative of a group of intellectuals in the United States led by James T. Shotwell, a member of the US delegation to the Paris peace conference, a Council session held in June 1924 produced an official document entitled *Outlawry of Aggressive War*. Known as the 'Shotwell project', its central thesis was the definition of 'aggressive war' as an international crime, accompanied by an analytical specification of the various acts of aggression and the sanctions (essentially economic) to be taken against the aggressor.[25] A state was deemed an aggressor for being the first to have recourse to

---

25.   The first three articles of this project read:

Art. 1. The High Contracting parties solemnly declare that aggressive war is an international crime. They severally undertake not to be guilty of its commission. Art. 2. A State engaging in war for other than purposes of defence commits the international crime described in art.1. Art. 3. The Permanent Court of International Justice shall have jurisdiction on the complaint of any signatory, to make a judgement to the effect that the international crime described in art. 1 has or has not in any given case been committed'.

See Schmitt, *Nomos of the Earth*, p. 372.

hostile military action, with no provision for any *justa causa* for going to war.

The Geneva protocol of 1924 was not adopted, partly on account of the opposition of the British government. Nevertheless, the US advocates of the *outlawry of aggressive war* did not throw in the towel, and under the so-called Kellogg-Briand Pact signed in Paris they succeeded in obtaining the absolute prohibition of war as a political instrument available to nations. This Pact—essentially the brainchild of the United States—was signed in Paris in August 1928 by the delegates of fifteen nations, including the major powers that had won the Great War. By 1939, over sixty states had ratified the Pact, including Germany, Italy and Japan. It is considered, and not only by Carl Schmitt, the normative marker of an irreversible mutation in international law, and of a new conception of war that had gained international consensus. There can be no doubt, for example, that the experience of international criminal jurisdiction, starting with the Nuremberg trials against the Nazi criminals, took this pact as a decisive normative premise.[26] In the preamble and the two articles of the Pact, the signatory nations recognize their 'solemn duty' to 'promote the welfare of mankind', committing themselves to a 'frank renunciation of war as an instrument of national policy', condemning 'recourse to war for the solution of international controversies', and hence recognizing that the 'solution of all disputes or conflicts which may arise among them, shall never be sought except by pacific means'. Naturally, within the space of a few years, the outbreak of the Second World War gave the lie to these high-minded intentions, and the whole gamut of problems posed by peace and war came to a head once again, in more dramatic terms than ever.

In the summer of 1944, as World War II was coming to an end with its cortège of tens of millions of victims—among them millions of Jews and hundreds of thousands of Rom and Sinti exterminated by the Nazis—the representatives of the governments of the United States, Britain, the Soviet Union and China gathered at Dumbarton Oaks, near Washington, DC, to lay the foundations of a new international organization. With few exceptions, the project drawn up at

---

26. On this topic see L. Gross, 'The Criminality of Aggressive War', *American Political Science Review*, 41 (2), 1947, pp. 208ff.

Dumbarton Oaks contained all the essential elements of what was to become the Charter of the United Nations. When, in April 1945, the Conference of the United Nations met in San Francisco to approve the Charter of the new organization, the fifty or so states that had accepted the invitation of the sponsoring governments, in the persons of Roosevelt, Churchill and Stalin, found themselves confronted by a veritable ultimatum: either they accepted the guidelines laid down by the major powers at Dumbarton Oaks, or they would be excluded from the treaty.[27] With only a single exception—Article 51 on the right of states to legitimate defence—every attempt to avoid having the workings of the new organization depend on the categorical decisions of the major powers was thwarted. The pursuit of power on the part of the United States, Britain and the Soviet Union predominated over the sovereignty of all the other nations, and any allusion to peoples, nations or ethnic groups with no political representation at the conference was simply ignored.

The Security Council is invested with the full decision-making powers of the United Nations: it is not, like the Council of the League of Nations, a purely deliberative organ. One whole chapter of the Charter, the Seventh, is devoted to the scope for organization and military direction attributed to this organ once it has decided on an international enforcement action.[28] The Security Council does not deliberate unanimously, as was the case for the Council of the

---

27. See B. Conforti, *Le Nazioni Unite*, Padova: Cedam, 1994, pp. 1–6; R.C. Hilderbrand, *Dumbarton Oaks: The Origins of the United Nations and the Search for Postwar Security*, Chapel Hill: University of North Carolina Press, 1990; R.B. Russell, *A History of the United Nations Charter: The Role of the United States 1940–1945*, Washington, DC: The Brookings Institution, 1958. The appendix of the latter gives a substantial historical and documentary reconstruction which includes the texts of the 'United States Tentative Proposals for a General International Organization' (pp. 995–1,006), the 'Dumbarton Oaks Proposals for the Establishment of a General International Organization' (pp. 1,019–28) and an eloquent 'Guide to Evolution of Charter Articles' (pp. 1,067–72).

28. See in particular articles 42, 43, 45, 46 and 47. As is well known, most of the measures in Chapter Seven of the Charter, intended to regulate and organize the deployment of armed force under the control of the Security Council, have never been enforced. In particular art. 47, concerning the institution of a Military Staff Council made up of the Chiefs of Staff of the permanent members of the Security Council.

League of Nations, but decides on the basis of a qualified majority and on condition that no contrary vote is cast by any of the five permanent members recognised in Article 23 of the Charter—namely the victorious powers in the Second World War, France included. Lastly, in spite of being invested with vast discretionary powers for politico-military intervention,[29] the members of the Security Council are not obliged to abstain when it comes to consideration of the use of force to solve controversies in which they themselves are involved, as had been the case with the League of Nations.[30] It follows that the five permanent members of the Security Council can, both *de jure* and *de facto*, take advantage of the powers of this organ, while their power of veto makes them immune to any initiatives that might be directed against them.[31]

The structure of the United Nations was established according to

---

29. On the need for a delimitation of the powers of the Security Council so as to contrast its tendency to operate *ultra vires*, also on the basis of the (untenable) doctrine of its implied powers, see G. Arangio-Ruiz, 'Nazioni Unite e legalità internazionale', in *L'Onu: cinquant'anni di attività e prospettive per il futuro*, Atti dei Convegni SIOI, Roma: SIOI, 1996, pp. 387–415.

30. As Hans Morgenthau has pointed out, the Holy Alliance was patently an international government of the great powers, whereas the League of Nations was an international government of the great powers tempered by the counsel and consensus of all the nations that belonged to it: in principle, thanks to the requisite of unanimity, they could oppose the initiatives of the great powers. The United Nations, in its turn, is an international government of the great powers which, in constitutional terms, is identical to that of the Holy Alliance, being wholly autocratic while purporting to be open and moderate like the League of Nations. The Security Council is, in reality, a Holy Alliance of the twentieth century, and its five permanent members are a Holy Alliance within the Holy Alliance (H. Morgenthau, *Politics among Nations*, New York: Knopf, 1960, p. 480).

31. It is common knowledge that both superpowers have repeatedly violated the principles set out in the preamble to the UN Charter, protecting both themselves and their allies by systematic use of the right of veto in the Security Council. Each has engaged in lengthy armed conflicts, the United States in Vietnam and the Soviet Union in Afghanistan. They have also carried out specific military operations on their own initiative, including interventions in Guatemala (1954), Lebanon (1958), Cuba (1961), San Domingo (1965), Grenada (1983), Libya (1986) and Panama (1989) by the United States, and the Soviet Union's military activity in Eastern Europe in 1956 and 1968. In only one case was the United States condemned by the International Court of Justice, for aiding the Nicaraguan Contras, but the US government was able to neutralize the Court's decision by using its veto.

the idea that a stable and universal peace could be ensured by the over-whelming military force of the major powers, always available for use against any possible 'aggressor state'. Peace, as Winston Churchill told the House of Commons on 24 May 1944, would be guaranteed by the 'overwhelming military power' of the new 'world organization'.[32] Wars of aggression are legally proscribed right from the preamble to the Charter, with war being styled a 'scourge' from which the United Nations intends to free humankind for ever. And the use of force by states is explicitly forbidden by the fourth section of Article 2, while Article 39 authorizes the Security Council to take measures, implying the use of force if necessary, against a state which violates or threatens to violate international peace.

In order to realize this aim, the Charter provided for the insti-tution of a permanent army under the authority of the Security Council and a Military Staff Council made up of the chiefs of staff of the permanent members of the Security Council. This was conceived, at least in theory, as an international police force through which the major powers would carry out their role as 'peace lords': in fact, their power of military intervention was not subjected to any precise legal limits, and the sovereignty of all the other nations was thereby drastically curtailed. Nor was there any provision for sanc-tions if the peace should be violated with acts of aggression carried out not by an intermediate or minor power, but by one of the major powers which had won the world war.[33] Moreover, in such cases not only was the transgressor able to fall back on the power of veto, but the permanent army at the service of the Security Council (thus in reality an instrument of its permanent members) would have had, as

---

32. Quoted by Kelsen in *Peace through Law*, p. 67.

33. Blatant discrimination is immediately apparent if one compares the reaction of the United Nations to Iraq's invasion of Kuwait in 1990 with its radically different reaction to the attack launched by the United States and Great Britain on Iraq in 2003. At the instigation of the United States, the first action was countered with one of the most overwhelming military expeditions in human history, with the unconditional assent of the Security Council. Moreover, following its defeat, Iraq was subjected—again backed by a consensus of the Security Council—to onerous economic and territorial sanctions. Nothing of the sort happened, or indeed could have happened, in the face of the aggression against and invasion of Iraq by the United States and Britain in 2003.

it were, to fight against itself or divide into two opposing factions, one at war with the other. In practice, the power of veto and the absence of the obligation to abstain when involved in a controversy requiring the use of force made it impossible for a conflict among the permanent members to be regulated by means of coercion against their will.

In all likelihood, it was this opacity concerning its basic functioning that gave rise to what most observers denounce as the most serious distortion in the normative framework of the United Nations to have emerged in its first sixty years of existence. This is the non-application of the provisions of Chapter 7 of the Charter—in particular articles 43 and 47, regarding the constitution of a military contingent under the authority of the Security Council. As a result, it has become customary for the Security Council to delegate the use of force to the major powers whenever this is deemed necessary, contracting out the power of making 'legitimate' recourse to warfare, even in its most aggressive and devastating forms—precisely that form of warfare which the United Nations claimed to have 'outlawed' for ever.

As has been ably demonstrated, over the last few decades the Security Council has limited itself to distributing 'letters of marque', giving a free hand to those major powers that were interested in conducting military operations of peace enforcement, or indeed insisted on doing so.[34] The patina of international legality conferred each time has, we might say, simply transformed the pirates into privateers. The paradigm for this, as Richard Falk has argued,[35] can be found in the Gulf War of 1991, and the same has occurred in Somalia, Rwanda, and Haiti, and in the war of Bosnia-Herzegovina (1991–95) as well as, a posteriori, in the war over Kosovo (1999). In all these cases, as Gaetano Arangio-Ruiz has emphasized, any nation which declared itself ready and willing to do so was authorized to use its military forces, under its own command, while on the part of

---

34. Luigi Condorelli, contribution to roundtable 'La riforma del Consiglio di Sicurezza', *Relazioni internazionali*, 59, 1995, p. 69. See also my *Cosmopolis: Prospects for World Government*, Cambridge: Polity Press, 1997, p. 174.

35. See R.A. Falk, 'Reflections on the Gulf War Experience: Force and War in the United Nations System', *Juridisk Tidskrift* 3 (1), 1991, p. 122.

the Security Council there has been 'no effective direct exercise of military coercion'.[36] In reality, the Security Council has renounced its primary function—the control and limitation of the use of international force—and shown itself ready not only to authorize the use of force beyond the provisions of the Charter, but also to legitimize *ex post facto* the military conduct of the major powers, including the use of quasi-nuclear weapons of mass destruction such as 'fuel-air explosives' and the murderous daisy-cutter bombs, quite apart from countenancing the extermination of innocent civilians.

On top of all this, in the UN Charter we find no definition of the notion of a 'war of aggression', and this, at least in theoretical terms, makes the Security Council the unchallengeable arbiter in resorting to or renouncing the use of force against aggressor states that violate or threaten to violate world peace. There is no reference to such a definition even in Article 51, which authorizes a state that has come under attack by another state to resist with the use of force until such time as the Security Council shall intervene. From the text of the Article one can merely deduce that the aggression must consist in an 'armed attack', not simply a threat of attack, and this should at least rule out the idea—resolutely defended by the United States and Israel—of the legitimacy of 'preventive or pre-emptive self-defence'.[37] In reality, the lack of a precise notion of 'war of aggression', as the voluminous literature devoted to interpreting Article 51 and the innumerable theoretical and practical controversies which have resulted go to show, has rendered this Article a favourite tool in the hands of the major powers to justify their wars, in the name of an ever more elastic notion of 'self-defence'.[38]

---

36. See Arangio-Ruiz, 'Nazioni Unite e legalità internazionale', p. 401.

37. See R.A. Falk, 'Why International Law Matters', in the survey 'War, Law and Global Order', in Jura Gentium Journal, at www.juragentium. unifi.it.

38. See A. Cassese, *International Law*, pp. 354–7. The normative principle by which an 'aggressor' must be implicitly recognized as any state that is the first to use force against another state—a principle that can be indirectly inferred from the UN Charter—ignores, among other things, the significant number of cases of indirect aggression, consisting for example in the political, economic and military support granted to forces within another state that threaten its territorial integrity or political independence (see A. Cassese, *Lineamenti di diritto internazionale penale*, Bologna: il Mulino, 2005, p. 151). Furthermore, this principle ignores cases in which it is not a state but, for example, an international criminal organization that threatens a state's

Very belatedly, in December 1974, the UN General Assembly attempted to fill this normative vacuum by issuing Resolution 3314 (XXIX), giving an elaborate definition of 'aggression'. Aggression is referred to in the preamble as 'the most serious and dangerous form of the illegal use of force',[39] while Article 1 describes it in lapidary fashion as 'the use of armed force by a State against the sovereignty, territorial integrity or political independence of another State'.[40] Article 3 gives a wide-ranging analytical specification of possible modes of aggression.[41] However, an important caveat is introduced

---

territorial integrity or political independence. And, above all, it leaves unresolved the highly delicate problem of the timing of the response of a state under attack if the military initiative—whether in progress or when its preparation is nearing completion—is based on missiles, which may be long-range, with or without nuclear warheads.

39. The English text of the Resolution can be consulted in the survey 'War, Law and Global Order' in *Jura Gentium Journal*, at www.juragentium.unifi.it.

40. The original English text of Article 1 reads: 'Aggression is the use of armed force by a State against the sovereignty, territorial integrity or political independence of another State, or in any other manner inconsistent with the Charter of the United Nations, as set out in this Definition.'

41. Article 3 of the Resolution states:

Any of the following acts, regardless of a declaration of war, shall, subject to and in accordance with the provisions of article 2, qualify as an act of aggression: (a) The invasion or attack by the armed forces of a State of the territory of another State, or any military occupation, however temporary, resulting from such invasion or attack, or any annexation by the use of force of the territory of another State or part thereof; (b) Bombardment by the armed forces of a State against the territory of another State or the use of any weapons by a State against the territory of another State; (c) The blockade of the ports or coasts of a State by the armed forces of another State; (d) An attack by the armed forces of a State on the land, sea or air forces, or marine and air fleets of another State; (e) The use of armed forces of one State which are within the territory of another State with the agreement of the receiving State, in contravention of the conditions provided for in the agreement or any extension of their presence in such territory beyond the termination of the agreement; (f) The action of a State in allowing its territory, which it has placed at the disposal of another State, to be used by that other State for perpetrating an act of aggression against a third State; (g) The sending by or on behalf of a State of armed bands, groups, irregulars or mercenaries, which carry out acts of armed force against another State of such gravity as to amount to the acts listed above, or its substantial involvement therein.

in Article 2, where it is specified that aggression is not to be automatically imputed to the state that is the first to use military force against another state. The Security Council, taking into account the circumstances, and whether the consequences of the attack are of sufficient gravity, may decide that the first to use force is not in fact guilty of the crime of aggression.[42]

As has been observed, this definition—produced by the General Assembly and not the Security Council, and hence not mandatory—is incomplete, and was always intended to be so.[43] Article 4 actually states that it is not to be regarded as exhaustive, since the crime of aggression can be combined with other alleged transgressions in war at the discretion of the Security Council.[44] Moreover—and this is a particularly grave omission—the resolution does not contemplate any sanction against those committing a crime of aggression. Article 5 limits itself to two utterly banal considerations in the wake of the sentence pronounced by the Nuremberg Tribunal, namely that 'a war of aggression is a crime against international peace' and that it incurs 'international responsibility'.[45]

Antonio Cassese has argued that, in this and other cases, one can see the tendency of the major powers to ensure that the notions of 'act of aggression' and 'war of aggression' should not be clearly defined, thereby making it impossible to enforce the provision laid down in Article 2, section 4 of the UN Charter forbidding nations to use force. In his view, this tendency prevailed because the major powers,

---

42. Article 2 provides clarification:

The first use of armed force by a State in contravention of the Charter shall constitute prima facie evidence of an act of aggression although the Security Council may, in conformity with the Charter, conclude that a determination that an act of aggression has been committed would not be justified in the light of other relevant circumstances, including the fact that the acts concerned or their consequences are not of sufficient gravity.

43. See Cassese, *Lineamenti di diritto internazionale penale*, pp. 148–9.

44. Article 4 reads: 'The acts enumerated above are not exhaustive and the Security Council may determine that other acts constitute aggression under the provisions of the Charter.'

45. Article 5 states, 'A war of aggression is a crime against international peace. Aggression gives rise to international responsibility.'

when it comes to actively applying this measure, aim to keep a large degree of freedom of action both at the individual level, and collectively through the United Nations Security Council. The definition of 'aggression' has been left in a sort of limbo with respect to its characterization both as a state crime and as an international crime imputable to individuals.[46]

More generally, Giorgio Gaja has pointed out the existence of an 'evident paradox': while the prohibition of the use of force is a fundamental principle of international law, and violation of this principle is considered one of the most serious examples of 'international crime', it is practically unknown for one state to ask for sanctions to be imposed on another state or its citizens on the basis of an accusation of aggression.[47] The criminalization of aggressive war has thus failed to produce any significant developments—not in normative terms, not in the structure of the international legal system, and still less in dissuading nations from having recourse to the arbitrary use of force.

War as a crime for which individuals are indictable

The new concept of war that gained ground in the first decades of the twentieth century did not just postulate a war of aggression as an international crime imputable to states: it also introduced, as we have seen, the possibility of individuals being indicted for this and other international crimes. And this has played a fundamental role in moulding international criminal justice.

Up to the end of the Second World War, international institutions had never prosecuted individuals in law. Indeed, from the dawn of modern international law and its founding fathers Hugo Grotius, Alberico Gentili and Baltasar Ayala, internationalist doctrine had excluded the possibility of individuals being considered subjects in the international legal order, whether in conjunction with, or in

---

46. See Cassese, *Lineamenti di diritto internazionale penale*, p. 148.

47. See G. Gaja, 'The Long Journey towards Repressing Aggression', in A. Cassese, P. Gaeta and J.R.W.D. Jones, eds, *The Rome Statute of the International Criminal Court: A Commentary*, Oxford: Oxford University Press, 2002, pp. 427–8.

place of, the nation-states. International courts of justice had never been invested with obligatory jurisdiction, and had in fact been confined to relatively marginal issues. To maintain a world order, the major powers had had recourse to political and military force, treaties and diplomacy, rather than to legal instruments. This was the case, in particular, for the Holy Alliance, the League of Nations and the United Nations.

From the first decades of the twentieth century, commentators in the West began to argue the case for extending the judicial function to the international arena. As we have noted—and as Carl Schmitt insisted—the dress rehearsal for this radical doctrinal departure was the incrimination of Kaiser Wilhelm II of Hohenzollern as a war criminal at the end of the First World War. In its indictment of the venerable emperor, Article 227 of the Versailles Treaty accused him of 'supreme offence against international morality and the sanctity of treaties', a formula dictated by Wilson.[48] This accusation, with its rhetorical and scrupulously non-legal language, did not refer to the traditional notion of 'war crimes', involving violation of the so-called *jus in bello*. Such a violation concerned the conduct of belligerents that infringed the norms of the 'law of warfare', meaning the proper conduct of war on land or at sea, the rights of prisoners, and so on.

Having achieved victory in the First World War, the Entente allies were determined to criminalize and punish warfare as such—specifically as an act or series of acts of aggression—and insisted that individuals, cited by name, be held responsible for this crime.[49] Article 227 required that the kaiser should stand trial, together with high-level German political and military figures, before an international court composed of judges representing the five victorious powers (Britain, France, Italy, Japan and the United States). Furthermore, other articles in the Treaty required Germany—although no such obligation was to be found anywhere in either international treaties or customary law—to hand over some 900 named individuals

---

48. As is well known, this formula was proposed by President Wilson against the advice of his secretary of state, Robert Lansing, who was opposed to the indictment of the kaiser and the setting up of an international Tribunal.

49. Schmitt, *Nomos of the Earth*, pp. 260–9.

accused of violating laws and war customs, so that they too could be tried.[50]

As is well known, the trial of Kaiser Wilhelm II and his collaborators never took place. He had taken refuge in Holland, and that country refused to extradite him, rightly arguing that there was nothing in international law that could countenance the incrimination of a head of state as being personally responsible for an international misdemeanour. According to the international legal order as it stood, the only subject in law was the state: only a state could be indicted for international wrongdoing, and any sanctions imposed, whether economic, financial, territorial, military or other, had nothing to do with criminal law. For its part, the German government refused to hand over the 900 individuals, but did consent to having them tried on German soil, in front of the Supreme Court in Leipzig, which was agreed to by the victorious powers. But only a few of the accused actually stood trial, and only light sentences were handed down. Yet, in spite of this paltry result, the whole affair had significant consequences in normative terms. Article 3 of the Fourth Hague Convention, 1907, stated that only states—not individuals—could be called to answer for violations of the law of warfare, whereas the precedent set by the Versailles Treaty made this principle partially inoperative.[51]

The real origin of international criminal jurisdiction can be identified with the institution, in 1945 and 1946 respectively, of the Nuremberg and Tokyo Tribunals. The creation of these two criminal courts had been anticipated, in the theoretical sphere, by Hans Kelsen's essay *Peace through Law*, which appeared in 1944. Kelsen set out an institutional strategy for attaining peace, borrowing from Kant (notably the celebrated pages in *Zum ewigen Frieden*) the ideal of perpetual peace, with federalism as a model, and indeed the idea of making

---

50. On this topic, see my *Invoking Humanity: War, Law and Global Order*, London/New York: Continuum, 2002, pp. 102–6.

51. See A.J. Kochavi, *Prelude to Nuremberg: Allied War Crimes Policy and the Question of Punishment*, Chapel Hill: University of North Carolina Press, 1998; J.W. Willis, *Prologue to Nuremberg: The Policy and Diplomacy of Punishing War Criminals of the First World War*, Westport, CT: Greenwood, 1982; S. Lener, 'Dal mancato giudizio del Kaiser al processo di Norimberga', *Civiltà Cattolica* 97 (1), 1946.

individuals, as well as states, subjects in international law.[52] Kelsen maintained that, in the aftermath of the Second World War, his project for a 'permanent league for the maintenance of peace' stood a good chance of being accepted by the victorious major powers. In his project, one important innovation was grafted on to the old model of the League of Nations—namely the attribution of a central role to judicial, as opposed to normative and executive, functions.

In Kelsen's opinion, the principal cause for the failure of the League of Nations lay in the fact that at the summit of its power structure was a Council representing a sort of worldwide political government, rather than a Court of Justice. In the light of his normativism, this was a serious 'error of construction' because it meant that the international order lacked any neutral and impartial judicial authority. Peace could only be guaranteed by a court of justice able to settle international controversies by applying international law objectively, free of any political conditioning.[53] There was one other aspect which Kelsen, true to the Kantian conception of international law as 'cosmopolitan law' (*Weltbürgerrecht*), considered crucial: it was necessary to establish the individual penal responsibility of whoever violated international law in carrying out government activities or directing military operations. The court was to indict individual citizens who were guilty of war crimes, and their countries were to be held responsible for making them available to the court.[54]

It was this sort of legal internationalism, albeit in a very different form to that contemplated by Kelsen, which guided the victors—the United States, the Soviet Union, Britain and France—in instituting the Nuremberg International Military Tribunal. Agreement was reached in London on 8 August 1945, just two days after the atomic bomb was dropped on Hiroshima, and two days before the bombing of Nagasaki. The Tribunal held its opening session in November 1945, and hearings continued until October 1946. Of the twenty-two

---

52. See Kelsen, *Peace through Law*, pp. 13–5.

53. Kelsen makes no secret of the fact that the greatest difficulty lies in the need to create an international police force, autonomous and independent of the armed forces of the various countries, able to enforce the application of the Court's sentences. See H. Kelsen, *Law and Peace in International Relations*, Cambridge, MA: Harvard University Press, 1948, pp. 145–68.

54. See Kelsen, *Peace through Law*, pp. 71ff, 87–8.

accused, three were cleared, six were convicted and given life imprisonment or shorter prison sentences, and ten were given the death sentence, which was carried out immediately. For the first time in the history of humankind, a war of aggression was considered not as a generic breach of international law involving the liability of the state qua state, but as an authentic 'international crime' for which individuals too were held penally responsible. Article 6(a) of the Tribunal's Statute gave an explicit definition of 'crimes against peace', placing them under the jurisdiction of the court alongside 'war crimes' and 'crimes against humanity'. They consisted in actions such as 'planning, preparation, initiation, or waging of a war of aggression, or a war in violation of international treaties, agreements, or assurances, or participation in a common plan or conspiracy for the accomplishment of any of the foregoing'.[55] Robert Jackson, chief US prosecutor to the Nuremberg Tribunal, had this to say in his opening speech to the court:

Any resort to war—to any kind of a war—is a resort to means that are inherently criminal. War inevitably is a course of killings, assaults, deprivations of liberty, and destruction of property. An honestly defensive war is, of course, legal and saves those lawfully conducting it from criminality. But inherently criminal acts cannot be defended by showing that those who committed them were engaged in a war, when war itself is illegal. The very minimum legal consequence of the treaties making aggressive wars illegal is to strip those who incite or wage them of every defense the law ever gave, and to leave war-makers subject to judgment by the usually accepted principles of the law of crime.[56]

In one of the best-known passages of the trial's summing up, war is declared to be 'essentially an evil thing':

---

55. See A. Roberts and R. Guelff, eds, *Documents on the Laws of War*, Oxford: Oxford University Press, 2000, p. 177.

56. H. Kelsen cites this passage and subjects it to a formalistic critique in contradiction with his general advocacy of the primacy of international law with respect to internal law. 'Will the Judgment in the Nuremberg Trial Constitute a Precedent in International Law?' *International Law Quarterly* 1 (2), 1947, pp. 153–71, at p. 156.

Its consequences are not confined to the belligerent states alone, but affect the whole world. To initiate a war of aggression is not only an international crime; it is the *supreme international crime*, differing from other war crimes only in that it contains within itself the accumulated evil of the whole.[57]

In the text of the Nuremberg sentence and in the intentions of the Tribunal judges, a war of aggression as the prominent instance of the category of 'crimes against peace' does indeed seem to be clearly conceptualized, even if it is set down in very general terms and without specifying the subjective elements in the criminal conduct.[58] Aggressive war—i.e., a war that is not purely defensive—is not only an international crime but, as we have seen, is the 'supreme international crime' inasmuch as it is the root of all the negative consequences of warfare. All who incite to warfare or decide to go to war or fight are indictable for this 'supreme crime', because they are personally responsible for killings, acts of aggression, limitations of liberty and the destruction of property. Whoever knowingly fights an illegal war relinquishes any claim to legal immunity or extenuating circumstances: he or she is simply a criminal to be subjected to judicial punishment.

Thus we are confronted by a notion of war opposed *toto caelo* to that of the European warfare limited by the *jus publicum Europaeum*. In the latter conception, war was seen as the sovereign right of states, with antagonistic relations between states being regulated and limited by law, and hence rendered legal. By virtue of Resolution 95(1) of the UN General Assembly, incorporating the

---

57. See the Avalon Project of the Yale Law School: Judgment of the International Military Tribunal, at www.yale.edu/lawweb/avalon/imt/proc/judcont.htm. My italics. On this topic, see also M. Mandel, *How America Gets Away with Murder: Illegal Wars, Collateral Damage and Crimes Against Humanity*, London: Pluto Press, 2004.

58. Gaja ('Long Journey', p. 435) emphasizes that no attempt is made to specify the subjective elements either in Resolution 3314 (XXIX) of the United Nations General Assembly, 1974: 'the General Assembly resolution fails to give any indication of essential elements of the crime such as which individuals are criminally liable and what sort of mental element is required for the same purpose'; on the topic of the subjective elements of the crime of aggression and the distinction between 'direct' and 'specific' malice, see Cassese, *Lineamenti di diritto internazionale penale*, pp. 154–6.

principles set out in the Statute and the judgement of the Nuremberg Tribunal, the new notion of war may be considered as confirmed by a customary international norm. In common with every other principle which the UN Commission on International Law derived from the Statute and the sentence of the Tribunal, the new legal conception of warfare is valid *erga omnes*.[59] Among these principles, we can single out individual responsibility for violating criminal norms of international law, the non-extenuating nature of acting in obedience to higher orders, and the concepts of 'crimes against peace', 'war crimes' and 'crimes against humanity'.

The 'dual-standard system' of international criminal justice

For decades, the principles established by the Tribunals of Nuremberg and Tokyo were not put into effect. Only once was an attempt made to cite the Nuremberg trial as an international legal precedent: in August 1949 Ethiopia asked Italy to extradite the marshals Pietro Badoglio and Rodolfo Graziani as war criminals. Ethiopia wanted to bring them before an international tribunal made up of a majority of non-Ethiopian judges which would have followed the principles and procedures laid down in the Statute of the Nuremberg Tribunal. As one might expect, this attempt met with no success.[60]

The two international Tribunals have come in for scathing criticism, notably by Hannah Arendt, Bert Röling, Hedley Bull[61] and Hans

---

59. For the text of the 'Principles of International Law Recognized in the Statute of the Nüremberg Tribunal and in the Judgment of the Tribunal', 1950, see *International Humanitarian Law: Treaties and Documents*, at www.icrc.org/ ihl.nsf/FULL/390. See also P.C. Jessup, 'The Crime of Aggression and the Future of International Law', *Political Science Quarterly* 62 (1), 1947. Another pertinent international document, albeit devoid of any binding juridical efficacy, is the 'Draft Code of Crimes against Peace and Security of Mankind', adopted in 1996 by the United Nations Commission for international law. The definition of 'aggression' as an international crime presented in this document has been described by Cassese as disappointing on account of its circular logic (Cassese, *Lineamenti di diritto internazionale penale*, p. 149).

60. See C. Miglioli, *La sanzione nel diritto internazionale*, Milano: Giuffrè, 1951, p. 69.

61. H. Arendt, *Eichmann in Jerusalem: A Report on the Banality of Evil*, New York: The Viking Press, 1963. Bert Röling has argued that the post-war international

Kelsen. The severest critique of all, which has found almost universal consensus, is the one formulated by Kelsen. The punishment of war criminals—not only Nazis—was supposed to be an act of justice and not the continuation of hostilities by means purporting to be judicial, but in fact betraying the desire for revenge. For Kelsen, it was incompatible with the function of justice that only the defeated nations were obliged to submit their citizens to the jurisdiction of a criminal court. The victorious nations should also have accepted that citizens of theirs who had committed war crimes should be brought to trial. And such a trial should take place in front of a proper international court in all senses, meaning an independent, impartial body with wide-ranging jurisdiction, not the tribunal of the military occupiers with its highly selective competence.[62] In a famous essay, Kelsen argued forcefully, for these and other reasons, that the Nuremberg trial was not to be taken as a legal precedent, and could not be considered as a model to be imitated.[63]

It was not only Kelsen who was in no doubt that the Allies had also been guilty of serious violations of international law, and that the principle must be respected by which the same conduct must be judged according to the same legal criteria. But the *tu quoque*

---

trials were used by the victors for propaganda ends and to conceal crimes they themselves had committed—see B.V.A. Röling, *The Nuremberg and the Tokyo Trials in Retrospect*, in C. Bassiouni and U.P. Nanda, eds, *A Treatise on International Criminal Law*, Springfield: Charles C. Thomas, 1973. For his part, Hedley Bull (*The Anarchical Society*, London: Macmillan, 1977, p. 89) has indicated that the symbolic function of the trials was obscured by the selective nature of their pronouncements. See also R. Quadri, *Diritto internazionale pubblico*, Napoli: Liguori, 1974.

62.   See Kelsen, *Peace through Law*, pp. 110–5. Kelsen believed that, by invading Poland and declaring war on Japan, the Soviet Union committed war crimes which were indictable before an international Tribunal.

63.   See H. Kelsen, 'Will the Judgment in the Nuremberg Trial Constitute a Precedent in International Law?', p. 171:

If the principles applied in the Nuremberg trial were to become a precedent, then, after the next war, the governments of the victorious States would try the members of the governments of the vanquished States for having committed crimes determined unilaterally and with retroactive force by the former. Let us hope that there is no such precedent.

Kelsen returns to this topic in *Principles of International Law*, New York: Holt, Rinehart & Winston, 1967, third edn, pp. 215–20.

argument, often used by the defence counsel of the accused, was systematically rejected by the court, on the grounds that, according to its Statute, it was competent to judge only German war crimes, and none which might have been committed by the Allies. For this reason, any line of argument or testimony which highlighted crimes committed by the victorious powers was deemed 'irrelevant' by the court, and opposed or ruled out of court.[64]

In spite of this series of criticisms, almost half a century after the experience of the Nuremberg and Tokyo Tribunals, international criminal jurisdiction has been revived in the form of the ad hoc International Criminal Tribunals convened at The Hague for the former Yugoslavia (ICTY, 1993) and at Arusha for Rwanda (ICTR, 1994). The institution of these Tribunals by the UN Security Council was itself controversial.[65] But there is one crucial novelty: although the statutes for these tribunals were drawn up taking the principles of Nuremberg as precedent, the competence of the prosecutors and judges is restricted to crimes of *jus in bello*—i.e. war crimes, crimes against humanity and the crime of genocide. As we have seen, the competence of the Nuremberg Tribunal concerned above all 'crimes against peace', with a war of aggression being designated as 'the supreme international crime' deserving the death sentence, and yet this case in point does not figure in the statutes of the two ad hoc Tribunals. As we shall see, it is also substantially lacking in the statute of the International Criminal Court (ICC), itself based in The Hague.[66]

64.   See A.-M. de Zayas, 'Der Nürnberger Prozess', in A. Demand, ed., *Macht und Recht. Grosse Prozesse in der Geschichte*, München: Beck'sche Verlagsbuchhandlung, 1990. See also C. Ginsburg and V.N. Kudriatsev, eds, *The Nuremberg Trial and International Law*, Dordrecht: Kluwer, 1990.

65.   See Zolo, *Invoking Humanity*, pp. 106–9.

66.   In the statute of the International Tribunal for the former Yugoslavia, four Articles (2–5) are devoted to specifying the competence of the Court, as are three (2–4) in the statute of the International Tribunal for Rwanda. On international crimes and the competence of international criminal jurisdiction, see S. Zappalà, *La giustizia penale internazionale*, Bologna: il Mulino, 2005, pp. 17–47. On the Tribunal of Arusha, whose activity proved to have little effect on the process of pacification and repristination of normal life, see D. Shraga and R. Zacklin, 'The International Criminal Tribunal for Rwanda', *European Journal for International Law* 7 (4), 1996, pp. 501–18; G. Cataldi, 'Il Consiglio di Sicurezza delle Nazioni Unite e la questione

Furthermore, in terms of war crimes and crimes against humanity, the Geneva Conventions, drawn up in 1949, created a particularly ambitious repressive system. Every country which ratifies the Conventions is obliged to search for, arrest and put on trial people accused of serious violations of international law, or else to hand them over to another state requiring their extradition, on the basis of the principle *aut dedere aut judicare*. What is more, the Geneva Conventions introduced the highly innovative notion of 'universal jurisdiction', which enables any contracting state to try somebody irrespective of their nationality, the nationality of the victim, or where the crime was committed.[67] And lastly, under the Convention on the Non-Applicability of Statutory Limitations to War Crimes and Crimes Against Humanity adopted by the UN General Assembly and introduced in November 1970, war crimes and crimes against humanity have been declared imprescriptible.[68] None of this has ever been contemplated for the crime of aggression.[69]

In practice, a dual-standard system of international criminal justice has come about in which a justice 'made to measure' for the major world powers and their victorious leaders operates alongside a separate justice for the defeated and downtrodden. In particular, international crimes of *jus in bello*, which are normally considered less serious than the crime of aggression, have been prosecuted relentlessly and in some cases punished with great harshness, in particular by the Hague Tribunal for the former Yugoslavia. At

---

del Ruanda', in P. Picone, ed., *Interventi delle Nazioni Unite e diritto internazionale*, Padova: Cedam, 1995, pp. 445–61; I. Bottigliero, 'Il rapporto della commissione di esperti sul Ruanda e l'istituzione di un tribunale internazionale penale', *La comunità internazionale* 4 (4), 1994, pp. 760–8.

67.   Applications of this innovation have been few but of a high profile, including the incrimination of the Chilean general Augusto Pinochet by the Spanish magistracy and of Israeli leader Ariel Sharon by the Belgian magistracy.

68.   See the 'Convention on Non-Applicability of Statutory Limitations to War Crimes and Crimes Against Humanity of the United Nations General Assembly', which came into force on 11 November 1970.

69.   Giorgio Gaja ('Long Journey', p. 429) has once again pointed out the paradox whereby, 'while repression was partially provided for crimes against humanity through the adoption of the 1948 Genocide Convention and for war crimes under the 1949 Geneva Conventions, no parallel initiative was taken with regard to crimes against peace'.

the same time, aggressive war, a crime predominantly committed by the political and military authorities of the major powers, has been systematically ignored. Even though it was described at the Nuremberg Tribunal as the 'supreme international crime', those responsible for such crimes retain impunity, occupying the summit of the pyramid of international power. On this subject, Antonio Cassese has pointed out that

> Not surprisingly, since 1946 there have been no national or international trials for alleged crimes of aggression, although undisputedly in many instances States have engaged in acts of aggression, and in a few cases the Security Council has determined that such acts were committed by States.[70]

We can illustrate three main instances of this normative and judicial pathology which the adepts of the internationalist doctrine have tended to overlook.

The International Criminal Tribunal for the Former Yugoslavia.

The first instance concerns the new ad hoc criminal Tribunals. The conduct of the Hague Tribunal—and its Chief Prosecutor's Office in particular—during the Kosovo war unleashed by NATO in March 1999 against the Yugoslav Federal Republic, provides an eloquent example.

The NATO attack, agreed without the authorization of the Security Council and ignoring any reference to international law, has been judged by the most authoritative Western international jurists as a serious breach of the UN Charter.[71] Moreover, the military intervention was condemned by such major powers as the Russian Federation, India and China, who were sceptical of the 'humanitarian' motivations adduced by the aggressors. The Security Council chose not to declare the military attack illegal and punish it, and

---

70. See Cassese, *Lineamenti di diritto internazionale penale*, pp. 149–50. Cassese recalls that the Security Council has labelled as 'acts of aggression' some of the military actions and raids carried out by Israel against the Palestine Liberation Organization (PLO) and some of the attacks launched by South Africa on Angola.

71. Among them Michael Glennon, Bruno Simma and Antonio Cassese. See Zolo, *Invoking Humanity*, pp. 66–81.

in any case would not have been able to, in view of the inevitable veto from the United States, as well as Britain and probably France. For its part, thanks to its 'special' nature and selective competence, the Hague Tribunal not only placed both aggressors (the political and military authorities of NATO) and victims (the citizens of the Yugoslav Republic) on the same legal standing, but actually established a close collaboration with the aggressors.

To appreciate the gravity of this conduct we have to bear in mind at least two circumstances. First of all, the Hague Tribunal had been pushed for, equipped, assisted and amply financed by the United States. Secondly, in the last stages of the war in Bosnia, a close collaboration on judicial matters had developed between the Chief Prosecutor's Office and the NATO forces deployed in the former Yugoslavia. The military personnel of the NATO contingents Implementation Force (IFOR) and Stabilization Force (SFOR) acted as a police force, carrying out investigative activities, pursuing incriminated persons, and proceeding to arrest them on behalf of the Tribunal. Following the NATO attack on the Yugoslav Republic in March 1999, not only was this collaboration not terminated, but the Prosecutor's Office of the Tribunal actually formalized and intensified its dealings with NATO authorities at the highest level, going so far as to improvise an indictment of the president, Slobodan Milošević, together with other leading members of the Yugoslav government, while the NATO bombing was still raging.

But that is not all. Under the Tribunal's Statute the Chief Prosecutor's Office was able to disregard the fact that NATO's leading political and military authorities could be held responsible for the crime of 'aggressive war', but it also ignored the violations of the international law of warfare committed by NATO military personnel during the seventy-eight days of uninterrupted bombing, carried out in more than 10,000 raids by up to 1,000 Allied planes. The Hague Tribunal had complete jurisdictional competence with respect to these violations, and it was its clear duty to investigate, and where appropriate indict, those responsible.[72]

Three formal denunciations were in fact presented to the Tribunal— by a delegation from the Russian parliament, by the Belgrade

---

72. Ibid., pp. 109–14.

government, and by a group of authoritative Canadian jurists led by Michael Mandel—but the chief prosecutor, Carla del Ponte, decided to dismiss them as manifestly unfounded, showing no scruples about placing international justice at the service of those powers on which the Tribunal was both politically and financially dependent. It is no secret that Pentagon sources described as 'outrageous' the mere suggestion that the political and military commanders-in-chief of NATO could be subject to criminal investigation.

One particular issue in the denunciations had been the attack carried out by NATO bombers on the Belgrade television station on the night of 23–24 April 1999, in which some twenty journalists and other employees had died, leaving many wounded. Two other serious crimes were denounced: firstly the use of around 1,400 cluster bombs, in violation of the international treaty prohibiting the use of anti-personnel mines, to which all the countries involved in NATO's military action were parties, with the sole exception of the United States.[73] Secondly, NATO was accused of making use of depleted uranium missiles. NATO secretary-general, George Robertson, had to admit that the A10 tank-buster bombers deployed by the United States had dropped more than 30,000 of these missiles on Yugoslav territory, in particular in Kosovo. On striking a solid body, these warheads explode and disperse uranium in the form of a fine radio-active powder. This powder contaminates the soil, water and air and enters the food chain, producing an increase in environmental radio-activity which can be responsible for malignant tumours, leukaemias, foetal malformations and childhood diseases. Yet the Prosecutor's Office of the Tribunal felt no need to investigate.

The legal motivations adduced by the chief prosecutor to justify the dismissal of these grave accusations refer to NATO's overall 'responsible conduct', which was such that its use of force would never have resulted in 'civilian victims directly or indirectly'; to the absence of intention to harm; and to the entirely exceptional nature of the occasional technical errors or failures in communication

---

73. A high percentage of the devices scattered by cluster bombs remain on the terrain unexploded, and are thus in every respect equivalent to anti-personnel mines. Moreover, such mines above all kill or maim minors, as was overwhelmingly the case in both Kosovo and Serbia.

(for example, the bombing 'by mistake' of the Chinese embassy in Belgrade).[74]

With respect to this whole sorry business, Antonio Cassese has spoken of the persistence of a 'Nuremberg syndrome' by which international criminal jurisdiction perpetuates the model of the 'justice of the victors'.[75] And it is surely an alarming paradox[76] that, while the defeated ex-presidents of the Yugoslav Republic and Iraq have been imprisoned and made to stand trial by special Tribunals backed and financed by the United States and their closest allies, the heads of state and leaders of the Western powers that have waged wars of aggression, and stand guilty both of killing thousands of innocent people—30,000 in the 2003 attack on Iraq alone—and of other crimes recognized in penal codes the world over, and which indeed carry the death penalty in the United States, have not been made to pay the price for their actions.[77] Indeed, these are precisely the people who are in practice acting as the prosecution.

Conclusion

An analogous instance of the 'dual-standard system' of international justice which punishes the crimes of *jus in bello*—war crimes and crimes against humanity, in addition to genocide—while ignoring the

---

74. See Carla del Ponte's statements to the Security Council on 2 June 2000, at www.un.org/icty/pressreal/p510-e.htm.

75. See A. Cassese, 'Il processo a Saddam e i nobili fini della giustizia', *La Repubblica*, 19 October 2005, p. 23: 'when it came to ascertaining whether NATO military personnel had committed war crimes in Serbia in 1999, the Chief Prosecutor in The Hague [Carla del Ponte] preferred to avoid opening an investigation'.

76. On this topic see M. Mandel, *How America Gets Away with Murder*, pp. 6–7.

77. The US army, for example, used napalm and white phosphorus in Iraq during the attack on Fallujah in November 2004, injuring and killing thousands of civilians. Indiscriminate use was made of white phosphorus in the various districts of the city—in the absence of any direct reporting, thanks to a news blackout imposed by the US high command. This emerges from an investigation of 'Rainews 24', 'Fallujah. La strage nascosta', conducted by the journalist Sigfrido Ranucci, featuring testimony from US ex-servicemen and footage of the phosphorus bombing raids and their effects not only on Iraqi resistance fighters but also on civilians, including women and children.

crime of aggressive war concerns of the Statute of the ICC, approved in Rome in July 1998 and in force since March 2003.[78] This Statute, unlike the statutes of the ad hoc Tribunals, includes the crime of aggression in the list of 'the most serious crimes of concern to the international community' over which the Court exercises jurisdiction (Article 5). Yet the second section of the same article provides that the Court

> shall exercise jurisdiction over the crime of aggression once a provision is adopted in accordance with articles 121 and 123 defining the crime and setting out the conditions under which the Court shall exercise jurisdiction with respect to this crime.[79]

In practice, the Statute states that the court cannot exercise jurisdiction over the crime of aggression until the assembly of nations which have ratified the Statute has adopted an amendment to the Statute itself defining the crime of aggression; and before this can happen, at least seven years must pass from the date on which the Statute comes into force.[80] It is clear that this ambiguous formulation was adopted to disguise insuperable differences of opinion concerning the 'crime of aggression' during the negotiations on the Statute of Rome.[81] On the one hand, numerous Arab and African countries were in favour of adopting the definition given in the Resolution of the UN General Assembly of 1974, if necessary in a more detailed and comprehensive formulation. On the other hand, there were nations such as the

78. See 'Statuto di Roma della Corte penale internazionale', *Rivista di studi politici internazionali* 66 (1), 1999, pp. 25–95. On this topic, see also G. Vassalli, 'Statuto di Roma. Note sull'istituzione di una Corte Penale Internazionale', ibid, pp. 9–24. Comprehensive documentation can be found on the UN website, at www.un.org/law/icc.

79. Art. 5. The Court shall exercise jurisdiction over the crime of aggression once a provision is adopted in accordance with articles 121 and 123 defining the crime and setting out the conditions under which the Court shall exercise jurisdiction with respect to this crime.

See A. Roberts and R. Guelff, eds, *Documents on the Laws of War*, Oxford: Oxford University Press, 2000, p. 673.

80. This delay is prescribed in Article 121 of the Statute of Rome.

81. See Gaja, 'Long Journey', pp. 430–2.

United States that were adamant that the Resolution was not to be taken as a normative basis for defining the crime of aggression—while yet other countries, including Germany, insisted on the need for a formulation that was technically more rigorous, above all in terms of penal guarantees.[82]

However, the most profound disagreement regarded the relative powers of the court and the UN Security Council. The United States, in opposition to the majority of the nations taking part in the negotiations, was bent on subordinating the activity of the Court with respect to the crime of aggression to the decisions of the Security Council.[83] In other words, the Court was not to carry out investigations into the responsibility of individuals for the crime of aggression without the consent of the Security Council, and specifically without a resolution declaring the existence of aggression. In practice, this would subordinate the initiatives of the Court prosecutor to the will of the permanent members of the Security Council and, in particular, to that 'Washington consensus' which, according to a tradition that admits of no exceptions, is certain to be applied in any case in relation to citizens of the United States.[84]

As is well known, this position corresponds to the general efforts made by the United States to limit the powers and autonomy of the Court, efforts that have led among other things to the 'constitutional' contamination between executive and judicial functions introduced by Article 16 of the Statute. This Article confers upon the Security Council the power to have an initiative of the Court prosecutor suspended for a year (and, since the request can be repeated indefinitely, potentially forever) if a resolution based on the provisions of Chapter VII of the UN Charter deems it to be inopportune. This Chapter enumerates the initiatives that the Security Council can undertake in reacting, either pacifically or with the use

---

82. See Cassese, *Lineamenti di diritto internazionale penale*, p. 150.

83. See P. Mori, *L'istituzionalizzazione della giurisdizione penale internazionale*, Torino: Giappichelli, 2001, pp. 57ff; W. Shabas, *An Introduction to the International Criminal Court*, Cambridge: Cambridge University Press, 2001.

84. I give the expression 'Washington consensus' a meaning which does not differ from, but is simply broader than, its common usage in international economic and financial literature—for example in J.E. Stiglitz, *Globalization and its Discontents*, New York: W.W. Norton & Co., 2002.

of force, to violations of peace and acts of aggression.[85] Not satisfied with this result, the United States has failed to ratify the Court's Statute, and has been working for years, with considerable success, to hamper its activity, in particular by exploiting both Article 16 and Article 98 of the Statute.[86]

The final outcome, as Giorgio Gaja has argued, is that the definition of a war of aggression as an international crime, which figures in Article 5 of the Statute of Rome, is destined to remain devoid of any practical significance if the ICC is not endowed with jurisdictional competence on the question. According to a realistic conception of international law, an act for which there is no operative instrument of repression cannot be considered criminal conduct.[87] In the opinion of Gaja, it is all too likely that, on the topic of wars of aggression, the ICC will go on being denied a jurisdictional power with any autonomy vis-à-vis the resolutions of the UN Security Council.[88]

A sort of magical normative transubstantiation

Finally, there is a third instance of the 'dual-standard system' of international criminal justice, concerning the relationship between the crime of aggression and territorial occupation as the outcome of that aggression. According to the prevailing internationalist doctrine, which diligently applies the discipline of 'military occupation' introduced by the Fourth Geneva Convention of 1949, the occupation of a territory constitutes a case in international law irrespective of

---

85.   See the text of Article 16:

No investigation or prosecution may be commenced or proceeded with under this Statute for a period of 12 months after the Security Council, in a resolution adopted under Chapter VII of the Charter of the United Nations, has requested the court to that effect; that request may be renewed by the Council under the same conditions.

86.   Article 98 permits a state not to hand over to the Court the citizen of another state (present on the territory of the first state and whom the Court intends to bring to trial) if a treaty exists between the two states preventing such an extradition.

87.   See Gaja, 'Long Journey', pp. 431–2.

88.   Ibid., pp. 440–1. See also W.A. Schabas, *An Introduction to the International Criminal Court*, Cambridge: Cambridge University Press, 2001, p. 31 ('there is no guarantee that its [the crime of aggression] presence in article 5.1 may only be pure symbolism').

whether the use of force that has led to the occupation is deemed legal or criminal.[89] This doctrine is derived from the so-called 'principle of effectiveness', whereby international law cannot realistically ignore the fact that force—not legality—is the principal source of its legitimation, since there is no 'supranational' authority able to exercise coercion to enforce the normative dimension of law.[90]

Thus, in particular when it comes to the law of warfare, the international legal system would be largely restricted to merely registering—and hence legitimizing—the status quo. In a strictly 'realist' perspective, international law is seen as a 'scientific', 'non-evaluative' discipline that takes account of the normative orientations introduced by each new victorious strategy adopted by the major powers. It is they who 'make' international law, while the science of international law exists to formalize the successive decisions taken by the major powers as the new 'rules of the game'. From this 'realist' perspective, it is obvious that a power that has invaded a territory using armed force and brought it under control is legitimately exercising the rights that the Fourth Geneva Convention grants to victors vis-à-vis the conquered.

Other authors, among them Benedetto Conforti,[91] have argued, on the basis of the so-called 'Stimson doctrine' and a series of pronouncements by the UN General Assembly,[92] that the principle

---

89.   On the topic of military occupation and its legal regulation, see the extensive historical and theoretical survey in J.H.W. Verzijl, *International Law in Historical Perspective*, Part IX–A, 'The Laws of War', Alphen aan den Rijn (Netherlands): Sijthoff & Noordhoff, 1978, pp. 150–64, 167–290. See also K. Nabulsi, *Traditions of War: Occupation, Resistance, and the Law*, Oxford: Oxford University Press, 1999.

90.   See Cassese, *International Law*, pp. 12–13, 46; Cassese, *Il diritto internazionale nel mondo contemporaneo*, Bologna: il Mulino, 1984, pp. 34–5.

91.   See B. Conforti, *Diritto internazionale*, Napoli: Editoriale Scientifica, 1997, pp. 199–202. In his classic *Völkerrechts* (Wien: Springer Verlag, 1957), Alfred Verdross argued that the principle of effectiveness can only operate when the normative framework of international law is being observed: 'If the principle of effectiveness were to be valid without any restrictions, this would lead to the dissolution of the whole international legal order' (p. 116). On this topic see also L. Oppenheim and L. Lauterpacht, *International Law*, 1, London: Longmans, Green & Co, 1948, pp. 142–3.

92.   The so-called 'Stimson doctrine', named after US Secretary of State H.L. Stimson, who formulated it in 1932, proposed denying recognition to territorial expansion based on violence or serious violations of international law. On the

of effectiveness is correctly invoked only if it is a question of legally recognizing a mere de facto situation such as, for example, the occupation of a territory which does not belong to or is not claimed by anybody, and is thus an international *res nullius*. In this case, the de facto situation can be recognized without force having to prevail over legality. Conforti maintains, however, that the dictum *ex facto oritur jus* ('law originating in fact') should not be extended uncritically—even though this is the direction of current international practice—to cases in which the occupation of a territory has come about in violation of Article 2 of the UN Charter, which forbids the use of force, or in violation of the principle of the self-determination of peoples.[93] This has been the case, for example, in the occupation both of Arab territories by the state of Israel in 1967, and of Namibia, the former German colony assigned to South Africa following the First World War under a mandate from the League of Nations and illegally annexed by the government of Pretoria after the Second World War.

Nowadays, the most common cases of territorial occupation are of the first type, inasmuch as they do not take into account whether the use of force leading to occupation of the territory was legal or illegal: one only has to think of the military occupation endured by countries such as Kosovo, Afghanistan, Iraq and, above all, Palestine. The occupiers are major Western powers; or military alliances, like NATO, that are hegemonized by the Western powers; or regional forces with the backing of these powers, such as Israel. In all these cases, the military occupation has been the consequence of a war of aggression—in Iraq, one of horrendous proportions—and yet this circumstance has had no bearing on the definition of the legal relationship between the occupying authorities and the population of the occupied territories. This normative incongruity derives from a historical conjuncture which has left a mark as indelible as it is legally untenable. When it came to defining the regime in occupied

question of denying recognition to territorial acquisitions made through the illegal use of force, the General Assembly of the United Nations has made several pronouncements. See B.B. Ferencz, 'Defining Aggression: Where it Stands and Where it's Going', *American Journal of International Law* 66 (3), 1972, p. 502.

93.   See Conforti, *Diritto internazionale*, pp. 200–1.

territories, the Fourth Geneva Convention had to perform a difficult balancing act between the expectations of the nations that had been subjected to military occupation in the Second World War, who saw the problem from the point of view of the victims, and the nations that, without ever having endured occupation themselves, were the occupying powers at the moment of the armistice. The latter were determined to defend the interests of the occupiers, at the expense of the populations under occupation.

The Fourth Geneva Convention, which deals in general with the protection of civilians in wartime, contains in its third part a long series of articles—Articles 47 to 78—setting out provisions concerning not only the duties of the occupying power but also, and above all, its rights. Article 64, for example, lays down that the penal laws in force in the occupied territory can be repealed or suspended if the occupying authorities regard them as a threat to their security. Moreover, the occupiers have the right to introduce new laws in order

> to maintain the orderly government of the territory, and to ensure the security of the Occupying Power, of the members and property of the occupying forces or administration, and likewise of the establishments and lines of communication used by them.[94]

Other articles specify that the occupiers can set up their own criminal courts to try subjects of the occupied territory, handing down prison sentences and, in the case of crimes such as espionage,

---

94.   Article 64 reads:

The penal laws of the occupied territory shall remain in force, with the exception that they may be repealed or suspended by the Occupying Power in cases where they constitute a threat to its security or an obstacle to the application of the present Convention.... The Occupying Power may, however, subject the population of the occupied territory to provisions which are essential to enable the Occupying Power to fulfil its obligations under the present Convention, to maintain the orderly government of the territory, and to ensure the security of the Occupying Power, of the members and property of the occupying forces or administration, and likewise of the establishments and lines of communication used by them.

The English text of the Fourth Geneva Convention can be consulted in the *Jura Gentium Journal* survey, 'War, Law and Global Order'.

sabotage of the occupier's military installations, and premeditated homicide, also the death sentence, if this is contemplated in local legislation.

Thus we are confronted by a legal process in which, through a sort of magical normative transubstantiation, the fact that the armed aggression was successful, leading to the military occupation of another people's territory, produces an automatic act of indemnity for the 'supreme crime' committed by the aggressors, and makes the effects of their aggression legitimate. This is a case of legal incoherence which no invocation of the 'principle of effectiveness' should be able to remedy or attenuate in the least, unless one adopts the dictum, redolent of a radical legal realism, of *ex iniuria jus oritur* ('law originating in injury'). This would be tantamount to negating the normative character of the international legal order, and indeed denying its juridical nature altogether. If this dictum is rejected, as it is sure to be by anyone who has been the victim of military occupation, it becomes legitimate to argue that the armed aggression which has produced the occupation is a crime, making the occupation itself illegal. And it then follows that all the conduct and actions of the aggressors during their occupation of others' territory have to be considered illegal.

At this point, not only must the intentional killing of civilians be considered criminal—so too must the voluntary or involuntary killing of any person, whether in uniform or not, and the destruction of the civil infrastructures and resources of the occupied country. Naturally, all the coercive acts, including internment, prison sentences and the death sentence, applied by the aggressor-occupiers to the occupied, should be considered illegal—all the more so if the population of the occupied territories consider the occupation to be that of an enemy, from which they intend to free themselves. Furthermore, no 'right to legitimate defence' should be granted to soldiers of the occupying forces, for the simple reason that an aggressor can lay no claim to legitimate defence: the occupier should simply be obliged to withdraw, restoring the complete liberty of those attacked and recompensing them for the destruction and death caused.[95] Finally, armed resistance against the occupying forces—once

---

95. See Mandel, *How America Gets Away with Murder*, pp. 8–9.

again, the cases of Afghanistan, Iraq and Palestine spring to mind—should be considered legitimate even when carried out by irregular forces.[96] Our analysis of the dual process of the criminalization of war—with the political and military input of the United Nations on one hand and the judicial contribution of the international criminal courts on the other—has shown how the current international legal order is incapable of making the major world powers respect rules and procedures that could render warfare less destructive and sanguinary. The legal proscription of war has not produced an organic, coherent and comprehensive normative system, able to achieve, even if imperfectly, its declared objective: that pacification of the world which the system of Westphalia was unable to ensure.

The legal discipline of the phenomenon of war that came to prevail in the course of the twentieth century displays normative flaws and deontic incongruities of such gravity as to render it unfit for disciplining and restraining, in any degree, the international use of force. In terms of the prevention and repression of the illegal use of force, current international law is an 'evanescent' legal system—to use Hersh Lauterpacht's expression—which is unable to exercise effective normative and regulative functions. The *jus contra bellum* has proved to be no more efficacious than the *jus belli*.

As we have seen, this failure is due in the first place to the hierarchical structure of the UN Security Council. The legal 'surplus value' which the powers that emerged victorious from the Second World War have awarded themselves makes them immune from the process of the criminalization of aggressive war. In the second place, the failure must be ascribed to the hostility of the major powers towards any definition of the notions of 'aggression' and 'war of aggression' that would be likely to limit their sovereignty, including the unconditioned recourse to the use of force. Moreover, in the context of international criminal justice a systematic normative

---

96. Mandel is critical of Amnesty International and Human Rights Watch because, when the attack on Iraq was launched, these organizations sent brusque warnings to all the belligerents, recalling their duty to respect international war laws, but 'no one said a word about the illegality of the war itself and the crippling criminal responsibility of the heads of state who had started it' (Mandel, *How America Gets Away with Murder*, pp. 7, 8–9).

discrimination has been made between the 'supreme crime' of a war of aggression and the crimes of *jus in bello*, prosecuted by ad hoc Tribunals on behalf of the 'justice of the victors'. On the other hand, the very reluctance of the major powers to settle on a rigorous definition of the notion of a 'war of aggression'—and their readiness to sidestep any legal restriction on their military sovereignty—is a sign of the fragility of the fundamentally centralist, hierarchical and cosmopolitan institution of the United Nations. The proclamation 'world peace through world law',[97] with its debts to both Kant and Kelsen, implying the possibility of guaranteeing global peace by relying on universalistic legal and institutional instruments made available to the major powers, has revealed the true nature of its idealistic and normative abstraction as well as—and this is the most serious point—its political ambiguity. It is what, following the political realism of Hans Morgenthau, has been called the 'cosmopolitan model of the Holy Alliance'.[98]

In addition to all this, we can entertain serious doubts as to the efficacy of international criminal justice—whether it is applied to punish the vanquished or, in a purely academic hypothesis, the victors—as an instrument of direct or indirect prevention of war, and hence of global pacification. In reality, there is no guarantee that a judicial activity that metes out even the most severely retributive and exemplary sanctions (the Hague Tribunal actually imposed prison sentences of forty-five and forty-six years, as well as life imprisonment)[99] has any effect on the macro-structural dimensions of war—i.e. on the profound motives underlying human aggressive-ness, conflict and armed violence. When so much is being made of international criminal justice, one

---

97.   So runs the title of the famous volume, G. Clark and L.B. Sohn, *World Peace through World Law*, Cambridge, MA: Harvard University Press, 1960.

98.   See Zolo, *Cosmopolis*, pp. 1–18.

99.   In March 2000 the Hague Tribunal sentenced the Croat-Bosnian general Tihomir Blaskic to forty-five years' imprisonment. In Zagabria thousands of Croats held a protest demonstration in front of the US embassy, evidently holding this country responsible for the Tribunal's repressive activity (see 'Protest in Zagreb', *International Herald Tribune*, 7 March 2000, p. 7). On appeal the sentence was most surprisingly reduced by nine years. The Serbo-Bosnian general Radislav Krstic was sentenced in the first instance to forty-six years' imprisonment, subsequently reduced to thirty-five. Several life sentences were also handed down.

would do well perhaps, with Hedley Bull, to come out strongly in favour of diplomacy, above all when implemented preventively.[100]

From the point of view of the major powers, the Security Council, the international criminal jurisdiction and the whole discipline of the law of warfare are of use if they serve to legitimize *ex post facto* the results of wars which the powers themselves had decided unilaterally to wage. The United Nations, with its plethoric bureaucracy, cohort of academic jurists and ever-increasing number of self-styled 'non-governmental organizations', operating in reality at the service of their governments, defers to the victors and their brand of justice. Modern warfare has been transformed into a global 'humanitarian' and 'preventive' war in which the major Western powers wield ever more sophisticated and uncontrollable instruments of mass destruction, which will shortly also encroach on outer space. And they do so in the name of a 'just war' against the new enemies of humanity, or 'new cannibals': those organizations of 'global terrorism' which counter the nihilism of the West's abuse of power and military superiority with their own bloody nihilism. Carl Schmitt's apocalyptic prophecy of the advent of a 'global civil war', irrespective of its controversial motivations, seems to be approaching dramatic fulfilment. And there is also confirmation for the bitter adage of Radhabinod Pal, the Indian judge at the Tokyo Tribunal who was frequently at odds with the majority of the court: 'only a lost war is a crime'.[101]

---

100.   See H. Bull, *The Anarchical Society*, pp. 162–83, which lays great emphasis on the importance of diplomacy for maintaining world order. Judicial activity that is carried out as a sort of penal counterpoint to the military contest risks producing a symbolic reinforcement of sentiments of hostility and introducing formal constraints that run counter to the traditional functions of mediation fulfilled by diplomacy, both formal and informal.

101.   See R.B. Pal, 'The Dissenting Opinion of the Member for India', in R.J. Pritchard and S. Magbanua Zaide, eds, *The Tokyo War Crimes Trial: The Comprehensive Index and Guide to the Proceedings of the International Military Tribunal for the Far East*, New York & London: Garland Publishing, 1987, vol. 21, p. 128 ('When the conduct of nations is taken into account, the law will perhaps be found to be that only a lost war is a crime').

2

HUMANITARIAN WAR

Global security

The practice of justifying aggressive war as 'humanitarian intervention' derives from documents drawn up in the highest political and
military circles in the United States from the end of the 1980s. In
August 1990, in a speech delivered in Colorado, US President George
H.W. Bush outlined a project of world pacification styled the 'new
world order'. The thrust was that, having won the last world war—
the Cold War—the United States had a duty to oversee the future
development of international order and set out the principles and
rules that were to govern it.[1]

The following year, this project was elaborated in a policy document entitled *National Security Strategy of the United States*.[2] Early
in 1992, the strategic outlines announced by the president were further
developed in another text, *Defense Planning Guidance*. This important document was drawn up by a staff of officials in the Pentagon and
State Department, presided over by the deputy secretary of defense,
Paul Wolfowitz—a leading figure in the neoconservative movement
then embarking on a long and brilliant career which was to see him

---

1. A similar attitude characterized both Woodrow Wilson and his Fourteen
Points in 1918, at the end of the First World War, and Franklin D. Roosevelt and
Winston Churchill with the Atlantic Charter of 1941, anticipating victory in the
Second. See Zolo, *Cosmopolis: Prospects for World Government*, Cambridge: Polity
Press, 1997, in particular pp. 35–8, which I draw on in this chapter.

2. See President of the United States, *National Security Strategy of the United
States*, Washington: The White House, 1991.

installed as president of the World Bank.[3] In the meantime, an extensive specialized literature was pursuing the strategic and military
implications of the notion of 'global security' that lay at the core
of these documents. The fact that the world was no longer divided
up by the traditional ideological and military barriers did not mean
that threats to peace had ceased: they had become more insidious
and widespread, requiring different means for concentrating and
deploying international power and radically new defence strategies
that could ensure security on the global scale.[4]

The strategic insights that emerge from these documents, and
from *Defense Planning Guidance* in particular, are extraordinarily
illuminating, because they anticipate the essential traits of US
foreign policy during the final decade of last century. The collapse
of the Soviet empire and the end of the Cold War were seen as
ushering in a new era in which the danger of a large-scale nuclear
war has diminished. Thus the United States had within its grasp the
'extraordinary possibility' of building a just, pacific international
system based on the values of liberty, the rule of law, democracy
and the market economy. The foundations for this new world order
were to be a system of 'global security', reflecting the ever increasing
interdependence of economic, technological and communications
factors on the planetary scale. Such a system would require the close
cooperation of the nations in the three most highly industrialized
areas on the planet: North America, Europe and Japan. In view
of the increased complexity and interdependence of international
factors, the vital interests of the industrial countries were judged

---

3.   The document, *Defense Planning Guidance for the Fiscal Years 1994–1999*,
was published by the *New York Times* on 8 March 1992. The text was subsequently
re-elaborated by Paul Wolfowitz (see *New York Times*, 26 May 1992).

4.   See, among many others, P. Wolfowitz, 'An American Perspective', in E.
Grove, ed., *Global Security: North American, European and Japanese Interdependence
in the 1990s*, London: Brassey's, 1991, pp. 19–28; R. Art, 'A Defensible Defense:
America's Grand Strategy after the Cold War', *International Security* 15 (1), 1991,
pp. 5–53; J.L. Gaddis, 'Toward the Post–Cold War World', *Foreign Affairs* 70 (2),
1991, pp. 102–22; and R.F. Helms II and R.H. Dorff, eds, *The Persian Gulf Crisis:
Power in the Post–Cold War World*, Westport/London: Praeger, 1993. For a cautious
and questioning approach to the topic of 'collective security' after the end of the Cold
War, see T.G. Weiss, ed., *Collective Security in a Changing World*, Boulder/London:
Lynne Rienner Publishers, 1993.

to be more vulnerable than ever before, in particular with respect to their unhampered and regular access to energy sources, supplies of raw materials, liberty and security of movement by sea and air, and the stability of world markets (financial markets in particular). Finally, the industrialized nations were seen to be living under the combined threats of international terrorism and the proliferation of biological, chemical and nuclear weapons.

The organization of this system of global security involved two essential strategic innovations. In the first place, now that NATO was no longer committed to opposing the Warsaw Pact countries, following the Pact's dissolution, the defensive strategy of the alliance had to be revised. Its traditional geographical framework had to be expanded so as to counter the increasing risks of international disorder which might spring up in many different regional areas.[5] In a world that was no longer divided up into two blocs, the trans-Atlantic alliance which had underwritten the US military presence in Europe needed to be recast, with new functions being allocated to its massive military resources. The new 'Atlantic entente' had to be the expression of a strategy that was protective rather than defensive, expansive rather than merely reactive, dynamic and flexible rather than static and rigid. And the emphasis on security was not to be restricted to the military sphere, but extended to include the political and economic dimensions—not least in order to control the ongoing decomposition of the Soviet empire.[6] It was on the basis of these premises, and showing remarkably rapid strategic reflexes, that United States presented a 'new strategic concept' to the NATO summit held in Rome in November 1991. In the summit's closing declaration we find explicit reference to a new vocation for NATO that goes beyond the geographical limits of its traditional competence, defined in Article 5 of its Charter, to identify the need to pay greater attention to the 'global context', rather than merely the regional context of Europe and the Atlantic.[7]

5. On this topic see the article by NATO Secretary-General Manfred Wörner, 'Global Security: The Challenge for NATO', in Grove, ed., *Global Security*, pp. 100-5.

6. See Grove, ed., *Global Security*.

7. There is a copious literature on NATO and its most recent transformations. See, in addition to the relevant works already cited, the following essays: H. Scheer, 'L'irresistibile ascesa della Nato', in T. Di Francesco, ed., *La Nato nei Balcani*,

In the second place—and this is the crucial point—the strategy of global security requires the major powers, seen as responsible for world order, to regard the old principle, sanctioned at Westphalia, of non-interference in the domestic jurisdiction of nation-states as having been superseded. They are called on to exercise and legitimize their right and duty to undertake 'humanitarian intervention' whenever force is required to solve crises within individual nations, and particularly to prevent or put an end to serious violations of human rights.

Since the 1960s, various international institutions have referred to the principle of 'humanitarian intervention' as the right of the international community to intervene on a country's national territory in order to verify violations of human rights and bring aid to the mistreated population. During Carter's presidency, the defence of human rights was officially proposed as a juridically legitimate motive for interference in a nation's domestic affairs.[8] Nonetheless, it was in the 1990s that the perspective of humanitarian intervention became the key element in the strategy of the 'new world order', making ever stronger claims to ethical and juridical legitimacy. At the same time, there was a growing tendency in the West to refer to 'international humanitarian law' rather than the 'international law of war'. The latter, as is well known, was the outcome of a long process of adaptation and secularization of the ethico-religious principles of the doctrine of the *bellum justum* elaborated in Catholic theology. The new 'international humanitarian law' is presented as legitimizing—through economic measures, interventions of 'peace-

Roma: Editori Riuniti, 1999; L. Sorel, 'Il nuovo atlantismo contro l'Europa', *Diorama letterario* 20 (5), 1999, pp. 26–9; M. Tarchi, 'La guerra della Nato e le vecchie appartenenze', in M. Cabona, ed., *'Ditelo a Sparta': Serbia ed Europa contro l'aggressione della NATO*, Genova: Graphos, 1999, pp. 213–20; S. Silvestri, *Nato: la sfida delle incertezze*, in E. Berselli et al., *La pace e la guerra*, Milano: Il Sole 24 Ore, 1999, pp. 97–116; R. Menotti, 'Che cosa resta della NATO', *Limes*, supplement to issue 1 of 1999, pp. 123–34; A. Cagiati, 'La nuova Alleanza Atlantica', *Rivista di studi politici internazionali* 66 (3) 1999, pp. 339–47. See also dossier 4 of *Limes* 1999, largely devoted to the transformation of NATO and Italy's role in the organization, with interventions by, among others, F. Fubini, A. Desiderio, C. Pelanda, F. Mini, R. Menotti and A. Nativi.

8. See N. Albala, 'Limites du droit d'ingérence', *Manière de voir* 45 (1999), pp. 82–3.

enforcement', international criminal jurisdictions—situations in which the sovereignty of states may be subordinated to the international safeguarding of human rights.[9]

The legalization of humanitarian interventions

The theoretical premise for humanitarian intervention is that the international safeguarding of human rights takes precedence over state sovereignty, and indeed over the maintenance of peace and world order. A nation's 'external sovereignty'—in common with its 'domestic sovereignty' vis-à-vis its own citizens—cannot be considered an absolute, unlimited prerogative, particularly in the context of a planetary society in which the processes of integration are making for ever greater unity and functional interdependence. When a government rides roughshod over the fundamental rights of its citizens or commits crimes against humanity, the international community has the right and obligation to intervene. The upholding of international order requires the imposition of a minimum level of respect for human rights on all states without exception, if necessary through the use of force. This also means establishing severe sanctions to be applied against those countries responsible for persecuting religious, racial or ethnic minorities, as well as for war crimes, mass murder or rape, and indeed wholesale genocide.

In the context of the strategic tenets of the 'new world order' and the doctrine of human rights, the practice of humanitarian intervention gained ground rapidly during the closing decade of the last century, thanks to the initiatives of the Western world, and of the United States and Britain in particular. The Gulf War of 1991 brought matters to a head, forcing both supporters and opponents of military action against Iraq to pay attention not only to the question of 'peace-making', but also to that of 'humanitarian intervention'. This practice was reinforced in the immediate post-war phase, thanks to the activism of the US and British governments, which undertook

---

9. See F. Lattanzi, *Assistenza umanitaria e interventi di umanità*, Turin: Giappichelli, 1997; J. Gardam, ed., *Humanitarian Law*, Brookfield: Ashgate, 1999; R. Gutman and D. Rieff, *Crimes of War*, New York: Norton, 1999.

'humanitarian interventions' in both northern and southern Iraq with the tacit consent of the United Nations. This led to a limitation of the sovereignty of the Iraqi state, with the establishment on its territory— and progressive enlargement on the basis of unilateral decisions—of no-fly zones, ostensibly to protect the Kurdish minority in the north and the Shiite minority in the south.

From 1992 to 1994 the policy of humanitarian intervention was applied without any normative reference, ignoring even the UN Charter. The intervention of the United States, with some allies, in Somalia was initially motivated by the need to guarantee aid in the form of food and health provisions, but rapidly turned into a bloody military conflict whose aims became further and further removed from the institutional purposes of the United Nations, until they came to coincide with the interests of powerful oil companies. No less ambiguous, and tragically controversial, were the prospects, over many months, for an analogous 'humanitarian' intervention on the territory of the former Yugoslavia. In the end, the mission was in practice taken over by NATO forces. This organization, engendered during the Cold War, was made to seem like the military emanation of the United Nations, rather than a politico-military structure designed to safeguard the more or less legitimate interests of Western nations. NATO's military activity on the territory of the former Yugoslavia during the Bosnian war (1992–95) and above all the war for Kosovo (1999) became increasingly intrusive, with the tacit assent of the United Nations. The latter war definitively sanctioned the practice of humanitarian intervention, taking in the most explicit way possible the humanitarian motivation as *justa causa* for a war of aggression. In this case, it was argued that the use of international force for humanitarian motives was legitimate in opposition not only to the principle of non-interference in the domestic jurisdiction of a sovereign state, but also the UN Charter, the principles of the statute and sentence of the Nuremberg Tribunal, and indeed international customary law.[10]

Confronted by such a palpable eversion of international law, the United Nations did next to nothing, giving proof of its subordination to, if not patent complicity with, the Western powers. A

---

10.   See D. Zolo, *Invoking Humanity: War, Law and Global Order*, London: Continuum, 2002, in particular Chapter 3, pp. 66–98.

resolution censuring NATO's military intervention, presented to the Security Council by Russia, India and Belarus, was naturally rejected by the three Western powers holding the power of veto: the United States, Britain and France. Only three of the fifteen Council members—Russia, China and Namibia—dared to manifest their dissent by voting in favour. So it was that governments representing over two-thirds of the world's population could find no instrument of 'international democracy' able to give effective expression to their opposition to a 'humanitarian war'.

After a lengthy silence, UN Secretary-General Kofi Annan finally made a statement in which he endorsed the line of the United States (which, as everybody knew, had been instrumental in getting him elected as secretary-general). He had no qualms about declaring that, in instances of systematic and large-scale violation of human rights, humanitarian intervention could be pursued disregarding the principle of respect for states' sovereignty and non-interference in their domestic affairs. Indeed, addressing the General Assembly on 20 September 1999, Annan went so far as to justify the military intervention of NATO, in the absence of a mandate from the Security Council, in terms of a 'state of necessity'. He presented the use of force as the lesser evil in light of the risk of genocide resulting from the inertia of the international community. And, rather than make a stand for the institutional prerogatives of the United Nations as involving an absolute monopoly over the legitimate use of international force, as should have been his elementary duty, Kofi Annan insisted on the primacy of the protection of human rights and on the declining function of nation-states in the era of globalization.[11] In practice, the United Nations, through the mouthpiece of its secretary-general, legitimized a war of aggression simply because the aggressors presented it as 'humanitarian war'.

And what part did the Hague Court of Justice—the supreme judicial organ of the United Nations—play in all this? As is well known, this Court is not even endowed with an obligatory jurisdiction. It only had to declare its incompetence in order to reject the appeal presented by the Yugoslav Federation against the ten NATO countries that

---

11. See B. Guetta, 'Quando l'Onu mostra i muscoli', *La Repubblica*, 2 November 1999.

took part in the military attack.[12] Similarly, the International
Criminal Tribunal for the former Yugoslavia, created by the Security
Council at the instigation of the United States, declined to intervene
to censure the aggression being carried out by the NATO countries,
since it had no specific competence to judge crimes against peace. Its
statute, unlike that of the Nuremberg Tribunal, gave it competence
to judge only crimes of *jus in bello*— meaning war crimes, crimes
against humanity and genocide.[13]

The theoretical debate

Thus we see how the leading international institutions, starting with
the Security Council and General Secretariat of the United Nations,
have endorsed or legitimized a posteriori the 'humanitarian break-
through' imposed by the major Western power without raising the
slightest objection as to questions of principle—indeed conferring
upon it full international legality. And yet the case for considering
the safeguarding of human rights as prevailing over the integrity of
states' domestic jurisdiction, such as to justify the use of force, is
by no means proven. Doubt persists in situations where the use of
force has been authorized by the international institutions, and all
the more acutely in those where it has not been authorized, as was
the case in the 1999 war for Kosovo. In this instance, the humanitarian motivation was invoked as sufficient grounds for ethical and
juridical legitimation of the use of force, even outside the terms of
the United Nations Charter and international customary law.

The fourth section of Article 2 of the Charter obliges member
states to refrain from threatening or using force against the territorial integrity and political independence of any nation. There is
only one general exception to this prohibition: force can be used if
the Security Council, having ascertained the existence of a threat to
peace, a breach of peace or an act of aggression, decides that it is

---

12. For a comment on the decision of the International Criminal Court see
P.H.F. Bekker, 'Legality of Use of Force: Yugoslavia versus United States et al.',
Americam Journal of International Law 93 (4), 1999, pp. 925ff.

13. On the International Criminal Tribunal for the former Yugoslavia, see
Zolo, *Invoking Humanity*, pp. 99–132.

necessary, under its direction and control, to have recourse to force in order to re-establish international order (Articles 39 and 42). This general exception is accompanied by a more specific one: the right of a country to react in self-defence if attacked by another state or group of states (Article 51).

Some authors refuse to recognize the existence of a customary norm which, in contrast with the UN Charter and international and general law, confers on the Security Council the power to authorize the use of force in situations of humanitarian emergency.[14] A customary norm of this type should emerge from states' uniform behaviour and the general conviction that this practice is legal. However, the practice is not in the least uniform from the point of view of the sanctions imposed. In some cases, as for example in Somalia in 1992, there has been recourse to armed intervention; in others, such as Chechnya, it was considered sufficient to rely on a diplomatic measure, in the form of a (Platonic) censuring of the authorities in Moscow; in yet other cases—including the bloody repression of the Kurdish minority by Turkey—there was simply no reaction on the part of the international community. What is more, it is emphasized that even mere humanitarian assistance (provision of foodstuffs, medicines, aid workers, and so on) requires the agreement of the country intended to benefit from the aid. And such consent is also required, as should be common knowledge, for peace-keeping operations, to which, on occasion, 'humanitarian interventions' have been mistakenly assimilated, in particular during the 1992–95 war in Bosnia-Herzegovina.[15]

---

14. See, in this connection, B. Simma, 'NATO, the UN and the Use of Force: Legal Aspects', *European Journal of International Law* 10 (1), 1999; E. Garzón Valdés, 'Guerra e diritti umani', *Ragion pratica* 7 (13), 1999, pp. 25–49; M. Spinedi, 'Uso della forza da parte della NATO in Jugoslavia e diritto internazionale', *Quaderni Forum* 12 (3), 1998, pp. 23–31. In Simma's opinion,

> In contemporary international law, as codified in the 1969 Vienna Convention on the Law of Treaties (Articles 53 and 64), the prohibition enunciated in Article 2(4) of the Charter is part of *jus cogens*, i.e. it is accepted and recognized by the international community of states as a whole as a norm from which no derogation is permitted' (p. 3).

15. See C. Pinelli, 'Sul fondamento degli interventi armati a fini umanitari', in G. Cotturri, ed., *Guerra—individuo*, Milano: Angeli, 1999, p. 88; U. Villani, 'La guerra del Kosovo: una guerra umanitaria o un crimine internazionale?', *Volontari e*

We can add that, according to the International Court of Justice—
witness the famous sentence of 1986 concerning Nicaragua—the
ban on the use of force is part of international and customary law,
and violations of human rights do not justify armed intervention by
foreign countries in order to put a stop to them.[16]

With respect to the second argument—the legitimacy of the use
of force on humanitarian grounds even without the authorization
of the Security Council—the case in its favour has been argued by
Antonio Cassese, ex-president of the Hague Tribunal, with reference
to the war for Kosovo.[17] Cassese declared forcefully that NATO had
committed a serious breach of the UN Charter in making war on the
Yugoslav Federal Republic in the absence of the legal premises. And
yet he maintained that the state that had suffered the aggression—the
Yugoslav Federal Republic—was not deserving of any international
solidarity, nor any legal compensation. The use of force by NATO
was legitimate, although in breach of the UN Charter. The episode
of the war for Kosovo stands as proof, Cassese has written, that 'a
new legitimation is being created in international law for the use of
force'.[18] In his opinion, the attack was not an act of aggression, but
the first act of a legal international custom *in fieri*. In other words,
in the international community there is a normative tendency to
consider the use of force legitimate, even without a prior mandate
from the Security Council, when it is a case of putting a stop to
serious human rights violations.

Viewed in this light, NATO's military intervention acquired

---

terzo mondo 1–2, 1999, pp. 26–38.

16. See Spinedi, 'Uso della forza', pp. 23, 26–7.

17. See A. Cassese, '*Ex iniuria ius oritur*: Are We Moving towards International
Legitimation of Forcible Humanitarian Countermeasures in the World Community?',
European Journal of International Law 10 (1), 1999, pp. 23–5. Different opinions
have been expressed by such authors as B. Simma, 'NATO, the UN and the Use of
Force', pp. 1–6; C.M. Chinkin, 'Kosovo: A 'Good' or 'Bad' War?', *American Journal
of International Law* 93 (4), 1999, pp. 841–7; P. De Sena, 'Uso della forza a fini
umanitari, intervento in Jugoslavia e diritto internazionale', *Ragion pratica*, 7 (13),
1999, pp. 141–65; U. Villani, 'La guerra del Kosovo', pp. 30–1; Spinedi, 'Uso della
forza', pp. 30–1.

18. See A. Cassese, 'Le cinque regole per una guerra giusta', in U. Beck, N.
Bobbio, A. Cassese and D Zolo, eds, *L'ultima crociata? Ragioni e torti di una guerra
giusta*, Roma: I libri di Reset, 1999, p. 28.

not only ethical and humanitarian, but also legal legitimacy, as the expression of a sort of 'instant custom'. More generally, in the closing years of the last century, the hope, expressed by the German jurist Bruno Simma,[19] that NATO's breach of the UN Charter would remain an isolated case, was widely seen as misplaced. Any approach based on the belief that the Westphalian principle of respect for states' sovereignty would not be violated by the major powers was seen not just as unproductive, but as narrowly conservative and founded on wishful thinking. International law had to be brought up to date. The duty of jurists was not to oppose the current 'humanitarian' trend but rather to set out the conditions under which such a trend could give rise to an international legal regime capable of formulating a new framework for the legitimate use of force subject to general rules.[20]

This thesis can be—and has been—disputed on the basis that the doctrine of humanitarian war elaborated by Cassese offers no legal grounds for legitimizing a posteriori NATO's attack on the Yugoslav Republic, unless one intends to invoke the maxim *ex iniuria oritur ius*—which, as Norberto Bobbio was quick to observe, would in effect do away with the international rule of law.[21] The novelty of Cassese's doctrinal elaboration lies precisely in his demonstration that, prior to the NATO intervention, there was no customary trend in the international community to legitimize the use of force on

---

19. See B. Simma, 'NATO, the UN and the Use of Force'.

20. See A. Cassese, 'Zolo sbaglia, il diritto va aggiornato', in U. Beck et al., eds, *L'ultima crociata?*, pp. 34–8. Cassese set out to define the new 'humanitarian' claim of the legitimate use of force without the authorization of the Security Council. Deducing them from events in Kosovo, Cassese enumerates six conditions: 1. Highly serious violations of human rights take place within a state; 2. The impossibility or lack of will of the state to put a stop to the violations has been ascertained; 3. The Security Council is not able to undertake military intervention because of internal opposition; 4. Every possible peaceful solution has been tried; 5. The use of force has been decided upon by a group of states and the majority of the member-states of the United Nations are in favour; 6. The use of force must have limited objectives (see Cassese, '*Ex iniuria ius oritur*', p. 27). For a critique of this position, see my 'Il diritto internazionale e il Tribunale dell'Aia', in Cabona, ed., '*Ditelo a Sparta*', pp. 226–9.

21. See N. Bobbio, 'Perché questa guerra ricorda una crociata', interview by G. Bosetti, in U. Beck et al., eds, *L'ultima crociata?*, pp. 18–19. The topic was pursued by T. Mazzarese, 'Guerra e diritti: tra etica e retorica', *Ragion pratica* 7 (13), 1999, pp. 13–23.

humanitarian grounds without a Security Council mandate. Indeed, as I pointed out above, it cannot be maintained that there was a customary trend to legitimize the use of force on humanitarian grounds *even with* the authorization of the Security Council. In addition, one cannot simply ignore—unless one intends to identify the international community with the nineteen NATO member countries that went to war with the Yugoslav Republic—the dissent of countries with the demographic and political clout of Russia, India and China.

Nor does it appear that any factors have come to light since then suggesting that an indirect normative effect of NATO's 'humanitarian intervention' has been to inaugurate a new international custom—as Cassese himself, with commendable honesty, has recognized.[22] If we can speak of a current trend, we seem to be heading for a definitive abandonment of the monopoly on the legitimate use of force assigned to the UN Security Council. From now on, military force is to be directly deployed by alliances or individual states in order to safeguard collective interests, obviously according to each state's interpretation of those interests. In fact, the tendency is for a return to the 'anarchic' situation that preceded the foundation of the League of Nations and the United Nations during last century, with the likelihood of the major powers once again claiming legitimacy for their resort to force.[23] At least in the eighteenth and nineteenth centuries this claim, as Carl Schmitt showed, was subject to the formal limits and procedures set out in the European *jus publicum*.[24]

The universal safeguarding of subjective rights

The theoretical assumption underlying the doctrine of humanitarian intervention, as I have mentioned, is that safeguarding human rights has to be considered a principle of the international legal order that takes priority over state sovereignty. In both the institutional and the strictly legal domain, it is a question of replacing the

---

22. See A. Cassese, 'A Follow-Up: Forcible Humanitarian Countermeasures and *Opinio Necessitatis*', *European Journal of International Law* 10 (4), 1999, pp. 791–9.

23. See Spinedi, 'Uso della forza', pp. 30–1.

24. See C. Schmitt, *The Nomos of the Earth in the International Law of the Jus Publicum Europaeum*, New York: Telos Press Publishing, 2006, pp. 140–71.

goal of keeping the peace, which is at the core of the UN Charter, with the 'humanitarian' objective of the defence of human rights.

This functional transformation has implications of considerable theoretical significance: a criterion which is in principle universalistic—defence of the rights of all the members of the human race, irrespective of citizenship, cultural identity, religious beliefs, and so on—is supposed to supersede the particularistic principle of the sovereignty of states and the inviolability of their borders. This principle, which goes back to seventeenth-century Europe and the peace treaties of Westphalia, has been at the centre of the formation of international law, and indeed the development of the modern European state. It was reaffirmed during the last century by a long series of conventions and treaties, as well as in the Covenant of the League of Nations. In general it was also confirmed by the UN Charter, in its declaration in Article 2 of the 'sovereign equality of all its Members'.[25]

While the goal of the maintenance of peace and the international order is wholly compatible with the particularistic principle of the sovereignty of nation-states, the humanitarian objective tends instead to negate the sovereignty of states at its very roots in the name of a universalistic—or cosmopolitan—conception of international law and institutions. The humanitarian ideology, if taken at all seriously, requires that the current international order, until now based on the particularism of intergovernmental relations, should be transformed into a 'global humanitarian regime'. It implies, as its ultimate goal, a sort of *civitas maxima* which is politically unified and, in Habermas's Kantian aspiration, informed by a 'cosmopolitan law' (*Weltbürgerrecht*) which identifies as subjects of international law all human individuals, rather than states or states alone.[26]

The clash between these two philosophical options—universalism

---

25. On the notion of 'sovereign equality' and its ambiguity, see A. Cassese, *International Law in a Divided World*, Oxford: Oxford University Press, 1986; W. Levi, *Law and Politics in International Society*, Beverly Hills: Sage Publications, 1976, pp. 121–33.

26. See J. Habermas, 'Kants Idee des ewigen Friedens—aus dem historischen Abstand von 200 Jahren', *Kritische Justiz* 28, 1995, pp. 293–319, now in J. Habermas, *Die Einbeziehung des Anderen*, Frankfurt: Suhrkamp, 1996; J. Habermas, 'Bestialität und Humanität. Ein Krieg an der Grenze zwischen Recht und Moral', *Die Zeit* 18 (1999).

versus particularism—throws up some delicate problems of a general nature which merit careful thought. In the first place, the move towards a universalistic doctrine does not seem to be compatible with the current state of international law and institutions. The United Nations lacks a universal dimension for the simple reason that it was conceived and structured by the powers that emerged victorious from the Second World War to guarantee the newly founded world order (involving their own hegemony), rather than to promote or protect any universal values. It is the will of the governments of the member-states—not a world public opinion guided by a universal ethic—that gives legitimacy to the United Nations' decisions. Moreover, not only is the United Nations grounded in the particularistic will of the governments—be they democratic, despotic or totalitarian—of its member-states (rather than in the direct representation of 'the citizens of the world'); it is also characterized by the extreme particularism of the discrimination between permanent and non-permanent members of the Security Council. Even more crucially, the five permanent Council members hold the power of veto. In short, the international safeguarding of human rights is incompatible—on account of the necessary intervention in states' domestic affairs which it implies—with the sovereignty of nation-states and the principle of the self-determination of peoples. And it is even more incompatible with the hierarchical decision-making procedures of the United Nations.

This, surely, is the paradox that explains why the United Nations is currently at an impasse. The attempt to render it truly democratic and universalistic in the pursuit of a humanitarian goal—fostered by Secretary-General Kofi Annan—would mean a radical transformation of its structure, which is in practice an impossibility: to understand this, one has only to consider the repeated failures of projects of reform, the most recent being officially sponsored by Kofi Annan himself in March 2005.[27] At the same time, maintaining the

27. In March 2005 Kofi Annan placed before the UN General Assembly an appeal for reform of the United Nations entitled *In Larger Freedom*, which came to nothing. One of the proposals advanced by Kofi Annan and the sixteen members of the High-Level Panel he had appointed was that legitimacy of the use of force by the Security Council should also include the so-called 'collective international responsibility to protect'. The proposal aimed to legitimize the form of 'humanitarian

current format—starting with the right of veto for the permanent members of the Security Council—means definitively isolating it from the international arena and leaving it completely at the mercy of the Western powers, and above all of the United States. Following the end of the Cold War and the defeat of the Communist bloc, the US superpower continues to exercise the privilege of its veto in the Security Council, but no longer recognizes the veto of other powers.

Moreover, in the context of humanitarian intervention, a role of great symbolic as well as political and juridical significance has been played by the new international criminal courts. As is well known, fifty years on from the controversial experience of the Nuremberg and Tokyo Tribunals, the UN Security Council decided to set up two International Tribunals to deal with serious violations of international and humanitarian law, one for the former Yugoslavia and the other for Rwanda. The impetus for the institution of these courts came from the Western nations, and in particular the United States and Britain. As a result, alongside military limitations of states' sovereignty, judicial limitations of such sovereignty have been introduced by imposing the jurisdictional primacy of the international courts over the domestic criminal jurisdiction of the states involved.

Here, too, we can identify some delicate problems of a general nature, over and above the controversy concerning the international legality of the two special courts created by the Security Council and the contested doctrine of its 'implicit powers'.[28] The first problem concerns the function and autonomy of these international judicial institutions: not only were they created ad hoc—in violation of an elementary principle of the rule of law—but they operate in

---

war' carried out by the United States in Somalia, Haiti and the Balkans. See D. Zolo, 'Riformare le Nazioni Unite?', in G. Gozzi and G. Bongiovanni, eds, *Popoli e civiltà. Il pluralismo dei sistemi giuridici e le trasformazioni del diritto internazionale*, Bologna: Il Mulino, 2006.

28.   See G. Arangio-Ruitz, 'The Establishment of the International Criminal Tribunal for the Former Territory of Yugoslavia and the Doctrine of the Implied Powers of the United Nations', in F. Lattanzi, and E. Sciso, eds, *Dai Tribunali Penali Internazionali ad hoc ad una Corte permanente*, Napoli: Editoriale Scientifica, 1995; A. Bernardini, 'Il Tribunale penale internazionale per la ex Jugoslavia', *I diritti dell'uomo* 21 (1993), pp. 15–25; P. Palchetti, 'Il potere del Consiglio di Sicurezza di istituire il Tribunale Penale Internazionale', *Rivista di diritto internazionale* 79 (2) 1996 , pp. 143ff.

the absence of any context of international institutions that could represent the constitutional structure of a *Rechtsstaat*. Removed from such a context, the jurisdiction of these courts—in particular the powers of the chief prosecutor—appears excessively discretionary, and at the same time apt to play to the political aspirations of the powers that were instrumental in creating them. These powers are ready to provide military assistance, carrying out functions of criminal investigation on the court's behalf, and to finance them with suspicious munificence.[29] Here, too, universalism—meaning the neutrality and impartiality of the judicial function—collides with the particularistic origins of these institutions and their political dependence on the will of the major powers. Incidentally, in the case of Yugoslavia, those powers were engaged in a victorious military conflict in the very region of the Hague Court's territorial competence.

Then again, one must surely question the quality and efficacy as a deterrent of a criminal jurisdiction that operates according to highly discretionary criteria of selectivity, ignoring the equality of subjects in law; that systematically violates the principle *nulla culpa sine judicio*; and that ends by staging 'exemplary' trials, which often come down to ceremonies in which the accused are morally degraded, in a spirit of victimization and immolation that has precious little to do with a modern conception of criminal justice.[30]

Finally, we must ask ourselves whether modern warfare, with its weapons of mass destruction, can coherently be used by international institutions—or military alliances such as NATO—charged with protecting universal values like human rights. Here we are confronted by a true aporia: maintaining that all individuals are subjects of the international legal order, and are thus invested with inviolable and inalienable rights, means attributing to them first and foremost the right to life, recognised by Article 3 of the 1948 Universal Declaration of Human Rights. In the second place— again as laid down in the Declaration—they must be assured of the

---

29. See Zolo, *Invoking Humanity*, Chapter 4, pp. 99–132.

30. Hedley Bull was the first commentator to criticize these aspects of international criminal justice. See H. Bull, *The Anarchical Society*, London: Macmillan, 1977, p. 89.

fundamental rights of habeas corpus: nobody can be subjected to treatment which may harm their physical integrity, liberty, affective relationships or property, unless they have been found guilty of behaviour which was consciously in breach of the penal laws. Such a finding requires judicial procedures to be observed 'in a fair and public hearing by an independent and impartial tribunal'. Finally, Article 7 of the Declaration of Human Rights sanctions the right of all human beings to equal treatment before the law.

The legitimation of 'humanitarian war' is the equivalent of a contradictory negation of all these principles. In the case of the war for Kosovo, for example, in practice the death sentence was enforced on thousands of Yugoslav citizens, in the absence of any investigation of their personal responsibility. And the principle of equal treatment before the law was also violated: it should not be forgotten that in the former Yugoslavia the alleged humanitarian safeguarding of human rights was pursued simultaneously using two approaches that were mutually incompatible. The Hague Court applied the principle by which no one can be subjected to penal sanctions unless found responsible for crimes committed in person and knowingly. What is more, the statute of the Hague Court excludes the death sentence from the list of punishments it can inflict. This treatment, which does at least formally respect some important principles of the rule of law, was accorded to a tiny minority of citizens of the former Yugoslavia, often high-ranking members of the political or military hierarchy, accused of international wrongdoing. In contrast, thousands of simple citizens received very different treatment: lethal bombing raids, in which, as we have noted, murderous cluster bombs and depleted uranium missiles were also deployed.

One final theoretical question to have re-emerged forcefully with the practice of humanitarian intervention concerns the thesis, much in vogue among Western nations, of the universality of human rights, and hence of their universal and compulsory applicability. However, in the contemporary world this universality is highly controversial, both within and beyond the West.[31] The dispute relates in particular

---

31. See N. Bobbio, *L'età dei diritti*, Turin: Einaudi, 1990; L. Baccelli, *Il particolarismo dei diritti*, Rome: Carocci, 1999.

to the relationship between the individualistic philosophy underlying the Western doctrine of human rights and the broad spectrum of civilizations and cultures endowed with very different values. In that category, one can think, in particular, of countries in south-eastern and north-eastern Asia, with their predominantly Confucian culture, or sub-Saharan Africa, as well as, of course, the Islamic world.

In this respect, the dissension that characterized the second UN Conference on Human Rights, held in Vienna in June 1993, was very illuminating. On that occasion, two opposing conceptions came face to face: on one hand there was the Western doctrine of the universality and indivisibility of human rights, and on the other the positions of many countries in Latin America and Asia, with China in the vanguard. The latter nations insisted on the priority, in terms of human rights, of socio-economic development, the battle against poverty, and the release of Third World countries from the burden of international debt. They accused Western countries of seeking to use the ideology of humanitarian intervention to impose on the whole of humankind their economic supremacy, political system and world-view.

No less emblematic was the polemic that erupted in Singapore in April 1993 and led to the Bangkok Declaration concerning the affirmation of Asian values—order, social harmony, respect for authority, the family—in the face of the West's tendency to impose on Oriental cultures its own ethico-political values, together with science, technology and industry. The 'individualistic' doctrine of human rights was held to be in contrast with the ethos of Asiatic traditions, as well as of the ancient African and American cultures.[32] More than twenty years ago, Hedley Bull was indeed perspicacious in arguing that the Western ideology of humanitarian intervention to safeguard human rights lay firmly in the tradition of the West's 'civilizing mission'.[33]

---

32. On this topic see M.C. Davis, ed., *Human Rights and Chinese Values: Legal, Philosophical and Political Perspectives*, New York: Columbia University Press, 1995; W.T. de Bary and T. Weiming, eds, *Confucianism and Human Rights*, New York: Columbia University Press, 1998; E. Vitale, "Valori asiatici' e diritti umani', *Teoria politica* 15 (2–3), 1999, pp. 313–24; M. Bovero, 'Idiópolis', *Ragion pratica* 7 (13), 1999, pp. 101–6.

33. As Bull pointed out, this is a tradition which goes back to the beginning of the nineteenth century, when North Americans carried out military interventions in

There can be no doubt that there is a need today for the subjective rights of individuals to be safeguarded on the international—and not just national—scale, however illusory it is to think of setting up a sort of cosmopolitan *Rechtsstaat* designed to transcend the structures of nation-states. The challenge is to make the transnational interventions safeguarding subjective rights compatible with the diversity of cultures, with the identity and dignity of peoples, and with the integrity of the juridico-political structures with which they have endowed themselves. From this perspective, one can give no credit to the ambition of individual powers or military alliances such as NATO to set themselves up, in blatant violation of international law, as the custodians of human rights viewed as universal values, and hence to be safeguarded irrespective of states' domestic jurisdiction. And surely one must denounce as mere bluff their recourse to a humanitarian motivation to justify not only their wars of aggression but also the creation of international ad hoc criminal courts operating under their close supervision.

The affirmation of the humanitarian militarism of the United States and its closest allies has led to a genuine collapse of the international legal order, recognisable as both cause and consequence of the paralysis of the United Nations. *Rebus sic stantibus*, it is no exaggeration to speak of the failure of that 'juridical pacifism' which from Kant to Hans Kelsen, Norberto Bobbio and Jürgen Habermas has upheld international law and institutions as the chief—if not indeed the only—means for achieving peace and safeguarding fundamental human rights. Kelsen's formula 'peace through law' has come to be seen as an illusion redolent of the Age of Enlightenment, with its normative optimism and ingenuous cosmopolitan universalism. From the end of the Cold War to the present, the Western powers have not only made arbitrary use of military force, but have explicitly contested the international legal order in the name of their own unconditioned *jus ad bellum*. And this starkly negative record has to be seen as including also international criminal jurisdiction, the institutional innovation of the twentieth century. In the context of

---

Cuba and Europeans in the Ottoman Empire. See H. Bull, 'Human Rights and World Politics', in R. Pettman, ed., *Moral Claims in World Affairs*, London: Croom Helm, 1978, p. 81.

an ever-increasing concentration of international power, which is leading to something all too like an imperial world constitution, an international criminal court cannot but be a partisan instrument in the hands of the major powers. It is bound to exercise 'victors' justice'. Should it seek to avoid this role, as has been the case for the Hague International Criminal Court, its fate is sealed.

3

THE UNIVERSALITY OF RIGHTS
AND HUMANITARIAN WAR

Michael Ignatieff delivered his Tanner Lectures[1] on human rights at Princeton University in 2000—one year, that is, after the end of NATO's 'humanitarian war' against the Federal Republic of Yugoslavia, and one year before the terrorist attacks of 11 September 2001 that led to a series of preemptive wars by the United States against the 'axis of evil' (the attack on the Twin Towers, in fact, took place not far from the prestigious university in New Jersey that hosts these lectures). Thus an eminent Anglo-Saxon author took his stand on issues crucial to world order in highly dramatic circumstances, and this should be borne in mind in assessing the political as well as the theoretical significance of his lectures. This is the context in which I propose to discuss Ignatieff's treatment of 'humanitarian war'—meaning the legitimacy of the military interventions under-taken by the major Western powers to safeguard human rights. He essentially set out four theses:

1. The Western doctrine of human rights is meeting with exceptional success throughout the world, and not only in the West.
2. A rigorous approach to human rights recognizes that they do not address every legitimate expectation of human beings,

---

1. Now published in M. Ignatieff, *Human Rights as Politics and Idolatry*, Princeton: Princeton University Press, 2001.

but only those related to 'negative liberty'. The defence of
rights guarantees all individuals the capacity to act freely in
order to achieve rational goals. The basic premise underlying
the doctrine of human rights is political individualism and
the related primacy of individual rights, with respect not
only to social solidarity and political loyalty, but also to the
so-called 'collective rights', including the independence of
the nation of which the individual is a subject.

3. The doctrine of human rights, identified with the safeguarding of 'negative liberty', can justly lay claim to
   humanitarian universality. This gives it 'validity' beyond the
   sphere of Western culture and enables it to be legitimately
   proposed to civilizations and cultures around the world.

4. At present the universality of human rights is not matched
   by their universal defence worldwide, since it creates tension
   with the particularism of nation-states and the inviolability
   of their frontiers. Yet state sovereignty, even if inalienable in
   principle, cannot prevent military power from being used
   in certain instances to enforce the respect of human rights
   within a state's own borders, as occurred, legitimately, in
   Bosnia-Herzegovina, Kosovo and Iraq.

In the four sections that follow I offer a critical commentary on each
of these theses in turn.

Humanitarian fundamentalism

Ignatieff argues that the doctrine of human rights enjoys global
success even though it does not have a solid epistemological and
deontological grounding. This thesis is undoubtedly the original and
interesting feature of his Tanner Lectures. The most authoritative
international documents—see for example the European Union's
recent Charter of Fundamental Rights—take it for granted that the
so-called 'fundamental rights' can claim the prerogative of 'indivisibility and universality'.[2] This formula, officially introduced at the

---

2. For a critical evaluation of the 'Nice Charter', see D. Zolo 'Una 'pietra
miliare'?', *Diritto pubblico* 3, 2001, pp. 1,011–30.

UN Conference on Human Rights held in Vienna in 1993, has since been used polemically in the West against non-Western cultures—in particular those of Islamic, Hindu and Chinese–Confucian origin.[3] For the representatives of these cultures, human rights are closely bound up with the rational cornerstones of Western culture, as well as with the juridical formalism, individualism and liberalism that characterize the West.

On the theoretical level, there are authors following in Kant's footsteps, such as Jürgen Habermas and John Rawls, who maintain that human rights can be supplied with a rigorous cognitive and normative grounding. This means that they can be proposed to all humankind without falling into any form of cultural imperialism. For Habermas, the theory of human rights is to be interpreted as a distillation of the moral intuitions gradually accumulated by the universalistic religions and great metaphysical philosophies in the course of human history, making them a set of norms which can lay claim to a transcendental universality that goes well beyond the historical and cultural evolution of the West.[4]

Ignatieff takes issue with this 'secular religion', dismissing it as nothing other than a self-referential idolatry in which, he writes, humanism ends up by venerating itself. He maintains that the doctrine of human rights has its roots in Western tradition, and that it emerged in a particular historical period following violent social and political conflicts. Human rights did not establish themselves, as the disciples of Kant appear to believe, through the ecumenical convergence of irenic philosophies, or processes of ethical sublimation of political conflict and clashing social interests. For Ignatieff

---

3. In Vienna the thesis of the indivisibility and universality of rights was used by Western nations to counter the insistence of a large number of Asian and Latin American countries that 'collective rights' should take priority over individual rights.

4. John Rawls talks of an *overlapping consensus* as the basis for the pacific coexistence of humankind. In endorsing this position, Habermas asserts that the essential content of the moral principles embodied in international law is coherent with the normative substance of the great prophetic doctrines and metaphysical interpretations that have emerged in universal history. (J. Habermas, *Vergangenheit als Zukunft*, Zürich: Pendo Verlag, 1990). See also J. Habermas, 'Kants Idee des ewigen Friedens—aus dem historischen Abstand von 200 Jahren', *Kritische Justiz* 28, 1995, p. 307 (now also in J. Habermas, *Die Einbeziehung des Anderen*, Frankfurt: Suhrkamp Verlag, 1996).

there are no rational arguments that can demonstrate the universality of the doctrine of human rights if this is seen as a general
theory of justice and the 'good life': categories such as natural law,
or the religious ideas of creationism, or indeed the intrinsic moral
quality of the human person, are, to his way of thinking, 'idolatrous'
assumptions devoid of any rational grounding.[5]

Moreover, it is an illusion to think of the catalogue of human
rights as a unitary, coherent system of normative principles:
the fervid human rights activists who have taken the Universal
Declaration of 1948 as their ideological banner are simply not
aware of the profound tensions running through charters of 'fundamental rights'. The right of liberty and the right of property, for
example, are in conflict with social rights, based on the value of
equality, while the right to security poses an ever greater threat to the
right to privacy. And we could add that economic rights are at odds
with safeguarding the environment, while private ownership of the
mass media endangers citizens' intellectual integrity, in particular
in the case of minors. The idea that rights can operate, in Ronald
Dworkin's expression, as 'trump cards' in solving political conflicts
is ingenuous and false, because referring to rights often exacerbates
tensions rather than resolving them, in particular when the rights
themselves are mutually incompatible.[6]

Thus Ignatieff re-proposes some of the theses that the authoritative if lone voice of Norberto Bobbio has been propounding for
decades in Italy. In Bobbio's view, the doctrine of human rights
lacks both analytical precision and philosophical foundation.[7] The
rights listed in Western bills of rights have historically been subject
to continuous revision, are worded using inaccurate and semantically
ambiguous terms, are heterogeneous in nature and, above all, are
littered with deontic antinomies that frustrate any attempt to give
them an organic, consistent basis: 'rights that are fundamental
but antinomic cannot, none of them, have absolute foundations,

---

5. Ignatieff, *Human Rights*, pp. 53–4.

6. Ibid., p. 20.

7. See N. Bobbio, *L'età dei diritti*, Turin: Einaudi, 1990, pp. 5–16. Niklas
Luhmann is also sceptical concerning the universality of human rights. See N.
Luhmann, *Grundrechte als Institution*, Berlin: Dunker & Humblot, 1965. More
generally, see L. Baccelli, *Il particolarismo dei diritti*, Rome: Carocci, 1999.

foundations that make both a right and its opposite indisputable and inexorable'.[8]

As further support for these theses of both Ignatieff and Bobbio, we might add that the doctrine of human rights seems to lack criteria—to use a systemic lexicon—of cognitive self-regulation and self-planning. There is no question of being able to formulate conceptual maps to identify, define and catalogue rights in a precise fashion. While the well-known taxonomy put forward by Thomas H. Marshall—civil rights, political rights, social rights—undoubtedly has its uses, it reflects an historical and sociological approach. What is more, being firmly grounded in the last three centuries of British history, it completely ignores the 'new rights'.[9]

The 'catalogue of rights' tends to grow by accumulation or 'subsequent generations', with one right leading to another, or by interpolations based purely on contingent circumstances.[10] In fact there have been philosophers and jurists in the West who have advocated extending the theory of fundamental rights to human embryos, to non-human living beings, and even to inanimate objects. But it is obvious that the anomic expansion of the repertory of fundamental rights gives rise to an incontestable aporia: if everything is fundamental, then nothing is. Besides, it is evident that the fundamental rights cannot all be on an equal footing—with the same normative import—particularly when they are at odds with one another. As Alain Laquièze has pointed out, the more widely the predicate 'fundamental' is used, taking in an increasing volume of different rights, the greater the risk of a clash between the fundamental nature of rights and the need to make

8.   Bobbio, *L'età dei diritti*, p. 13

9.   See T.H. Marshall, 'Citizenship and Social Class', in T.H. Marshall, *Class, Citizenship, and Social Development*, Chicago: University of Chicago Press, 1964.

10.   Bobbio uses the expression 'generations' without any theoretical intent. In *Diritti dell'uomo e libertà fondamentali* (Bologna: Il Mulino, 1984), P. Barile limits himself to giving a compendium of positive constitutional law. Other authors have attempted a theoretical elaboration, including R. Alexy, *Theorie der Grundrechte*, Baden-Baden: Nomos Verlagsgesellschaft, 1985; J. Rawls, 'The Basic Liberties and Their Priorities', in S.M. McMurrin ed., *The Tanner Lectures on Human Values, vol. 3*, Salt Lake City: University of Utah Press, 1982, pp. 1–87; G. Peces-Barba Martínez, *Curso de derechos fundamentales*, Madrid: Eudema, 1991; L. Ferrajoli, *Diritti fondamentali*, Rome/Bari: Laterza, 2001.

them relative to one another and conditional on other, competing rights.[11]

The thesis of the philosophical grounding and normative universality of human rights is thus a dogmatic postulate of the doctrine of natural law and of ethical rationalism, which is not borne out on the theoretical level and can be contested with valid arguments by both historicist and realist Western philosophies, as well as by non-Western cultures. Bobbio went on to draw an important practical corollary from this conclusion: what is significant for the concrete implementation of human rights is not their assumed soundness and universal validity.[12] Indeed, the effort to provide this proof risks having the rights expressed in an intolerant and aggressive language. What really matters is that the subjective rights should enjoy a broad political consensus, and that the 'language of rights' should be disseminated as the expression of social expectations and claims. But such consensus—as Bobbio seems to be perfectly well aware—is a purely empirical datum, contingent on historical circumstances and difficult to confirm in rigorous terms: it does not give grounds for any universalistic claim or proselytising, and still less for the use of force. Moreover, the consensus and proliferation of bills of rights has not been matched—or has been matched only very partially and ambiguously—by concrete implementation of the rights themselves, even in the West. As Bobbio warns, it is one thing to demand one's rights and quite another to ensure their effective safeguarding.[13]

Ignatieff's position is much less clear-cut than that of Bobbio, and for all his professions of secularity it is redolent of moralism and paternalism. For Ignatieff, the doctrine of human rights derives from the basic unity of the human species and the moral intuition that each member of the species merits 'equal moral consideration', and

11. See A. Laquièze, 'État de droit and National Sovereignty in France', in P. Costa and D. Zolo, eds, The Rule of Law: History, Theory and Criticism, Dordrecht: Springer, 2007, pp. 261–91. Laquieze recalls that in France Etienne Picard proposed instituting a 'scale of fundamentality' ('L'émergence des droits fondamentaux en France', Actualité Juridique. Droit Administratif, 1998, special issue on 'Les Droits fondamentaux', pp. 6ff).

12. Bobbio, L'età dei diritti, pp. 14–16.

13. Ibid.

thus cannot be humiliated or subjected to unwarranted suffering.[14] The historical success of this idea has been the vehicle for humanity's moral progress, and it is this progress which confers plausibility and power on the Western doctrine of human rights. Ignatieff maintains that it can in fact be empirically verified, in historical and pragmatic terms, that whenever individuals are granted fundamental rights they are less likely to be discriminated against, oppressed or abused. The language of rights, born in the West, has spread worldwide because rights help the most vulnerable individuals against unjust and oppressive regimes,[15] and this, according to Ignatieff, represents the true reason for the de facto universalism and global diffusion of rights. Not unexpectedly, they represent a challenge above all for the theocratic, traditionalist and patriarchal regimes that proliferate in the non-Western world, and in particular in the sphere of Islam.

In my opinion it is here, in this moralistic and paternalistic ambiguity, that we can put our finger on the germ of that 'humanitarian fundamentalism' which, as we shall see, ends up by making the pragmatic and secularized universalism of Ignatieff coalesce with the religious universalism of the American neoconservatives who preach 'humanitarian war'.

Individualism and negative liberty

The safeguarding of human rights, according to Ignatieff, guarantees each individual 'free agency' for the achievement of rational ends.[16] The philosophical and political premise of the doctrine of human rights is political individualism, and its essential content is the defence of 'negative liberty', in the sense that Isaiah Berlin gave to this notion, in opposition to 'positive liberty'.

Now there is no doubt that individualism, as once again Bobbio has pointed out, is the general philosophical and political premise underlying the doctrine of human rights.[17] At the dawn of the

---

14. Ignatieff, *Human Rights*, pp. 3–4, 95.

15. Ibid, p. 7.

16. Ibid., p. 57 ('the capacity of each individual to achieve rational intentions without let or hindrance').

17. Bobbio, *L'età dei diritti*, pp. ix, 58ff.

Renaissance, individualist anthropology gave rise in Europe—
and, it must be noted, only in Europe—to an authentic inversion
of the relationship between individuals and political authority.
The organicist view of social life enshrined in the Aristotelian and
Aristotelian–Thomist traditions, which recognized the integration
of individuals in the political group as the very condition of their
humanity and rationality, was replaced by a conception grounded in
natural law.[18] Whereas previously the duties of subjects with respect
to political (and religious) authorities had been paramount, it was
now the citizen's rights which took priority, accompanied by the
public authority's duty to recognize and safeguard those rights, and
ultimately also to promote them.

In the modern European state (sovereign, national and secular)
the original deontic figure—duty—has given way to a new and
largely contrasting figure: that of individual expectations or claims
that are collectively recognized and safeguarded in the form of
'subjective rights'. They are viewed as *jus* rather than *lex*—in other
words, no longer as the 'objective law' of which sovereign *potestas* is
the expression and guarantee. The idea of a natural order characterized by harmony, rules and hierarchical structure waned, giving way
to the metaphysical and social supremacy of the human being, with
the individual 'conscience' as the repository of moral autonomy
and political liberty, albeit in a social context ordered by reason,
morality and the law.[19]

While this can be considered to be the philosophical and political
koine of modern Europe, which over the last two centuries has been
contrasted (to little effect) only with the most 'heretical' and radical
brands of Marxism, Ignatieff actually goes further. Taking his lead
from Isaiah Berlin, he not only endorses the classic liberal version
of European political individualism but, as we shall see, believes
that he can make the whole spectrum of subjective rights fit into the
normative domain of 'negative liberty'.

In the classic liberal tradition, based on the primacy of individual

---

18.   On this topic see M. Villey, *La formation de la pensée juridique moderne*,
Paris: Montchrestien, 1975.

19.   See E. Santoro, *Autonomy, Freedom and Rights*, Dordrecht: Kluwer
Academic Publisher, 2003.

liberty and private property, political liberty has been viewed essentially as the 'absence of constraints'—as a sphere free from political interference. In John Locke's *Second Treatise of Government*, just as in the equally celebrated pages of John Stuart Mill's essay *On Liberty*, liberty is identified with a set of rights that are 'not to be hindered' by the behaviour of others. In his famous contribution to this tradition, 'Two Concepts of Liberty', Berlin not only distinguishes 'liberal liberty' from the pre-modern idea of liberty as political citizenship, but contrasts it with 'positive liberty', in the various meanings that this notion has taken on in the last two centuries in the liberal-democratic and social-democratic traditions.[20]

The positive sense of the word 'liberty' derives from the aspiration of the individual to be 'master of himself': in other words, it is the desire to be not only free but 'autonomous', endowed with a personal identity and enabled to plan one's life and shape one's destiny. 'Positive liberty', in this sense, implies freedom from need as a condition for the freedom to participate, deeply and intensely, in social communication and interaction. And this requires subjects to possess a certain capacity for cognitive reflection so that they can evaluate the impact of acculturation and manage the pressures to conform that derive from the social environment.

It is clear that the set of normative requisites covered by the expression 'positive liberty' means that the individual can lay claim not only to the rights of personal freedom, but also to political and social rights—not to mention the so-called 'new rights' (gender equality, environmental values, the rights of foreigners and migrants, and so on). The legal endorsement of the fundamental rights of liberty on behalf of citizens who only possess an uncertain identity and precious little autonomy risks being mere window dressing. This is particularly true of today's high-tech societies, where the exercise of all the other rights is coming increasingly to depend on what we might term the one fundamental 'new right', namely *habeas mentem*: the ability of individuals to verify, filter and interpret the ever-increasing flow of multimedia information with which they have to contend.

20. See I. Berlin, 'Two Concepts of Liberty', now in I. Berlin, *Four Essays on Liberty*, Oxford: Oxford University Press, 1989.

But 'positive liberty' also requires, as Will Kymlicka has argued,[21] the safeguarding of the individual not as an abstract existential monad, but as a member of a cultural community; it is in the critical interaction with this community that identity is construed and the capacity for self-projection nurtured. Here we come up against the delicate and crucial dialectic between individual rights and 'collective rights', which no classical liberal theory (or 'theory of negative liberty') has been able to encompass or resolve. It is given short shrift by Ignatieff, who mechanically subordinates collective to individual rights.[22] It is in fact no coincidence if the whole theory of 'collective' or 'group' rights—the right to speak one's own language or practise one's own religion, for example; or the right to access the natural resources of the land on which one lives—is still gravely defective in Western jurisprudence. Some authors—Jürgen Habermas, among others—actually maintain that it is impossible or inopportune for such collective interests to be expressed in the positive form of rights pertaining to individual and/or collective subjects under national or international jurisdictions.[23]

The recognition and defence of 'collective rights'—as non-Western authors have been insisting for decades, for all the remonstrations of Amartya Sen[24]—remains an essential condition for the affirmation of individual rights, and at the same time is at odds with them. One only has to think of the protection of the identity and political autonomy of minority linguistic and cultural groups and 'state-less nations'; of the battle against socio-economic discrimination against whole categories of migrant workers; of the struggle against poverty and epidemic diseases in large areas of the

21.   See W. Kymlicka, *Liberalism, Community and Culture*, Oxford: Oxford University Press, 1998.

22.   Ignatieff, *Human Rights*, pp. 66–7.

23.   On this topic see J. Habermas, *Kampf um Anerkennung im demokratischen Rechtsstaat*, Frankfurt: Suhrkamp, 1996; E. Vitale, ed., *Diritti umani e diritti delle minoranze*, Turin: Rosenberg e Sellier, 2000; A. Facchi, *I diritti nell'Europa multiculturale*, Rome/Bari: Laterza, 2001, particularly pp. 21–36.

24.   Ignatieff refers to Sen, who maintains that no serious famine has ever occurred in countries with a democratic form of government and a relatively free press (Ignatieff, *Human Rights*, pp. 90–1). See A. Sen, *Development as Freedom*, New York: Anchor Books, 1999; A. Sen, *Human Rights and Asian Values*, at www.xitami.net/indowindows/das/godown/economy/Asasnval.htm.

globe; or of the liberation of economically backward countries from the yoke of international debt.[25]

For Berlin—and for his fellow liberal Ignatieff, who reiterates the same theses—these problems have no significant connection either with personal liberty or with its concomitant rights. On the contrary, in their view 'negative liberty' is the only political ideal compatible with an authentic conception of ethical and philosophical pluralism, and with the recognition of the insuperable fallibility of our philosophical and religious convictions. In opposing rationalistic metaphysics, with its proclamation of a 'positive liberty' for all humankind, Ignatieff advocates confining the whole range of individual (and, in practice, also collective) rights to that sphere covering personal integrity, economic activity and privacy, which must remain impervious to oppressive powers. However, as Amy Gutmann has acutely observed,[26] on the one hand this proposal neglects—or indeed dismisses—the expectations of a vast part of the world's inhabitants, and on the other it disavows an empirical truth that is difficult to dispute. It ignores the fact that the language of rights and the related claims set out in national and international documents have gone well beyond the mere liberty not to be hindered or oppressed.

Among recent declarations of rights we can cite the 1966 Covenant on Political and Civilian Rights; the Covenant on Economic, Social and Cultural Rights of the same year; the 1981 African Charter on Human and Peoples' Rights; the 1992 Islamic Tunis Declaration; and, bringing up the rear, the Charter of Fundamental Rights of the European Union (December 2000). To these we can add the lengthy series of international documents 'specifying' categories of individual and collective rights: the Convention on the Political Rights of Women (1952); the Convention on the Prevention and Punishment of the Crime of Genocide (1948); the Declaration of the Rights of the Child (1959); the Declaration on the Granting of Independence

---

25. On these topics, see in particular the *Banjul Charter on Human and People's Rights*, approved in 1981 by the Organization for African Unity, in which economic and social rights, viewed as the collective rights of peoples, clearly prevail over the civil and political rights of individuals; the same can be said of the *Islamic Declaration* issued in Tunis in 1992. See R.J. Vincent, *Human Rights and International Relations*, Cambridge: Cambridge University Press, 1986, pp. 39–44.

26. See A. Gutmann, 'Introduction' to Ignatieff, *Human Rights*, pp. xi–xiv.

to Colonial Countries and Peoples (1960); and the Declaration on the Elimination of All Forms of Racial Discrimination (1963).[27] It would be nonsense to claim that the normative language of these documents relates only, or even predominantly, to the rights of liberty and resistance to oppression. It clearly covers the whole gamut of civil, political, social, cultural and economic rights, and those relating to bioethics, the environment and the protection of personal information, as well as the so-called 'collective rights'.

As for the assertion of individual rights, we shall merely recall the epic struggle for equality conducted by the feminist movements, although we could also refer to the pacifist and environmentalist movements, whose claims go far beyond the proto-liberal mantra of 'liberty from hindrance'. And, turning to the 'collective rights', surely the resistance of the Palestinian people to decades of attempted ethnocide by the state of Israel, with the complicity of the Western world and indeed a part of the Arab world, is emblematic. Clearly, in Palestine we have a case of a people who are not willing to surrender their identity and dignity—epitomized notably by the tragic figure of the suicide bomber—for the more facile achievement of individual instances of personal integrity and private well-being.

The universality of rights of negative liberty

Still following in the footsteps of Berlin, Ignatieff has stripped the doctrine of human rights of its metaphysical and religious associations, and confined it to the normative domain of 'negative liberty'. To his way of thinking, human rights can thus lay claim to that 'minimalist universalism' which renders them compatible with a whole range of civilizations, cultures and religions. Human rights can meet with a universal consensus as a 'thin theory' which addresses merely what is juridically *right*, not what is *good* in absolute terms. A theory which limits itself to defining the minimal conditions for which life is worth living should apparently be welcomed and acted on with alacrity in every corner of the globe.[28]

---

27. It was Bobbio who highlighted the tendency of international charters to make a point of specifying rights; see Bobbio, *L'età dei diritti*, pp. 29–33.

28. Ignatieff, *Human Rights*, p. 56.

In this way, Ignatieff believes, human rights will stop being perceived by non-Western civilizations as a neo-imperialist intrusion, an imposition of the Western world's life style, values and world-view. Everywhere rights will become a 'local' force, strengthening the weakest elements of society against despotic regimes and oppressive social practices. It will be the oppressed who will rally with enthusiasm to the cause of rights, rather than Westerners having to impose it coercively. The language of rights will provide everyone with good arguments and effective tools for 'helping themselves', to protect themselves as individuals from injustice, and to exercise the right to 'choose the good life as they see fit'.[29]

Ignatieff explicitly rejects one stringent criticism that may be made of his individualistic approach: that of wanting to impose the Western conception of the individual on all the cultures on the planet. He simply stands the objection on its head: moral individualism is the prime ally of cultural diversity, because an individualistic philosophy cannot but come out in favour of the various ways in which each individual chooses to live his or her own life. It is thus precisely a rigorous individualistic approach that can reconcile the universalism of human rights with the pluralism of cultures and moralities. In this sense individualism represents, according to Ignatieff, the only viable response to the challenges launched against the universalism of rights by Islam and Chinese-Confucian culture, as well as by Western postmodernist cultural orientations with a fatal penchant for ethical relativism.[30]

In my opinion, this is a very weak line of defence. Its only merit is to acknowledge the criticisms coming from the non-Western world, above all in the wake of the celebrated Bangkok Declaration of 1993, of the universalist claims that are made for Western ethical and political values. But the few pages Ignatieff dedicates to the political culture of Islam and the question of 'Asian values' provide yet another instance of the ethnocentric prejudice of Western universalism and globalism. For all their enthusiasm for the normative unification of the world, Western globalists invariably betray their limited interest in—and scant information concerning—the

---

29. Ibid., pp. 7, 57.
30. Cf. M. Ignatieff, op. cit., pp. 57-8.

cultural, political and juridical traditions with which they mean (or ought) to enter into dialogue.

As is well known, Western universalism has already had some energetic critics both in the Islamic world—in particular within the revolutionary movement of Khomeini—and in sub-Saharan Africa. Today it is south-east and north-east Asia that are putting up the stiffest ideological resistance to Western juridical and political pressure. In countries such as Singapore, Malaysia and China, the countering of Western values with 'Asian values' has taken on particular vigour and prestige thanks to such charismatic leaders as Singapore's philosopher-king Lee Kuan Yew and Malaysian Prime Minister Mahathir Mohamad.[31]

These figures have declared quite openly that the political values of the modern West cannot be endorsed by Asian cultures. This refusal concerns in particular the liberal-democratic tradition and the doctrine of human rights. With its organic idea of the family and society, the Confucian tradition provides some 1.5 billion people with the most suitable ideological framework for limiting the anomic effects of the market economy and mitigating the disruptive pressures of Western individualism and liberalism.[32] Besides, the safeguarding of human rights and the principle of equality before the law are of little interest to populations that are still largely

31. The two young Chinese intellectuals Son Qiang and Zhang Xiaobo, who were leaders of the Tienanmen Square generation, produced an essay, which rapidly became a bestseller with the significant title *The China that Can Say No*. On this topic see M.C. Davis, ed., *Human Rights and Chinese Values: Legal, Philosophical and Political Perspectives*, New York: Columbia University Press, 1995; W.T. de Bary and T. Weiming, eds, *Confucianism and Human Rights*, New York: Columbia University Press, 1998; E. Vitale, "Valori asiatici' e diritti umani', *Teoria politica* 15 (2–3), 1999, pp. 313–24; M. Bovero, 'Idiópolis', *Ragion pratica* 7 (13), 1999, pp. 101–6; F. Monceri, *Altre globalizzazioni: Universalismo liberale e valori asiatici*, Catanzaro: Rubbettino, 2002.

32. The Japanese Shintaro Ishihara, the Malaysian Mahathir Mohamad, and the Chinese Son Qiang and Zhang Xiaobo are respectively the authors of *The Japan that Can Say No*, *The Asia that Can Say No*, and *The China that Can Say No*. An extensive bibliography on the topic of 'Asian values', edited by Flavia Monceri, can be found under 'Law and politics in postcolonial Asia' at the *Jura Gentium Journal* website: www.juragentium. unifi.it. See also the critique by A. Ehr-Soon Tay, "Asian Values' and the Rule of law', in Costa and Zolo, eds, *The Rule of Law*, pp. 565–86.

oppressed by poverty, and which until quite recently were subject to all the excesses of Western colonialism.

Other authors have pointed out that the Western concept of 'subjective right' is itself alien to the Confucian ethos. The Chinese jurist Chung-Sho Lo noted that there was no corresponding expression in the Chinese language.[33] When Western political and juridical texts began to be published in Asia in the second half of the nineteenth century, translators had to coin a new term, *chuan-li* (power-interest), in order to make some sense of the concept. In the Confucian–Mencian tradition, the dominating idea is not that of individual rights but rather that of a 'fundamental social relationship' (whether sovereign–subject, parents–children, husband–wife, first born–second born, friend–friend).

The basis of a trial as we know it, involving a juridical debate between prosecuting and defence counsel, is quite foreign to Confucian culture.[34] Rather than the exacerbated competition between individuals to be 'proved right' and win one's case by prevailing over the adversary, which is characteristic of Western legal formalism, in the Confucian tradition the aim of 'legal proceedings' is to arrive at reconciliation through compromise and amicable agreement. Indeed, François Jullien has argued that in Chinese culture there is no legal mediation, based on general, abstract rules and following established bureaucratic procedures, between the requirements of morality and the imperative of power.[35] The solution of controversies through transaction is based on the personalization of the single case, not on its formalistic depersonalization.

---

33. L. Chung Sho, 'Human Rights in the Chinese Tradition', in UNESCO, *Human Rights: Comments and Interpretations*, New York: Columbia University Press, 1949.

34. See L. Scillitani, 'Tra l'Occidente e la Cina: una via antropologica ai diritti dell'uomo', in A. Catania and L. Lombardi Vallauri, eds, *Concezioni del diritto e diritti umani: Confronti Oriente-Occidente*, Napoli: Edizioni Scientifiche Italiane, 2000, pp. 385–94.

35. F. Jullien, 'Un usage philosophique de la Chine', *Le débat*, October 1996, p. 191. See also R. Panikkar, 'La notion des droits de l'homme est-elle un concept occidental?' *Diogène* 120, 1982; D. Davidson, *Asian Values and Human Rights: A Confucian Communitarian Perspective*, Cambridge, MA: Harvard University Press, 1998; C. Taylor, 'Conditions of an Unforced Consensus on Human Rights', in J.R. Bauer and D.A. Bell, eds, *The East Asian Challenge for Human Rights*, Cambridge: Cambridge University Press, 1999; D.A. Bell, *East Meets West: Human Rights and Democracy in East Asia*, Princeton: Princeton University Press, 2000.

Far from dying out, this profoundly anti-individualist and anti-formalist juridical culture is currently being reinvigorated in a large number of Asiatic countries that have chosen to assert their political identity by putting social harmony, the family, respect for authority and the sense of responsibility incumbent on public officials before all other considerations. And a similar approach, although taking a very different form, can be recognized in a large part of the Islamic world and in the autochthonous cultures of Africa and the Americas. From this perspective, the West is perceived as the place where community values collapse under the pressure of unchecked individualism and a political conception that obliges the state to recognize an increasing number of individual rights in the absence of any obligation or bond of solidarity.

In attempting to counter these criticisms, Ignatieff has, to my mind, backed himself into a corner. In the first place he has ignored the elements that link the theory of human rights to the whole context of the Western world-view. In the current advance of globalization, this world-view tends to be duplicated and spread around the globe on the back of 'modernization' involving the market economy, the ambition to dominate nature, faith in technological progress, the optimization of production, the obsession with acquisition and consumerism, and the cult of speed. It makes little sense to suppose that the Western doctrine of human rights can prove acceptable outside the context of the world's Westernization, which to a large extent coincides with the spread of globalization. In the second place, Ignatieff has failed to consider the whole issue of the intercultural—rather than unilateral or 'humanitarian'—modalities for translating the Western language of rights into the languages of other civilizations and cultures. He would have done well to refer, for example, to the attempts of Raimon Panikkar and Otfried Höffe at identifying the 'homeomorphous equivalents' of the language of rights in non-Western cultures and setting up a 'transcendental dialogue' on this basis.[36]

In reality Ignatieff has tried to open up a 'pragmatic' road to humanitarian fundamentalism: he has applied epistemological and political filters to a typical product of Western culture

---

36. Baccelli, *Il particolarismo dei diritti*, pp. 147–8, 181–2.

in order to turn it into a commodity that can be more easily exported to the rest of humanity. Once confined to the 'negative liberty' of individualism, he is convinced that human rights can be offered to (suggested to, recommended to, or imposed upon using legal or military expedients) the world as a whole as a 'sterilized package', cleansed of its Western taint and value judgments, and fit for universal use. Paradoxically, he has achieved precisely the opposite. Without realizing it—and herein lies his ethnocentric ingenuousness—Ignatieff has actually condensed all that is 'Western' about the doctrine of human rights: both its constituent, indelible individualism and its more strictly liberal core component, represented by the rights of 'negative liberty'. One could add that, on the epistemological level, his claim that a normative theory of human rights may rest on prescriptive propositions so bereft of axiological and evaluative implications as to be endorsable in any ethico-religious context whatsoever is no less ingenuous.

Universalising humanitarian war

In his Lectures, Ignatieff devotes a lot of space to the topic of the coercive safeguarding of human rights, with particular reference to the use of military force for humanitarian ends—so-called 'humanitarian intervention'. He has no qualms about commending the punitive function of the international criminal Tribunals, in particular the one for the former Yugoslavia, while concealing its serious collusion with the political and military authorities of NATO and the United States.[37] Ignatieff's position on this crucial point—which is decisive for assessing the overall political thrust of his theses—is in contradiction with his whole approach to the question of human rights. However 'thin' his theory may be, however focused on the liberty and integrity of all human beings without exception, and however eloquent in its condemnation of hostile behaviour towards individuals on the part of (non-Western) authoritarian regimes, Ignatieff's universalism identifies *sic et simpliciter* with the wars of aggression which the United States and its European allies have

---

37. See Zolo, *Invoking Humanity*, pp. 99–132.

waged in recent years in the name of human rights, in particular in the Balkans. In fact he makes an explicit apology for these wars.[38]

For Ignatieff it is clear that when a (non-Western) nation endangers the life of its citizens and violates their fundamental rights, its sovereignty is not to be respected (by the Western powers). The so-called international community has the duty to intervene by applying sanctions and, in the most serious cases, by military means. 'There are no peaceful diplomatic remedies', he declares, in no uncertain terms, 'when we are dealing with a Hitler, a Stalin, a Saddam or a Pol Pot'.[39] Thus war—even the 'humanitarian war' illegally waged by NATO against the Yugoslav Republic—is legitimate and ethically irreprehensible if it claims the safeguarding of human rights as its motivation. It is a 'just war' par excellence because it pursues neither territorial conquest nor the definitive suppression of a state's sovereignty. In carrying out humanitarian intervention, Western nations have always used military power—and here Ignatieff conveniently forgets the military bases that the United States builds in the countries to which it extends humanitarian 'assistance', as in Kosovo—to bring peace, democracy and stability, whereupon they have promptly withdrawn.[40]

It is surprising that Ignatieff fails to devote a single line to the question of the compatibility of the use of weapons of mass destruction with the goal of protecting the fundamental rights of human individuals. He does not so much as allude to the problem of whether, in the name of the (alleged) protection of the fundamental rights of some individuals, it is legitimate to sacrifice the lives, physical integrity, property, feelings and values of (thousands of) innocent people, as happened in particular in the war for Kosovo. Nor does he ask himself in the name of what neutral and impartial supreme entity innocent persons can be sacrificed—an entity which of course must be universalist, in just the same way as human rights have to be universalist, invested with an authority that has to be pre-eminently moral rather than simply political.

---

38. Ignatieff, *Human Rights*, pp. 37–48. On the 'humanitarian war' for Kosovo, see Zolo, *Invoking Humanity*.

39. Ignatieff, *Human Rights*, p. 42.

40. Ibid, pp. 38–9.

Ignatieff forgets—and it is surely an unforgivable oversight on the part of a fervid apologist of 'negative liberty'—that modern warfare is itself the most radical negation of the rights of individuals, starting from the right to life. In fact modern war, conducted with ever more sophisticated and lethal weapons of mass destruction, is incommensurable with the categories of ethics and the law. Its *raison d'être* is to destroy—irrespective of any sense of proportion, discrimination or degree—the life, property and rights of individuals, with no regard to personal responsibility. It is, in practice, the implementation of a collective capital punishment on the basis of the presumed criminal responsibility of all a nation's citizens. In terms of its consequences, modern warfare cannot in fact be easily distinguished from terrorism. And it is clear that these arguments are all the more compelling when addressed to advocates of the universality of human rights.

Paradoxically, Ignatieff's one preoccupation is that the 'humanitarian' use of war should be prompt, effective and coherent, rather than belated and partial, as he claims was the case in Rwanda, Bosnia and Kosovo. Thus the humanitarian use of military force must not be conditioned by the political and strategic interests of the major powers, nor indeed subordinated to the requisites of international peace-keeping. To this end, he advocates reform of the United Nations so that the Security Council is authorized to make systematic use of force for humanitarian purposes, and not just for peace-keeping and in the interests of international law and order. 'Humanitarian wars' will be perfectly legitimate and indeed 'successful' once the universality of rights is matched by universal armed intervention in their protection. And this would avoid 'coalitions of the willing' finding themselves morally obliged to use force without paying heed to the authority of the United Nations, and thereby bringing this institution into disrepute.

However 'thin' it may be, Ignatieff's ethico-juridical universalism tends, like any universalism, to intolerance, aggressiveness, and denial of cultural diversity and the complexity of our world. The whole project of pragmatic 'secularization' of the doctrine of human rights that he proposes stands revealed as just one more acclamation of the use of international force by the major powers. In fact this conclusion is wholly in line with the 'humanitarian fundamentalism' currently informing the hegemonic strategies of the United States and its European allies, and which elicits the bloody response of terrorism the world over, with its radical component of suicide. Surely nothing is more 'idolatrous' (and tragically disingenuous) than the apology for aggressive war made by Western powers in the name of human rights.

PREVENTIVE GLOBAL WAR

Ancient war

The idea that war can be not only just but 'holy'—waged to carry out the will of God, according to his revelation and under his guidance—is as old as the monotheistic religions of the Mediterranean. The doctrine of 'holy war'—or 'obligatory holy war' (*milchemet mitzvà*)—is illustrated in some celebrated passages in the Bible, in particular in Deuteronomy, as war waged to annihilate the enemies of God's people. Holy war is not a war like any other, fought for particular interests and objectives: it is a theological and salvific war, and as such is not subject to any restrictions of a moral or legal nature. Defeating the enemy, destroying his cities, herds and fields, exterminating him down to the last man, woman and child and mutilating the corpses are sacred gestures which respond to God's own design. Shedding enemy blood is the sacrificial seal which, through the mediation of Moses and other Jewish leaders, binds Jehovah to his people and vice versa.[41]

The Hebrew doctrine of the holy war has influenced the theologies of war elaborated by Catholics, Muslims and Protestants down to the present.[42] Catholic monotheism—from Augustine

---

41. See D.J. Bederman, *International Law in Antiquity*, Cambridge: Cambridge University Press, 2001.

42. See J.B. Elshtain, ed., *Just War Theory*, Oxford: Basil Blackwell, 1992; R.F. Peters, *The Jihad in Classical and Modern Islam*, Princeton: Princeton University Press, 1995; P. Partner, *Il Dio degli eserciti. Islam e cristianesimo: le guerre sante*, Turin: Einaudi, 1997; J.T. Johnson, *The Holy War Idea in Western and Islamic Traditions*, University Park, PA: Pennsylvania State University Press, 1997.

of Tagaste to the *Decretum Gratiani*, Thomas Aquinas and the
Spanish scholastics such as Francisco de Vitoria, Francisco Suárez
and Juan Ginés de Sepúlveda—has partly incorporated the traditional Hebrew idea of the holy war, but has above all recast it
from a moralistic perspective. This gave rise to the doctrine of the
bellum justum, a doctrine which Western theologians and moral-
ists have continued to return to for over a millennium, and which
the teaching of the Roman Church has always confirmed (most
recently during the 'humanitarian war' waged by NATO against
the Yugoslav Federal Republic[43]).

A 'just war' was not directly instigated by God and carried out
by the faithful in obedience to the divine will—it was simply legitimate because it was waged respecting moral rules laid down by the
religious authority. Setting brusquely aside the evangelical principles
of mildness and charity, Catholic theology legitimized the shedding
of blood. The declared intent was to authorize Christians to fight
just wars decided on by the legitimate political authorities, and at
the same time to contribute to limiting and mitigating the fighting,
obliging the Christian kings to wage only wars justified by good
reasons, and to fight them using acceptable means.

The moral limitation regarded primarily the 'causes' that could
justify going to war (known as *jus ad bellum*), such as defence
against aggression, the reconquest of territories that had been
unjustly seized, or punishment of an aggressor. Furthermore the
war had to have been decided on by the competent authority with
'proper intention', and have peace as its objective. The conduct of
hostilities also had to be 'just' (*jus in bello*). Christian soldiers were
required to spare the lives and goods of non-combatants and respect
a criterion of proportion between the just objectives of the war and
the inevitable sacrifice of human lives that war involves.[44]

We can identify three fundamental aspects of the Christian

---

43.   During the 'Giubileo dei militari', celebrated in San Pietro in 2000, the pope
declared, clearly referring to the NATO war against the Yugoslav Federal Republic,
that armed 'humanitarian intervention' is legitimate when there are no other means
of defending human rights.

44.   See F.H., Russell, *The Just War in the Middle Ages*, Cambridge: Cambridge
University Press, 1975; W.V. O'Brien, *The Conduct of Just and Limited War*, New
York: Praeger, 1981.

re-elaboration of the Jewish doctrine of the 'holy war' designated as *bellum justum*:

1. This doctrine refers back to the empirical model of 'ancient war' as recently reconstructed by Franco Cardini.[45] It is a direct confrontation between two armies on a battlefield on land, with rare exceptions of naval battles fought in coastal waters but never on the high seas. It takes place in a clearly delimited geographical space, where only the lives of the combatants are at stake in a 'heroic' challenge which may observe precise chivalric rituals. The contribution of machines of war is marginal with respect to the physical strength, courage and tactical skill involved (for many centuries gunpowder was unknown). Destructiveness is restricted to the arena of confrontation, and the loss of human life is limited. Sometimes, especially after mercenary troops came into common use in late medieval times, a long battle could end without a single life being lost.

2. The doctrine of the 'just war' refers to the political and religious ethos of the *respublica christiana* and presupposes the presence of a stable *auctoritas spiritualis*. Endowed with political and legal authority, and ideally designated as universal, taking precedence over all Christian kings and princes, supreme authority was invested in the head of the Roman Catholic church. This was a monotheistic and 'imperial' authority, since the pope was responsible for consecrating the emperor, legitimizing his temporal power. As was already apparent in Augustine, the doctrine of the 'just war' clearly involves integrating Christianity and its religious authorities with the temporal structures of the Roman Empire and, following the latter's fall, of the 'universalist' political systems that succeeded it through the Middle Ages. Moreover, as Carl Schmitt pointed out,[46] the doctrine of the *bellum justum* was not designed merely

---

45. See F. Cardini, *Quell'antica festa crudele*, Milano: Mondadori, 1997.

46. See C. Schmitt, *The Nomos of the Earth in the International Law of the Jus Publicum Europaeum*, New York: Telos Press Publishing, 2006, pp. 119–25.

to limit war: it also distinguished between wars waged by Christians—between adversaries bound by the authority of the church and emperor—and 'feuds'. The latter were the wars waged against kings and peoples who persisted in denying the authority of the Church, such as the Turks, Arabs and Jews.

3. The crusades and wars of the missions, blessed by the Roman pontiff, were *eo ipso* 'just wars', and corresponded to the wars of conquest fought by the Israelites on the command of Jehovah, their one God. They were just and holy irrespective of whether they were wars of aggression or defence, anticipating or in response to attack by Saracen infidels. In the same way, any war conducted against Christendom was by definition an unjust war. Moreover—and this is a key point—in any war waged by Christendom against the infidels, the enemies could not be considered *justi hostes*, in the sense this expression came to acquire in modern international law. They were bandits or criminals who could be tortured and killed without any heed for moral or legal norms. The shedding of their blood was not displeasing to God. In other words, at the heart of the Catholic-Christian doctrine of the 'just war'—as in the Islamic doctrine of the jihad—we can recognize the essence of the Jewish doctrine of the 'holy war'. It was no coincidence if war against the Turks, Arabs and Jews was referred to as *bellum justissimum*, and sometimes even as *bellum sacrum*.

The persistence of the essence of the Jewish 'holy war' at the heart of the Catholic doctrine of the 'just war' is evidence of a common trait that has characterized relations between the peoples of the Mesopotamian, Mediterranean and European regions down the ages. In this tradition, the international order was given a 'spatially discriminatory' character. This discrimination has had no difficulty in coexisting with the universalist and humanitarian ideal—with its Stoic, Christian and Enlightenment origins—of the moral unity of humanity and the equal dignity of its members (an idea, as is well known, that was to be enshrined in the 1948 Universal Declaration of Human Rights drawn up in the aftermath of the Second World

War). From the ancient rules to the *jus gentium* of the Romans, the Islamic *sijar* and the Catholic doctrine of the *bellum justum*, the legal discipline of the relations between peoples—including the regulation of war—has applied exclusively to the domain of 'civilization', by turns Hebrew, Greek, Roman, Christian, Arabo-Islamic, modern, liberal-democratic, and so on. All 'barbarians'—be they gentiles, idolaters, infidels, Turks, Moors, blacks, savages, cannibals, pirates, or whatever else—were rigorously excluded.[47] In the Mediterranean area in particular, this ideological distinction had a direct geographical, political and military transposition, designating inviolable boundaries between one country and another, or between land and sea. The 'barbarians' and the 'infidels' were considered extraneous to the realm of civilization and law, and thus alien to human society: their lives, property and institutions merited no respect or legal tutelage. In the legal sphere humanitarian universalism, which is constantly reiterated as a matter of principle, stops short at the ideal boundaries of the 'monotheism'—today we might say 'fundamentalism'—of a particular religion or civilization.

This prevalence of 'spatial discrimination' also characterized the theological school of Salamanca, including the celebrated humanitarian universalism of Francisco de Vitoria. The extermination of millions of native Americans in the course of the conquest of the New World was justified by Catholic theologians either by their referring, as Sepúlveda did, to the Aristotelian doctrine of the natural character of slavery[48] or, as in the case of Vitoria, by recognizing the right of the Iberian empires to disseminate the Catholic verity in the 'new space' of the Americas as *justa causa belli*.[49]

In the context of European colonial expansion too, at the turn of the twentieth century, there were Catholic theologians who made a point of legitimizing the wars of aggression against 'idolatrous' and

---

47. Ibid., pp. 92–100; P. Frezza, 'Ius gentium', *Revue Internationale Droits Antiquité* 2 (2), 1949 (Mélanges De Visscher, 1); M. Khadduri, *The Islamic Law of Nations: Shaybani's Siyar*, Baltimore: Johns Hopkins University Press, 1966.

48. See J.G. de Sepúlveda, *Democrates Secundus, sive de iustis belli causis apud Indos*, 1545, bilingual edn by M. Menendez y Pelayo, *Boletin de la Real Academia de la Historia*, Madrid, 1892.

49. See F. de Vitoria, *Relectio de Indis*, 1538, ed. L. Pereña and J. Pérez Prendes, Madrid: Consejo Superior de Investigación Científica, 1967.

'uncivil' peoples on other continents as 'just wars'. In the 1930s, for example, *La civiltà cattolica*, an authoritative organ of the Society of Jesus, argued that the Ethiopian people, incapable of adequately cultivating the land and endowed with scant demographic potential, were guilty of a grave violation of natural law in not giving up their territory spontaneously to the Italian people, forcing the latter to resort to military operations in order to exercise their right to expansion.[50]

Modern war

It was not until the ethical, theological and universalist premises of the doctrine of the *bellum justum* were abandoned, in the second half of the seventeenth century, that the modern international legal system—meaning inter-state law—could establish itself in Europe. The collapse of religious unity in Europe saw the emergence of the 'Westphalian' system of modern European states at the close of the Thirty Years War. The first truly modern international order arose out of the ashes of the political and spiritual universalism of the Roman Church and the Holy Roman Empire, and was based on the pluralism of national, territorial and sovereign states. The sovereignty of a state was expressed both within its borders, as *suprema potestas*, meaning exclusive discretionary powers for the state organs with respect to citizens, and outside, as absolute international independence for the political authorities of the state. The nation-state was established as *superiorem non reconoscens*, meaning that it no longer attributed any political or legal authority to entities outside its own territorial and normative province.

As is well known, this state-based model became universal from the beginning of the twentieth century, as the international community expanded in a complex sequence of political and economic developments. Some of the main factors were the emergence of the power of the United States and Japan; the spread of technology, of information and of Western lifestyles; increasing freedom of trade

---

50. See A. Messineo, 'Propagazione della civiltà ed espansione coloniale', *La civiltà cattolica* 2, 1936; A. Messineo, 'Necessità di vita e diritto di espansione', *La civiltà cattolica* 3, 1936.

and maritime traffic; and, last but by no means least, the introduction of weapons of mass destruction.[51] Alongside these processes, international law took on the features of a pluralistic and universal legal order—matching the universalism celebrated at Geneva—and remained substantially unchanged until the end of the Second World War, when it was subject to a partial revision with the drawing up of the UN Charter in 1945. In spite of its proclamation of the 'sovereign equality of all its Members',[52] in setting up the Security Council the Charter created an organ that disposes of sweeping powers of intervention and is controlled—*de jure* as well as *de facto*—by the five powers that emerged victorious from the war.

In legal terms, the model of Westphalia, in its initial purity, was characterized by the fact that no collective entities other than, or superior to, nation-states were recognized as international subjects. There was no legislator or government at the international level with the power to issue laws and enforce them with a validity *erga omnes* (in relation to all). The only source of international law was the sovereign authority of states insofar as they stipulated bilateral or multilateral treaties, or recognized the validity of customary norms or general principles. No obligatory jurisdiction was contemplated, endowed either with the power to verify violations of the law or with an international police force . Moreover, international law had nothing to do with a state's political structure; nor was it competent to judge the conduct of the state authorities vis-à-vis their own citizens. No other state and no international organization could interfere in the domestic affairs and jurisdiction of a sovereign state.[53]

In this normative framework, which was radically different to the ancient and medieval order, the phenomenon of war and the instruments of its legitimation and limitation underwent profound

---

51. On the growth of the international community, see the classic H. Bull and A. Watson, *The Expansion of International Society*, Oxford: Clarendon Press, 1984.

52. On the notion of 'sovereign equality' and its ambiguity, see A. Cassese, *International Law in a Divided World*, Oxford: Oxford University Press, 1986; W. Levi, *Law and Politics in International Society*, Beverly Hills: Sage Publicatons, 1976, pp. 121–33.

53. See A. Cassese, *Il diritto internazionale nel mondo contemporaneo*, Bologna: il Mulino, 1984.

changes. Taking it for granted that, in the absence of a superior, universal authority, each contendent was able to uphold the ethical and legal legitimacy of its wars—*bellum utrimque justum* ('war just for both sides')—modern international law no longer considered the 'justice' of war. Instead, attention was focused on the definition of rules and formal procedures disciplining the conduct of warfare. The use of force was ritualized in order to limit the most destructive effects of conflicts between European states. The ultimate objective of law-makers was to construct a system of collective security based on pacts which, while not renouncing the use of force to underwrite the international order, ruled out war in the sense of a 'private' recourse to the use of force on the part of any individual state.

In the transition to the pluralistic regime of modern international law, the ancient doctrine of the *bellum justum* did not completely vanish. Reference to 'just causes' of war did disappear, together with the archaic provision relating to the moral intentions of the belligerents. There was no place any more for the moralistic idea that it is always possible, when confronted with an armed conflict involving two contendents, to establish with universally valid ethical arguments which of the two was in the right and which in the wrong. The peremptory pronouncement of moral judgements was replaced by the flexibility of diplomatic mediation. And the 'sacred' or 'holy' motivation for war disappeared, even though, as we have seen, the 'spatial discrimination' between 'civilized' and 'barbarian' peoples was not by any means superseded. Wars against the latter—in particular the colonial wars at the turn of the twentieth century— were waged without limitations and using every available means, including chemical weapons such as mustard gas, first used by Italy in East Africa, against civilians as well as enemy forces.

On the contrary, the principle of *jus in bello* governing the conduct of war has been maintained, and indeed extended, albeit in a laicized, state-based version. Carl Schmitt was instrumental in calling attention to the merits of the pluralistic system of *jus publicum Europaeum*. He praised it as an international legal order committed to 'mettre la guerre en forme' without seeking to negate or outlaw it. Indeed, in Schmitt's opinion the European law of war had been effective as *temperamentum belli* ('moderation of war') precisely because it did not aspire to negate war juridically

or condemn it in moral terms.[54] War was ritualized by a complex
of diplomatic procedures, such as the declaration of war and the
conclusion of peace. Furthermore, once the discriminatory notion
of unilateral justification for going to war had been superseded, the
right to neutrality for third-party states, and hence their inviolability, was given formal recognition. Above all, numerous bilateral
and multilateral treaties were stipulated—through to the Hague
Conventions of 1949 and subsequent protocols—in order to protect
the victims of war, and in particular non-combatant civilians, and
to prohibit the use of unnecessarily destructive and dangerous
weapons.

The problem of the growing number of civilian victims in modern
warfare—along with that of the disproportion between military
objectives and the scale of carnage and destruction—is nonetheless
becoming increasingly serious. The human and social consequences
of war are prolonged long after the end of the armed conflict:
permanent mutilation, disintegration of family life, poverty, corruption, violence, hatred, devastation and pollution of the environment
all make for an ever more intolerable aftermath. The old model of
a land-based war between armies confronting each other on the
battlefield has been completely superseded. War between states has
extended to the sea, the oceans and the skies, with ever more
sophisticated instruments of mass destruction being deployed. The
old norms of the *jus in bello* which imposed a distinction between
civilians and combatants (and due proportion between the gains
and devastation of war) are increasingly lost sight of, and in many
cases can no longer apply.

The tragedy of the First World War, with its millions of dead and
wholesale devastation, brought about a drastic change in the global
legal order. War was seen, in particular by jurists in the United
States, as a radical negation of legality, and they were determined
that international law must be no less radical in opposing war. Under
the influence of Wilsonian idealism, modern war was to be considered a crime, for which not only states but even single individuals
could be held responsible, the latter being implicitly 'promoted' to
the status of subjects in international law. This paved the way for the

---

54. Schmitt, *Nomos of the Earth*, pp. 240–8.

controversial experience of international criminal jurisdiction, from the Tribunals of Nuremberg and Tokyo to those of the Hague and Arusha, through to the International Criminal Court.[55] The indictment of Kaiser Wilhelm II von Hohenzollern as a war criminal at the end of the First World War was the first sensational expression of this new direction. And the Kellogg-Briand Pact, stipulated in 1928, marked the formal consecration of this normative trend, which set out to banish war from the international legal order.

Finally, as the Second World War came to an end and the glare of the atomic explosions in Hiroshima and Nagasaki was still fading, war was defined in the Charter of the United Nations as a 'scourge' which a united international community had to erase from human history. Force was only to be used by the Security Council, and solely in order to guarantee peace or punish violations of peace by an aggressor. In December 1946, at the instigation of the General Assembly of the United Nations, the measures that had been applied by the Nuremberg Tribunal against the Nazi criminals were raised to the status of general principles of international law. Solemn endorsement was thus given to measures, stipulated in the Charter, which branded a state's use of (or threat to use) military force as aggression, irrespective of any question of *justa causa*. Only one exception was contemplated, set out in Article 51 of the United Nations Charter: if a state come under military attack on its territory and was forced to resist. In a situation of self-defence, it was legitimate for the state to use force while awaiting the intervention of the Security Council.

From modern war to global war

The two preceding sections have provided a lengthy prelude to my central thesis in this chapter: in the final decade of last century, with the end of the Cold War and of the two hegemonic power blocs, both the phenomenon of war and the rhetoric of its justification underwent a rapid change. This change can be adequately interpreted only in the context of the ongoing transformation in the financial, economic, political, legal and information spheres

---

55. See Zolo, *Invoking Humanity*, pp. 99–132.

that goes under the name of 'globalization'. The evolution of war and its ideological props has been speeded up, not 'caused', by the terrorist attack of 11 September 2001, which led to the United States and its closest allies waging wars on Afghanistan and Iraq. In fact 11 September occupies only a marginal place in this analytical framework. I emphasize this point because some interesting recent philosophical and political interpretations—for example, Carlo Galli's book *La guerra globale*[56]—take 11 September as a crucial watershed, if not indeed as the turning point between a modern and a global era.

The last few years have seen a transition from 'modern war' to 'global war'. A crucial component of this transformation has been the Western powers' reappropriation of the notion of 'preventive war', theorized and practised by the United States against the so-called 'rogue states' and organizations of global terrorism. This transition relates to the morphology of the 'new warfare', meaning its strategic dimension and destructive potential, both of which have attained a global scale. But it also involves an authentic eversion of current international law, since the Charter of the United Nations and general international law are profoundly incompatible with the notion of 'preventive war'. And to this must be added the large-scale regression to old rhetorical models for the justification of war, including major elements of the 'imperial' doctrine of the *bellum justum* and its theological and sacrificial ethos, based on the Bible: the 'holy war' to be waged against barbarians and infidels. Today, in the context of globalized mass communications, this rhetorical weapon has become an exceptionally significant tool of warfare.

A global 'just war'

The new warfare is 'global' first of all in the strategic sense, since it features events that are de-spatialized and take place on the planetary scale, with no temporal limits. In global war, states do not compete for specific territorial spaces or localized resources. Its prime exponent—the United States—orients the strategy of global war towards universal objectives such as 'global security' and the

---

56. See C. Galli, *La guerra globale*, Rome/Bari: Laterza, 2002.

'new world order', rather than the conquest of geopolitical spaces to be occupied and annexed in one form or another as additions to its own territory. Global war is waged to decide who is to prevail as leader in the worldwide system of international relations, and thus who will set the systemic rules of competition between the major powers, wield the political power to shape processes of the distribution of resources, and impose their own world-view, sense of order and indeed 'language', according to the maxim *Caesar dominus et supra grammaticam*[57] ('the emperor also holds sway over thought and expression'). NATO's attack on the Yugoslav Federal Republic was literally a 'war from the sky' in which the assailants relied on a network of satellite monitoring and espionage which constituted a permanent electronic counterpart to the war. The territorial dimension was rendered completely irrelevant through the use of selective bombing from such a height that the attackers did not risk even minimal loss of human life.

As emerges from a series of documents produced by the White House and the State Department, starting with the fundamental *Defense Planning Guidance* of 1992,[58] armed force is employed in the pursuit of a stable world order in a context of the increasing interdependence of international factors and the enhanced vulnerability of the industrialized nations. The elements perceived as being at risk are: free and regular access to energy sources, primarily oil and gas for fuel; availability of raw materials; freedom and security of air and sea traffic; stability of world markets, and in particular financial markets. In addition, the industrialized nations feel under threat from international terrorism and the proliferation of biological, chemical and nuclear weapons. Thus, what is actually at stake is the progress of globalization, in a context of growing political and economic asymmetry in international relations.

---

57. See C. Schmitt, 'Völkerrechtliche Formen des modernen Imperialismus', *Auslandsstudien* 8, 1933, now in C. Schmitt, *Positionen und Begriffe im Kampf mit Weimer, Genf, Versailles 1923–1939*, Hamburg: Hanseatische Verlagsanstalt, 1940, pp. 179–80.

58. The document can be found in the survey *War, Law and Global Order*, on the *Jura Gentium* journal website, at www.juragentium.unifi.it. See also D. Zolo, *Cosmopolis: Prospects for World Government*, Cambridge: Polity Press, 1997, esp. Chapter 2, pp. 19–52.

Global stability must be guaranteed—this is the crux of the matter—without affecting the mechanisms of worldwide distribution of wealth, which are opening up an ever-wider rift between rich and poor countries. And a global war of aggression, whether it is called 'humanitarian war' or 'war against terrorism', is a necessary expedient to achieve this goal. Being a global power, the United States is the only nation able to 'project power' on the planetary scale. Its interests, responsibilities and tasks are global, and it must therefore extend its influence to the world as a whole, reinforcing 'America's global leadership role'.[59] In so doing it will both strengthen domestic security and safeguard and promote its own 'vital interests' in the international arena.

But the new war is 'global' also in a symbolic sense—first of all on account of the Western powers' constant reference to universal values. War is justified in the name not of specific interests or particular goals, but from a superior and impartial standpoint of values which they maintain to be, or to have the potential of being, shared by humanity at large. The Weberian 'polytheism' of morals and religious faiths is systematically denied by the theoreticians of global war. They set a monotheistic view of the world—in particular the fervidly Christian outlook of the neoconservative ideologues of the United States—against the pluralism of values, diversity of cultures and complexity of the world as we know it. While declaring that they are combating the inhuman and blood-thirsty ideology of global terrorism, in reality the 'neocon' (and 'theocon') ideologues reject everything which stands in the way of Western monotheism. They show particular zeal in combating the culture of Islam, which seeks to resist the process of Westernization of the world which is what 'globalization' largely comes down to. It is unilateral war by the 'forces of good'—to adopt George W. Bush's elementary rhetoric—against the 'axis of evil'. It is 'humanitarian war' against the enemies of humanity, who deny the universality of such values as liberty, democracy, human rights and, of course, the market economy.

---

59. See the *Quadrennial Defense Review Report*, distributed by the US Department of State on 30 September 2001, in the survey *War, Law and Global Order*, on the *Jura Gentium* journal website, at www.juragentium.unifi.it.

These justifications for war appear regressive with respect to the whole tenor of modern international law, inasmuch as they once again invoke 'just causes' for the international use of force, according to the Catholic and imperial doctrine of the *bellum justum*. And it is significant that this doctrine was revived in the last decades of the twentieth century exclusively by authors in the United States, principally the philosopher and Zionist militant Michael Walzer. Walzer came to public attention for his part in an overtly ethical and theological document, signed and circulated by sixty eminent intellectuals in the United States, proclaiming the war declared by the Bush administration against 'the axis of evil' to be a 'just war'.[60] For Walzer, it was fundamental that this just war on terrorism should be preceded by ideological, economic and political initiatives designed to prevent the spread of terrorist cells and isolate and punish the states that gave them support.[61] And it is no less significant that in his book *Just and Unjust Wars* Walzer argued that, in cases of 'supreme emergency', when confronting an 'unusual and terrible' danger, for which one feels a profound moral repugnance because it represents the incarnation of the evil in the world and a radical threat to human values, no restriction of an ethical or legal nature can apply to whomever is confronted by this threat. Any means of preventive destruction, even the most terroristic and bloody, is morally legitimate.[62]

---

60. The document *What We're Fighting For*, drawn up in February 2002 by a large group of US intellectuals—including Michael Walzer, Samuel Huntington, Samuel G. Freedman, Francis Fukuyama, Amitai Etzioni, Jean B. Elshtain, and Theda Skocpol—speaks out in the name of 'American values', proposed as universal, and presents the war decided by the US administration against terrorism as a 'just war'. The ethical justification concerns the war in Afghanistan and, albeit without any direct reference, also possible future wars, including an attack on Iraq. In the document no allusion is made either to international law or to the functions of such international institutions as the United Nations. The document is available at www.propositiononline.com/html/fighting_for.html.

61. On the theory of preventive warfare against terrorism elaborated by Walzer, see R.R. Dipert, *Preemptive War and the Epistemological Dimension of Morality of War*, at atlas.usafa.af.mil/jscope/JSCOPE05/Dipert05html; more generally, see M. Bothe, 'Terrorism and the Legality of Pre-emptive Force', *European Journal of International Law* 14, 2003; F. Vander, *Kant, Schmitt e la guerra preventiva: Diritto e politica nell'epoca del conflitto globale*, Roma: Manifestolibri, 2004.

62. See M. Walzer, *Just and Unjust Wars*, New York: Basic Books, 1992.

The global use of force—whatever its strategic objective, declared or covert—is justified in the name of a sort of humanitarian fundamentalism which stresses the duty of Western nations to safeguard human rights in every corner of the globe. The normative universalism of human rights must be matched by the universalism of their military protection, as Michael Ignatieff has argued.[63] And, crucially, this means abandoning the traditional Westphalian principle of non-interference in the domestic affairs of states and adopting a principle which is its diametric opposite: the United States and Western powers have a duty to intervene with the use of force whenever they deem it necessary to put an end to the violation of fundamental rights within a state and, if necessary, to overthrow its political regime. This is the imperial monotheism of 'humanitarian war', upheld by the classical 'cosmopolitan' belief in the necessary decline of the pluralism of national sovereignties and the emergence of a globalized world under the responsibility and guidance of a single superpower.

Imperial universalism, the Catholic 'just war' doctrine and the biblical mystique of the 'holy war' come together in a discriminatory conception of the global space. Whoever denies the hegemony of Western values, by recourse to terrorism, belongs to the horde of the new barbarians and the new infidels: the enemies of humanity against which it is necessary to wage a war that is global, just and holy all at the same time.

A global preventive war

After 11 September 2001, global war became a 'global preventive war', in the form of a 'war against terrorism'. In a series of major strategic documents such as the *Quadrennial Defense Review Report*,[64] released by the Defense Department in September 2001, and the *National Security Strategy of the United States of America*,[65]

---

63. See M. Ignatieff, *Human Rights as Politics and Idolatry*, Princeton: Princeton University Press, 2001.

64. Department of Defense, *Quadrennial Defense Review Report*, 30 September 2001, at www.defenselink.mil/pubs/qdr2001.pdf.

65. The White House, *National Security Strategy of the United States of America*, Washington, DC, 17 September 2002, available in the section *War, Law and Global Order* on the *Jura Gentium* journal website, at www.juragentium.unifi.it.

dated September 2002, the US administration set out the significance it intended to attribute to the notion of 'preventive war'. The
notion is used in two senses, one concerning overall strategy, and the
other more specific.

A global democratic revolution

Firstly, the strategy of preventive war coincides with the global
hegemonic design of the United States and finds expression in the
constant threat to use force, in patent violation of the UN Charter,
which forbids not only the use of force but also its threatened use.
The fundamental outlines of this strategy of permanent threat
of war are clearly illustrated in the *Quadrennial Defense Review
Report*. Although this document was made public within a few
weeks of the attack on the Twin Towers, with a few amendments to
adapt it to the latest circumstances, it was the product of a lengthy
period of gestation. It reaffirms the right of the US administration
to denounce sovereign states unilaterally, without the need for any
legal procedure, as 'rogue states' to be marginalized in the international community. They can be subjected to political pressure,
to compulsory inspections designed to secure their preventive
disarmament, to explicit military threats, and even, ultimately,
as was the case for Afghanistan and Iraq, to military attack. The
United Nations is viewed not as an international organism existing
as a universal forum, but as an institution that is politically and mili-
tarily subordinated to the US administration. It is fair game for the
systematic exertion of pressure, and even for military diktat, and we
have even reached the point where the *Report* could declare quite
openly that the decision to attack Iraq would be taken in any case,
with or without a resolution of the Security Council.

Secondly, it is argued that the United States has to elaborate
a global strategy able to exploit the 'asymmetrical advantages'
it enjoys in terms of nuclear resources, intelligence and technological supremacy worldwide. The objective is to consolidate its
planetary hegemony, securing a stable military presence in the heart
of Central Asia. This will ensure control over the immense energy
resources contained in the territories of the ex-Soviet Republics of the
Caucasian, Caspian and trans-Caspian area—Georgia, Azerbaijan,

Turkmenistan, Uzbekistan and Tajikistan, as well, of course, as Afghanistan and Pakistan—and make it possible to complete the encirclement of Russia, to the west, and China, to the east, with both conventional and nuclear weapons.

The response to global terrorism has to be prepared in terms of military prevention, so as to make the US armed forces a 'total force' that can prevent terrorist groups and rogue states from using nuclear, chemical or biological weapons. The United States must reinforce its global system of military bases and open new ones in certain 'critical areas', so as to preclude their hostile domination and forestall the risk of their fostering collusion with terrorism. These areas include the Balkans, and in particular the Asian continent, stretching from the Middle East to Central Asia, from the Gulf of Bengal to the Sea of Japan and Korea, along what the *Report* refers to as the East Asian Littoral, in which it includes south-east Asia. If necessary, as a preventive political and military measure, a change of regime may be effected in a hostile state, involving temporary occupation of its territory, until the strategic objectives of the United States have been achieved.

This preventive rationale is matched by the ideological campaign launched by the Bush administration, presenting the military occupation of Iraq as the beginning of a 'global democratic revolution' affecting first of all the Middle East and the Islamic world, in a strategy designated as the 'broader Middle East'.[66] The chief aim of this strategy, which has been adopted by NATO, is that of controlling the whole region stretching from Morocco and Mauritania to Afghanistan and Pakistan by means of political, economic and surveillance initiatives. As well as encompassing one of the richest concentrations of energy resources in the world, this region is highly unstable, and the forcing ground for global terrorism. At its heart is the conflict between the state of Israel and the Palestinian people, but there is also the phenomenon of suicide terrorism. This phenomenon represents an intolerable global challenge, being the epitome of the rejection of Western values and

---

66. The strategy of the 'broader Middle East' was officially presented by President Bush at the G8 summit of 8–9 June 2004 at Sea Island, in Georgia; see US Department of State, Fact Sheet, *Broader Middle East and North Africa Initiative*, at www.state.gov/e/eb/rls/fs/33380.htm.

the resistance of the world of Islam to the neo-colonial strategy of the United States and the regional hegemony of Israel.[67] The (failed) project of the 'road map', drawn up by the Sharon government and the Bush administration, aimed to solve the Palestinian question according to the preventive strategy of the military 'democratization' of the Middle East. Above all, it pursued the line of negating a territorial 'spatiality' and identity for the Palestinian people, and of ruthlessly repressing their resistance.

Preemptive self-defence

In a second, more specific sense, formulated in particular in the *National Security Strategy of the United States of America*, 'preventive war' refers to the topic of self-defence. Article 51 of the UN Charter provides for the use of force by a state under military attack by another state. The established interpretation of this article, considered a cornerstone of the UN Charter, is that the right to self-defence authorizes a state to use force—while awaiting the intervention of the Security Council—in the presence of a military attack that is not merely threatened or regarded as imminent, but is actually in progress ('if an armed attack occurs').[68] A state's recourse to arms in self-defence is thus legitimate only if it is 'subsequent' to an attack and not 'preventive', however one interprets the latter term. This interpretation highlights the absolutely exceptional character of Article 51 with respect to the general principle set out in the fourth section of Article 2 of the Charter, which forbids states from using force or threatening to do so. Thus any military action by one state against another is forbidden, without exception, unless the former is actually being attacked.

The interpretation required by the White House document—which is careful to avoid any explicit reference to the UN Charter—is

---

67. For this argument, see A.M. Dershowitz, *Why Terrorism Works: Understanding the Threat, Responding to the Challenge*, New Haven: Yale University Press, 2002.

68. Article 51 reads: 'Nothing in the present Charter shall impair the inherent right of individual or collective self-defence if an armed attack occurs against a Member of the United Nations, until the Security Council has taken measures necessary to maintain international peace and security'.

subversive of this discipline in two distinct respects: it claims legitimacy for the unilateral use of force not only in the presence of a simple threat of attack by another state—so-called 'pre-emptive self-defence'—but also in the absence of an imminent threat or specific prospect of attack. War can be legitimately begun if there is the conviction that military conflict, although not imminent, is inevitable and that delay would involve a greater risk. The document is very clear on this point:

> Traditional concepts of deterrence will not work against a terrorist enemy whose avowed tactics are wanton destruction and the targeting of innocents; whose so-called soldiers seek martyrdom in death ... For centuries, international law recognized that nations need not suffer an attack before they can lawfully take action to defend themselves against forces that present an imminent danger of attack. Legal scholars and international jurists often conditioned the legitimacy of pre-emption on the existence of an imminent threat—most often a visible mobilization of armies, navies, and air forces preparing to attack. We must adapt the concept of imminent threat to the capabilities and objectives of today's adversaries. Rogue states and terrorists do not seek to attack us using conventional means. They know such attacks would fail ... The United States has long maintained the option of pre-emptive actions to counter a sufficient threat to our national security. The greater the threat, the greater is the risk of inaction—and the more compelling the case for taking anticipatory action to defend ourselves, even if uncertainty remains as to the time and place of the enemy's attack. To forestall or prevent such hostile acts by our adversaries, the United States will, if necessary, act pre-emptively.[69]

Thus the pre-emptive and unilateral use of force by the United States is reckoned to be made legitimate merely by the situation of emergency

---

69. See White House, *National Security Strategy of the United States of America*, section V.

generated by the phenomenon of global terrorism. On this point, too, the document is perfectly explicit: 'While the United States will constantly strive to enlist the support of the international community, we will not hesitate to act alone, if necessary, to exercise our right to self-defense by acting pre-emptively against such terrorism.'[70]

It is hardly necessary to point out that the proscription of the pre-emptive and unilateral use of military force is the cornerstone on which the whole structure of the UN Charter is built. A war of aggression—the most serious violation of the international legal order—coincides exactly with the pre-emptive and unilateral use of force by a state. Moreover, it is precisely the notion of aggression that distinguishes current international law from the ancient and medieval military ethic. As we have seen, both the Hebrew 'holy war' and the Catholic 'just war' legitimized the preventive use of force against the enemies of the people of God. In this case, medieval Scholastics, including Francisco de Vitoria, spoke of just aggression or *bellum justum offensivum*.[71] The doctrine of 'preventive war' theorized and practised by President Bush and his Western allies thus denotes a grave regression, for it means doing away with the very notion of 'war of aggression'.

In this context, it can be said that the war unleashed by the United States and Great Britain against Iraq in 2003, with the dramatic falsifications used to motivate it, its massive employment of weapons of mass destruction, its overwhelming ideological campaign, massacres of civilians, military occupation of the country, the depredation of its energy resources, the control by the occupiers of Iraq's political and legal structures, and the

---

70. Ibid., section III. On 1 June 2003 President Bush confirmed this doctrine: 'We must take the battle to the enemy, disrupt his plans and confront the worst threats before they emerge. In the world we have entered the only path to safety is the path of action. And this nation will act.' (*The National Strategy for Combating Terrorism*, Washington, 2003, p. 11). On the distinction between 'preventive war' and 'pre-emptive war', see R. Falk's essay, *Why International Law Matters*, in the section *War, Law and Global Order* on the *Jura Gentium Journal* website, at www.juragentium.unifi.it.

71. Schmitt, *Nomos of the Earth*, pp. 119–25.

fragmentation of the territory, is a paradigmatic case of the illegal and terroristic nature of 'preventive global war' waged against global terrorism.

5

EMPIRE AND WAR

In this chapter I present a linguistic survey and critical analysis of those uses of the notion of 'empire' which crop up increasingly often in Western writing on the political sciences and international studies. The following reflections are intended to help clarify the theoretical and political concept of 'empire', showing that its use, under certain conditions, is in fact justified. This is no mere academic exercise in lexicography. The re-emergence of the notion of 'empire' is one of the indications of the profound transformation of international political relations, associated with the processes of global integration and the emergence of phenomena of increasing polarization of power and wealth across the planet.[1]

At the same time, the autonomy of sovereign states is being transferred to new international actors—military, political, economic, judicial—such as NATO, the G8, the European Union, the World Bank, the International Monetary Fund, the international criminal courts, and so on. This transnational arena is seeing the emergence of the hegemony of the major Western powers, led by the United States of America. And the United States is increasingly fulfilling the role of a 'global' imperial power, placing itself above international law, and in particular the law of warfare. Not only does the United States resort to the use of force in blatant violation of international law, but it can count on receiving legal sanction for the new status quo from the international institutions. This endorsement comes in the form both of a normative legitimation of the outcome

---

1. See D. Zolo, *Globalization: An Overview*, Colchester: ECPR, 2007.

of wars of aggression passed off as humanitarian interventions or preventive wars against 'global terrorism', and of recourse to ad hoc international criminal justice. From the Hague Tribunal for the former Yugoslavia to the Special Tribunal designated as 'for Iraq', but actually imposed by the United States, the 'Nuremberg model' is being perpetuated: a 'victors' justice' applied by the major powers to the vanquished and the oppressed.

These phenomena underwent a marked acceleration in the late 1980s, following the end of the Cold War, the collapse of the Soviet Union, the passing of the duopolistic division of the world, the affirmation of the United States as the sole planetary superpower, and the spread of terrorism on an international scale. They received a further acceleration after 11 September 2001, and the wars of aggression conducted by the United States against Afghanistan and Iraq.

A methodological caveat

The term 'empire' as currently used in the West is rather different to the uses of 'empire' and 'imperialism' that characterized Marxist theory, and tended to prevail during the twentieth century.[2] Recent usage has been less ambitious in political terms and less elaborate theoretically. As a result, 'empire' has come to symbolize and communicate some key geopolitical issues. We should note, however, that not all authors regard 'empire' as the most appropriate conceptual tool to denote the present state of international relations, or to foster an adequate understanding and interpretation of the current situation.

Michael Doyle, for example, insists on maintaining a clear distinction between the notions of 'formal' and 'informal' empire, with only the latter being applicable to the contemporary world. In 'formal empire', represented essentially by the Roman model, dominion is exercised by means of territorial annexation, with the administration of the annexed territories being delegated to colonial governors backed up by garrison troops and local collaborators. By

---

2. See R. Owen and B. Sutcliff, eds, *Studies in the Theory of Imperialism*, London: Longman, 1972.

contrast, 'informal empire', based on the Athenian model, denotes the exercise of power over neighbouring territories and in the face of legally independent regimes through the manipulation and corruption of the local political classes.[3]

Other theorists of international relations, such as Robert Gilpin, Kenneth Waltz and Robert Keohane, argue that the concept of 'hegemony' is more useful than that of 'empire'. Keohane, in particular, has won considerable support for the notion of 'hegemonic stability'. This posits the supremacy of one or more major powers as a stabilizing element in international relations, a supremacy which implies none of the permanent, aggressive expansionism intrinsic to the classic model of imperialism.[4] Other authors maintain that the term 'empire' should only be used of the universalistic political formations which preceded the genesis, in seventeenth-century Europe, of the Westphalian system of sovereign states. The current predominance of economic power and cultural influence over political and military power, it is argued, makes it advisable to abandon the imperial model, or at least to proceed to its radical reformulation.[5] Yet there are also commentators—including, as we shall see, Alain de Benoist—who follow Carl Schmitt in considering it legitimate to use the term 'empire' in connection with the imperialistic extension of the 'Monroe doctrine', which the United States has pursued since the era of Wilson's cosmopolitan credo, and which they see as continuing to exert a profound influence on the expansionist strategies of the American superpower.[6]

---

3. See A.W. Doyle, *Empires*, Ithaca, NY: Cornell University Press, 1986.

4. See R.O. Keohane, *After Hegemony: Cooperation and Discord in the World Political Economy*, Princeton: Princeton University Press, 1984, pp. 31ff., 49–64, 83–4; R.O. Keohane, *Neorealism and Its Critics*, New York: Columbia University Press, 1986; K.N. Waltz, *Theory of International Politics*, New York: Newbery Award Records, 1979; R. Gilpin, *War and Change in World Politics*, Cambridge: Cambridge University Press, 1981. On the alternative between the notions of 'hegemony' and 'empire', see V.E. Parsi, 'L'impero come fato? Gli Stati Uniti e l'ordine globale', *Filosofia politica* 16 (1), 2002, 1, pp. 87, 92–3.

5. See D. Lieven, *Empire: The Russian Empire and Its Rivals*, London: John Murray, 2000, p. 9.

6. See C. Schmitt, 'Völkerrechtliche Formen des modernen Imperialismus', *Auslandsstudien* 8 (1933), now in C. Schmitt, *Positionen und Begriffe im Kampf mit Weimar, Genf, Versailles 1923–1939*, Hamburg: Hanseatische Verlagsanstalt,

Thus we need to be clear about the general meaning of 'empire' in Western political culture today. In this context the term takes on a semantic value and symbolic scope that can be crystallized in an authentic paradigm. For all the variations in detail, this imperial paradigm alludes to a political form characterized by three morphological and functional characteristics:

1. Imperial sovereignty implies a very strong political control that is centralized and expanding. Through it, the empire exercises *absolute* power over the populations residing on its territory. This direct power is complemented by a substantial sphere of political, economic and cultural influence in territories that are more or less contiguous, including other political formations that nominally conserve their formal sovereignty, although in practice this is limited. From this point of view, as Carl Schmitt has argued, the 'Monroe doctrine', initially applied on the American subcontinent and subsequently extended throughout the world, has been a typical expression of imperial expansionism.[7]

2. The centralism and absolutism of the structures of imperial power—imperial authority is by definition *legibus solutus* ('beyond the law') at the international level, while in the domestic sphere its power is 'non-representative'— are matched by a broad pluralism of ethnic groups, communities, cultures, idioms and religious beliefs which are quite distinct one from the other. The central power maintains a control which can be more or less stringent, but

1940; C. Schmitt, 'Völkerrechtliche Grossraumordnung mit Interventionsverbot für raumfremde Mächte. Ein Beitrag zum Reichsbegriff im Völkerrecht', *Schriften des Instituts für Politik und Internationales Recht an der Universität Kiel 7*, 1939, now in C. Schmitt, *Staat, Grossraum, Nomos*, ed. G. Maschke, Berlin: Duncker & Humblot, 1995; C. Schmitt, *Der Nomos der Erde im Völkerrecht des Jus Publicum Europaeum*, Berlin: Duncker und Humblot, 1974. On Schmitt's theory of imperialism and the associated idea of *Grossraumordnung*, see P.P. Portinaro, *La crisi dello Jus Publicum Europaeum*, Milano: Edizioni di Comunità, 1982, pp. 188–202.

7. See C. Schmitt, *The Nomos of the Earth in the International Law of the Jus Publicum Europaeum*, New York: Telos Press, 2006.

which in any case does not threaten the identity or relative cultural autonomy of the territories it dominates. In this specific sense, the model of the Ottoman Empire stands as paradigmatic, with its institution of the *millet* and widespread confessional tolerance.[8] The combination of anti-egalitarian absolutism and ethno-cultural pluralism denotes empire, as opposed to the representative and national character of the European *Rechtsstaat*.

3. The imperial ideology is pacifist and universalist. Empire is conceived as a perennial entity: it is a supreme power, guaranteeing peace, security and stability for all peoples on earth. The *pax imperialis* is by definition a stable and universal peace: the only possible reason for having recourse to military force is the promotion of such peace. The emperor is the sole ruler who by divine mandate (or the workings of providence) holds sway, in fact or potentially, over the whole world: sole *basileus*, sole *logos*, sole *nomos*. The emperor as *imperator* is the supreme military commander; as *pontifex maximus* he is the chief priest; as *princeps* he exercises sovereign justice. The imperial regime considers and imposes itself as a monocratic, monotheistic and mono-normative regime.

Clearly the structures, praxis and ideology of the Roman Empire in its evolution from Augustus to Constantine[9] are the remote but defining model for this imperial paradigm, even in the somewhat 'informal' version identified by Doyle. To gain a complete picture of this archetype one would obviously have to make a study of the imperial experiences that succeeded one another in Europe after the fall of the Roman Empire, taking it as a more or less direct model, including

---

8. The term 'millet' indicated a religious community which fulfilled the role of a decentralized administrative unit in the empire. See G. Prévélakis, *Les Balkans: Cultures et géopolitique*, Paris: Nathan, 1994. See also Chapter 1 ('Imperial Mapping and Balkan Nationalism') of D. Zolo, *Invoking Humanity: War, Law and Global Order*, London/New York: Continuum International, 2002, pp. 7–36.

9. See G. Poma, 'L'impero romano: ideologia e prassi', *Filosofia politica* 16 (1), 2002, 1, pp. 5–35; C.M. Wells, *The Roman Empire*, London: Fontana Press, 1992; P. Veyne, *The Roman Empire*, Cambridge, MA: Belknap Press, 1997.

such political formations as the Holy Roman Empire, the Byzantine Empire, the Ottoman Empire and the Spanish Empire.[10] There seems to be instead no direct influence of ancient—Middle Eastern, Mesopotamian or Chinese—empires. And it would also seem that the 'informal' Roman paradigm owes little also to the experience of the Napoleonic Empire,[11] or indeed to the colonial empires—whether the pioneers, such as the British, or more recent ones.[12]

To my mind, we can identify four uses of 'empire'—corresponding to the Roman archetype, with its 'informal' attenuation—in contemporary political science and international studies. This will cover the Marxist notion of 'imperialism', which deserves to be included in view of the currency of some neo-Marxist doctrines in international relations in the 1960s and '70s.

Neo-Marxist accounts of imperialism and empire

The notion of 'empire' implied in Marxist theories of imperialism, featuring the class-based conception of history and a 'materialist' critique of the capitalist economy, is still to be found in the Western political sciences.[13] In this sense, 'empire' has been largely severed from any historical context and inserted into a philosophy of history that views imperialism as the necessary outcome of the development of the capitalist economy.

---

10. See E. Bussi, *Il diritto pubblico del Sacro romano impero alla fine dell'VIII secolo*, Milano: Giuffrè, 1957–59; G. Ostrogorski, *Geschichte des byzantinischen Staates*, München: Beck, 1940; D. Kitsikis, *L'Empire ottoman*, Paris: Presses Universitaires de France, 1985; A. Musi, 'L'impero spagnolo', *Filosofia politica* 16 (1), 2002, pp. 37–61; F. Braudel, *La Méditerranée et le monde méditerranéen à l'lépoque de Philippe II*, Paris: Colin, 1982.

11. See E. Di Rienzo, 'L'impero-nazione di Napoleone Bonaparte', *Filosofia politica* 16 (1), 2002, pp. 63–82.

12. See W.J. Mommsen, *Das Zeitalter des Imperialismus*, Frankfurt: Fisher Bücherei, 1969; R.F. Betts, *The False Dawn: European Imperialism in the Nineteenth Century*, Minneapolis: University of Minnesota Press, 1975

13. See, among many other texts, P. Bourdieu, *Contre-feux 2*, Paris: Liber, 2001; L. Boltanski and E. Chiapello, *Le nouvel esprit du capitalisme*, Paris: Gallimard, 1999; A. Callinicos, ed., *Marxism and the New Imperialism*, London: Bookmarks, 1994; U. Allegretti, M. Dinucci and D. Gallo, *La strategia dell'Impero*, S. Domenico di Fiesole: Edizioni Cultura della Pace, 1992.

Nowadays, this doctrine of imperialism enjoys much less of a consensus than in even the quite recent past. Its theory of empire is called into question above all for its reliance on an economic 'causality' which is deemed to make the passage from capitalism to imperialism a necessary condition for the development (or survival) of the market economy. Imperialism, in this sense, fosters the expansion of the market economy beyond its natural environment—the sphere of the Western industrialized nations—so that it can draw the labour force in the industrially undeveloped nations into its mechanisms of exploitation. From this point of view, the phenomena of imperialism and colonialism are strictly interconnected. For Lenin, as is well known, the 'causal factor' was the tendency for the rate of profit to fall and for competition among capitalists to increase, while Rosa Luxemburg attributed it to underconsumption due to the impoverishment of the European proletariat.

Much more significant in contemporary debate in the political sciences are the neo-Marxist doctrines of capitalistic development and its imperialist consequences, such as Paul Baran and Paul Sweezy's theory of monopolistic capital, the 'dependency theory' elaborated, among others, by André Gunder Frank, and Immanuel Wallerstein's theory of a 'world-system'.[14] With respect to Marxist-Leninist orthodoxy, in these neo-Marxist versions the notion of 'empire' tends to take on characteristics that are considerably closer to the Roman archetype outlined above. Baran and Sweezy, for example, link the imperialistic evolution of concentrated, centralized, 'monopolistic' capitalism to the political (rather than economic) necessity of the industrially advanced nations to plough surplus capital into military investments. They identify a pyramidal hierarchy in the nations that make up the capitalist system, with the countries higher up exploiting those below them, until the lowest country of all is left with no one to exploit. The top of the pyramid is the 'imperial metropolis', while the lower echelons constitute the

---

14. See P.A. Baran and P.M. Sweezy, *Monopoly Capital: An Essay on the American Economic and Social Order*, New York: Monthly Review Press, 1966; A.G. Frank, *Capitalism and Under-development in Latin America*, New York: Monthly Review Press, 1969; I. Wallerstein, *The Modern World System*, New York: Academic Press, 1974; I. Wallerstein, *The Capitalist World Economy*, Cambridge: Cambridge University Press, 1979.

'colonial periphery'. The militarist vocation of the United States—
which occupies the whole of the metropolitan space—derives from
the onus on the systematic use of its armed forces to maintain, and
whenever possible strengthen, its position of leadership in the hierarchy of exploitation.[15]

Of course, the neo-Marxist versions of imperialism have also
come in for criticism. For liberal authors such as Robert Gilpin or
Joseph Stiglitz, the widening gap between rich and poor countries
does not depend on forms of 'imperialistic' oppression, whether
formal or informal. Economic globalization and the opening up of
markets worldwide cannot be interpreted in the light of the imperial
'hierarchy' of capitalist exploitation. The increasing polarization in
the distribution of global resources depends on the different degrees
of productivity in the national economic systems, and thus on the
levels of culture, technical qualification, administrative competence
and capacity for initiative that characterize the various nations. In
the view of Gilpin and Stiglitz, it is necessary to intervene on these
parameters, as well as in the regulation of international commer-
cial exchanges and movements of capital. To this end, the policies
adopted over the last few decades by the international economic
institutions, primarily the International Monetary Fund and the
World Bank, all subject to the 'Washington consensus',[16] need to be
radically revised.

An imperial Europe?

Carl Schmitt's formulation of 'empire' has a standard-bearer today
in the so-called *nouvelle droite* in France, and in particular in the
person of Alain de Benoist. He, and the movement 'Groupement
de recherches et d'études pour la civilisation européenne' (*Grece*)
that has grown up around him, unequivocally reject nationalism and
liberalism in the name of both a cultural Europeanism and a 'localist
pluralism'. Hence the idea of an 'imperial Europe' encompassing a

---

15.   See Baran and Sweezy, *Monopoly Capital*.

16.   See R. Gilpin, *The Political Economy of International Relations*, Princeton:
Princeton University Press, 1987; J.E. Stiglitz, *Globalization and Its Discontents*, New
York: W.W. Norton & Company, 2002.

broad internal political plurality which is ethnic and regionalistic rather than nationalist. De Benoist rejects the Gaullist idea of a 'Europe of fatherlands'. He denounces liberalism and state-based nationalism as economic and ideological mechanisms that undermine all-important cultural rootedness and diversity. In the face of the Americanization of France and Europe, de Benoist evokes a 'pagan' culture that he traces back to this continent's Indo-European origins; and he accompanies his call for an imperial Europe with a harsh attack on the imperialism of the United States, depicted as the supreme expression of dehumanization, vulgarity and stupidity. An imperial Europe, he proclaims, must be achieved in opposition to the United States or not at all.[17]

For de Benoist, there are only two possible models for the construction of Europe: empire and nation. Of these, the concept of 'nation' has become too broad to regulate local problems and too limited to deal with global issues, particularly in the economic field. 'Empire, in the most traditional sense of the term,' he argues, 'is the only model that can reconcile the one and the many: it is the *politia* that accounts for the organic unity of its different parts, leaving their autonomy untouched.'[18] The drawback, he adds, is that since Maastricht there has been no sign of an autonomous, politically sovereign Europe determined to come up with the equivalent of what the 'Monroe doctrine' was for the United States (and here the influence of Schmitt can be seen particularly clearly). We are confronted with a Europe lacking any clear project, legitimacy or political identity.

There are undoubtedly interesting aspects of de Benoist's proposal, even though, as I hardly need to point out, the idea of an imperial Europe is highly unlikely to find favour either within the liberal tradition or with the liberal-democratic left wing in Europe. The imperial paradigm, as we have seen, implies an absolutist and anti-egalitarian conception of power, even though it can be tolerant and compatible with ethnic and cultural pluralism. Nor does there

---

17.   See A. De Benoist, *L'Impero interiore: Mito, autorità, potere nell'Europa moderna e contemporanea*, Firenze: Ponte alle Grazie, 1996; P.-A. Taguieff, *Sur la Nouvelle droite: Jalons d'une analyse critique*, Paris: Descartes & Cie, 1994.

18.   See Taguieff, *Sur la Nouvelle droite*, p. 115.

seem to be much of a future for the idea of a 'pagan'—as opposed to merely secular—Europe. For, while European culture is indeed the outcome of Greek philosophy, Roman law and the Enlightenment, it also draws on the three monotheisms that have flourished on the shores of the Mediterranean—chronologically speaking, Judaism, Christianity and, last but not least, Islam.

It can also be noted that when de Benoist, following Schmitt, refers to the model of the 'Monroe doctrine', it is not clear whether he is thinking of an 'imperial Europe' under the influence of one or more hegemonic states—presumably France and Germany—or whether his idea of empire conceives of the various European ethnic groupings on an equal footing, guaranteeing the fundamental rights of European citizens. Both positions sit awkwardly with the standard doctrine of the *nouvelle droite*.

Hardt and Negri: an apology for global empire

In their highly successful book *Empire*, Michael Hardt and Antonio Negri argue that the new 'world order' imposed by globalization has brought about the disappearance of the Westphalian system of sovereign states.[19] National states no longer exist, except as simulacra within the international legal order and institutions. The world is no longer governed by state-based political systems: rather, it is governed by a single power structure that has no significant analogy with the modern state as it originated in Europe. This structure is a decentralized and de-territorialized political system, which makes no reference to ethnic or national traditions and values, and whose political and normative substance is cosmopolitan and universalist. For these reasons, the authors believe that 'empire' is the most appropriate term to denote the new type of global power.

At the same time it would be wrong to imagine that empire—or its central and expanding core—is constituted by the United States and its closest Western allies. Neither the United States nor any other national state, Hardt and Negri insist, 'actually forms the

---

19. See M. Hardt and A. Negri, *Empire*, Cambridge, MA: Harvard College, 2000.

centre of the imperialist project'.[20] Global empire is quite a different pheomenon to classical imperialism, and it would be a serious theoretical error to confuse the one with the other.

This is a very delicate point, on both the theoretical and the political level, and has given rise to considerable discussion. It has been claimed that, in Hardt and Negri's perspective, 'empire' seems to dwindle to being no more than a sort of 'mental category', ubiquitously present inasmuch as it coincides with the new dimension of globality. But if everything is imperial, nothing is imperial. How are we to identify the supranational subjects who are invested with imperial interests or aspirations? Who is to be the target of anti-imperialist criticism and resistance? Who, if we exclude the political and military machinery of the major Western powers—the United States above all—exercises the imperial functions?[21]

There is a second aspect of Hardt and Negri's theory of empire that has also come in for criticism. Their analyses presuppose an implicit 'ontology'—namely the dialectic of history as theorized by Hegel, Marx and Lenin. In the opinion of the two authors, global empire represents an advance on the Westphalian system of sovereign states. Having put an end to nation-states and nationalism, empire has also dispensed with colonialism and classical imperialism, and opened up a cosmopolitan perspective which is bound to find a favourable reception.

According to Hardt and Negri, any attempt to resurrect the nation-state in opposition to the world's present imperial constitution would be to espouse a 'false and pernicious' ideology. The anti-globalization philosophy and the claims of environmentalists and localists are to be rejected as primitive, anti-dialectical positions and hence, in practice, 'reactionary'. Communists—and Hardt and Negri describe themselves as such—are by vocation universalist, cosmopolitan, 'catholic': their horizon is that of

---

20. Ibid., p. 10.

21. On this discussion see A. Negri and D. Zolo, 'L'Impero e la moltitudine: Dialogo con sul nuovo ordine della globalizzazione', *Reset* 73, 2002, pp. 8–19, now also in A. Negri, *Guide: Cinque lezioni su Impero e dintorni*, Milano: Raffaello Cortina, 2003, pp. 11–33. A complete version in English, longer than the one originally published in *Reset*, can be found in *Radical Philosophy* 120, 2003, pp. 23–37, ed. A. Bove and M. Mandarini.

humankind at large, of 'generic human nature' as Marx put it. During the twentieth century, the proletarian masses looked to the internationalization of political and social relations. Nowadays the 'global' powers of empire have to be controlled, but not demolished: the imperial constitution should be maintained and made to serve non-capitalist objectives. For Hardt and Negri, even if it is true that the technologies used in enforcing law and order are the quintessence of the imperial order, this order has nothing to do with the practices of dictatorships and totalitarianism that flourished during last century.

From the point of view of the transition to a communist society, the construction of empire is 'a step forward': empire 'is better than what came before' because 'it does away with the cruel regimes of modern power' and 'also increases the potential for liberation'.[22] We can recognize here a sort of imperial optimism whose roots, I would suggest, go back to the dialectical metaphysics of Hegel and Marx. As we shall see, this imperial optimism clashes with Schmitt's realism and anti-universalism, even though Schmitt too was ready to recognize the end of the state-based system of the *jus publicum Europaeum* and propose a world order based on the post-state notion of *Grossraum*.

Global empire and war

Michael Ignatieff has recently asserted that the United States is in fact an empire—an empire of a new type, based on the principles of the free market, human rights and democracy: an authentic 'discovery in the annals of political science'. Nonetheless, however significant the innovations and features of its global hegemony, the United States, in common with all past empires, still has to shoulder a heavy burden of commitments and responsibilities. These include the task of securing 'peace, stability, democratization and oil supplies' in the Middle East and Central Asia, from Egypt to Afghanistan.[23]

---

22. See Hardt and Negri, *Empire*, pp. 46, 188.

23. See M. Ignatieff, 'The Burden', *New York Times Magazine*, 5 January 2003.

The United States is currently fulfilling the role which in the past was performed first by the Ottoman Empire, and then by the colonial empires of France and Great Britain. This explains why, after defeating the Taliban regime and occupying Afghanistan, the United States had to intervene in Iraq to put a stop to the proliferation of weapons of mass destruction, forestall the action of terrorist networks, and overthrow a tyrannical regime. The 9/11 attack showed that unless the United States adopted an imperial foreign policy it would not be able to guarantee social peace and democratic values at home.

Some Italian authors have argued along similar lines to Ignatieff, without a specific theoretical or political agenda, but have reached a diametrically opposite political judgement, making them highly critical of the imperial hegemony of the United States.[24] Personally, albeit with some reservations concerning terminology and political theory, I believe it is correct to use the expression 'empire' (and 'global empire') with regard to the increasing economic, political and above all military hegemony of the trans-Atlantic superpower.

In putting forward this thesis, I acknowledge, though without adopting it directly as a theoretical premise, the realism and anti-normativism of Carl Schmitt's philosophy of international law, as set out in such texts as *Völkerrechtliche Formen des modernen Imperialismus* (1933) and *Völkerrechtliche Grossraumordnung mit Interventionsverbot für raumfremde Mächte* (1939), the latter reformulated in 1950 as *Der Nomos der Erde*.[25] First of all, in Schmitt's theory of empire, I believe that the critique of the United States' universalistic projection of the Monroe doctrine should be recognized as an important historical and theoretical contribution. Starting from the essentially particularistic and defensive idea of a pan-American *Grossraum*, the strategies pursued by the United States have gradually led to forms of expansionist intervention extending far beyond the theatre of the Caribbean and South America. This universalistic and globalistic (and hence imperial) projection of the Monroe

---

24. See, for example, M. Cacciari, 'Digressioni su Impero e tre Rome', *Micromega 5*, 2001; G. Chiesa, *La guerra infinita*, Milano: Feltrinelli, 2002.

25. Schmitt, *Nomos of the Earth*, pp. 189–90, 243–4.

doctrine found its most radical expression in Wilson's idealism, and had a decisive influence on the construction of the League of Nations. Planetary development, as Schmitt wrote in *Der Nomos der Erde*,

> has reached a clear dilemma between universalism and pluralism, between monopoly and polypoly. The question was whether the planet was mature enough for a global monopoly of a single power or whether a pluralism of coexisting *Großräume*, spheres of influence, and cultural spheres would determine the new international law of the earth.[26]

Secondly, one cannot deny Schmitt's perspicacity in denouncing, alongside the global and polymorphous dimension of the US empire, its tendency to attribute a global dimension to war, along with the intent to annihilate the enemy which had characterised the wars of religion. There can be no doubt that the United States has succeeded in imposing not only its economic and political hegemony but also its world-view as a monopoly, down to its very language and conceptual vocabulary.[27] At the same time, this superpower has taken on the mantle of a global empire, above all thanks to its absolute military supremacy, which has enabled it to assert itself as the guarantor of world order and *gendarme du monde*. Schmitt warned that, when one state disposes of overwhelming military force, the very notion of war is transformed: the objective of the conflict becomes the extermination of the enemy, and hostility is so fierce as to elude any limitation or regulation.[28] Only those who find themselves in conditions of irretrievable inferiority will appeal, in vain, to the provisions of international law against the crushing superiority of the adversary; while whoever can count on complete military supremacy will make invincibility the foundation for a *justa causa belli* and treat the enemy, in moral as well as legal terms, as a bandit and criminal:

---

26. Ibid., pp. 243–4.

27. On the tendency for US imperial domination to impose its lexicon, terminology and concepts on hegemonized peoples, see C. Schmitt, 'Völkerrechtliche Formen des modernen Imperialismus', pp. 179–80.

28. Schmitt, *Nomos of the Earth*, pp. 320–2.

The discriminatory concept of the enemy as a criminal and the attendant implication of *justa causa* run parallel to the intensification of the means of destruction and the disorientation of theaters of war. Intensification of the technical means of destruction opens the abyss of an equally destructive legal and moral discrimination.... Given the fact that war has been transformed into police action against troublemakers, criminals, and pests, justification of the methods of this 'police bombing' must be intensified. Thus one is compelled to push the discrimination of the opponent into the abyss.[29]

Thirdly, I believe that Schmitt's philosophy of international law merits attention when he argues that it will be difficult to achieve a reduction in international conflict and in the destructive nature of modern warfare acting through universalistic and 'de-spatialized' institutions like the League of Nations and the United Nations, which are engaged in a radical legal criminalization of war. On the contrary, world pacification will require the neo-regionalistic revival of the idea of *Grossraum*, and a reprise of multilateral negotiation between states as the normative basis and legitimation of the processes of regional integration, to set against US imperialism.

In the framework of this philosophy of law and international relations, Schmitt's stance in opposition to normativism and universalism converges with the anti-cosmopolitan positions of such 'neo-Grotian' theoreticians of international relations as Martin Wight and Hedley Bull.[30] Bull, in particular, has insisted on the need to recuperate normative categories that are less reminiscent of an Enlightenment and Jacobin conception of the international order. Opposing Kelsen's philosophy of the 'primacy of international law',[31] Bull has argued powerfully for ideas such as a balance of power

---

29.   Ibid., p. 321.

30.   See M. Wight, *Why is there no International Theory?* in H. Butterfield and M. Wight, eds, *Diplomatic Investigations*, London: George Allen & Unwin, 1969; H. Bull, *The Anarchical Society*, London: Macmillan, 1977.

31.   See D. Zolo, 'Hans Kelsen: International Peace through International Law', *European Journal of International Law* 9 (2), 1998.

between the major powers, preventive diplomacy, multilateral negotiations between states, and the *jus gentium*—meaning the complex
of international customs that has gradually established itself as a
means of making war less discriminatory and destructive, while not
of course actually eliminating it.[32]

As for international criminal justice, inaugurated with the
Tribunals of Nuremberg and Tokyo, Bull was among the first
to denounce its legal limitations and pacifist velleities. In *The
Anarchical Society* he emphasized the selective and 'exemplary'
nature of the victors' justice. He was convinced that these
characteristics violated the principle of the formal equality of
individuals before the law, and invested the jurisdiction of the
two international Tribunals with an archaic and sinister sacrificial function. In fact, penal repression was applied—with
recourse above all to the death sentence and a high degree of
discretionality—only to subjects who were deemed to be the most
responsible at the political level, or the most deeply involved in
criminal activities.[33]

In the light of what has been said in this chapter, it can be argued
that the power of the United States is an 'imperial' power in a
complex sense which differs in some ways from the 'Roman archetype'. This new definition must obviously take account of the
innovations that the processes of globalization and the consequent
transformations of war have introduced into international political
relations.

The power of the United States is an imperial power first and
foremost in a strategic sense, being a power which, thanks to its
absolute military superiority, can operate in a universalistic
prospective, enveloping the planet in the mesh of its military bases
and its satellite network of electronic espionage. In the most authoritative documents published by the Pentagon and the White House,

---

32.   See H. Bull, *The Anarchical Society*; H. Bull, 'Hans Kelsen and International
Law', in J.J.L. Tur and W. Twining, eds, *Essays on Kelsen*, Oxford: Oxford University
Press, 1986. On this topic see also A. Colombo, 'La società anarchica fra continuità e
crisi', *Rassegna italiana di sociologia* 2, 2003, pp. 237–55.

33.   See H. Bull, *The Anarchical Society*, p. 89.

the United States proclaims itself, as a 'global power', to be the only nation able to 'project power' on a planetary scale. Given its global interests, responsibilities and duties, it must extend and reinforce its 'global leadership role', meaning its supremacy in shaping the global processes of the allocation of wealth and power, in rendering its own world-view predominant, and in laying down the rules for the achievement of such a role.[34]

The power of the United States is an imperial power in a normative sense too, because it tends to ignore systematically the principles and rules of international law. The American superpower regards itself as exempt not only from the ban on aggressive war laid down in the UN Charter—the aggression against Iraq is a blatant case in point—but also from the norms of the law of warfare that have been developed by the modern international legal order, in particular in the Geneva Conventions of 1949, to safeguard civilian populations and prisoners of war. The infamous names Mazar-i-Sharif, Guantánamo, Abu Ghraib, Bagram and Fallujah immediately evoke crimes committed by the highest-ranking US political and military authorities over the last few years. The United States is the largest exporter of weapons and producer of atmospheric pollution in the world, and refuses to ratify conventions and treaties designed to limit the whole-sale destruction of human lives and the industrial devastation of the environment—to give just two examples: the Convention on Prohibition or Restrictions on the Use of Certain Conventional Weapons, outlawing the production and use of anti-personnel mines, and the Kyoto agreements on climate control. Furthermore, not only did the United States refuse to ratify the Rome Treaty approving the statute of the International Criminal Court in 1998, but it has been actively hindering its activities since its inception.

This behaviour shows how the power exercised by the United States is *legibus solutus*, standing outside and above international

---

34. See Department of Defense, *Quadrennial Defense Review Report*, 30 September 2001, at www.defenselink.mil/pubs/qdr2001.pdf; White House, *National Security Strategy of the United States of America*, 17 September 2002, on the *Jura Gentium Journal* website at www.juragentium.unifi.it.

law. An emperor makes his decisions case by case, and does not lay down normative principles of an absolute nature; nor will he abide by any general rules. Imperial power is incompatible both with the general character of law and with the formal equality of subjects in the international legal order. In this sense, the United States is the sovereign source of a new international law—a new 'Nomos of the Earth'—in a situation which the threat of global terrorism enables it to present as a global and permanent 'state of emergency'. The imperial authority of the United States administers global justice, defines the rights and wrongs of its subjects, lays down the conditions for inclusion of states among its faithful vassals or for their condemnation as 'rogue states', carries out functions of international policing against terrorism, sorts out local differences, and intervenes in controversies (even in the exquisitely Mediterranean dispute between Spain and Morocco over the 'parsley island'!). In brief, the United States operates for peace and international justice, and its subjects even invoke its imperial power to solve conflicts in a universal perspective, meaning impartially and far-sightedly.

And it is no less significant that we are witnessing a revival in Anglo-American culture of the medieval *bellum justum*—a typically imperial doctrine which presupposes the existence of a single power and authority that transcends all other authority. Truly paradigmatic in this respect is the previously mentioned document signed by sixty intellectuals in the United States which gave immediate endorsement to its campaign against the 'axis of evil' as a 'just war'.[35.] Is this not simply a return to the ancient Judeo-Christian belief that the shedding of the enemy's blood can be morally condoned, if not indeed extolled, because it reflects the will of God? The international policing carried out by the imperial power using weapons of mass destruction involves the shaping of public opinion by means of theological and ethical, rather than merely political, arguments. War is justified from a superior and impartial standpoint, in the name of values held to be shared by humanity at large. It is presented as the cardinal tool

---

35.   The document 'What We're Fighting For' can be found on the *Jura Gentium Journal* website at www.juragentium.unifi.it.

for safeguarding human rights and extending the liberty, democracy, security and well-being of all peoples. Global war has as its ultimate end the promotion of a global peace: by definition, the *pax imperialis* is a perpetual and universal peace.

6

THE REASONS BEHIND TERRORISM

Starting from the Gulf War in 1991, terrorism has proved able to organize itself so efficiently and extensively as to be seen as a threat to the world as a whole, and not just to the West. Can it be defeated? Is the 'war on terrorism', which the United States has devised and put into practice as a global preventive war, a plausible response?[1] Is it necessary to rely on pre-emptive military strikes, as in the recent wars against Afghanistan and Iraq? Or can we not try a completely different approach, rather than turning a blind eye to the reasons behind terrorism? Or again, have we simply to accept terrorism, and the collective insecurity it propagates, as a fact of life, making world peace a mere illusion? Was 9/11 the thin end of the wedge?

These are crucial questions for understanding the world we live in, and yet there is no hope of finding definitive, consensual answers—in the first place because there is no consensus concerning the notion of terrorism, but also because so-called 'global terrorism' is not in fact a homogeneous phenomenon. The term alludes to a sort of planet-wide plot of evil against good, particularly as presented by such Western Manicheans as Alan Dershowitz[2] and Michael Walzer,[3] and in Italy figures like Oriana Fallaci and Marcello Pera. While it

---

1. See White House, *National Security Strategy of the United States of America*, 17 September 2002, on the *Jura Gentium Journal* website at www.juragentium.unifi.it.

2. See A.M. Dershowitz, *Why Terrorism Works: Understanding the Threat, Responding to the Challenge*, New Haven: Yale University Press, 2002. Benjamin Netanyahu has publicly sung the praises of this book and its author, commending his uncommon intellectual brilliance and moral courage.

3. M. Walzer, *Just and Unjust Wars*, New York: Basic Books, 1992.

is true that nowadays the Arab-Islamic world is the main bastion of terrorism, it is nonetheless easy enough to demonstrate that there is no single worldwide terrorist organization—a ubiquitous al-Qaeda, dominated by Osama bin Laden—and that terrorism is not an exclusive emanation of so-called Islamic fundamentalism. In reality, rather than a single, generalized 'terrorism', there are many different ones, which express themselves in different forms and contexts. For example, the Tamil Tigers who fought until recently in Sri Lanka for the liberation of Tamil Eelam and have systematic recourse to terrorism, have no links with the world of Islam: they are a Hindu minority in opposition to the country's Buddhist majority.

There is widespread intellectual and normative uncertainty, in spite of the fact that no less than twelve international conventions have been signed in the attempt to establish a common approach to terrorism. The uncertainty prevails both in international positive law itself and among its theoreticians. It is hardly a coincidence that the need for a rigorous definition of international terrorism was one of the central issues in the recent project for reforming the United Nations, drawn up—to no avail—by the High-Level Panel appointed by Kofi Annan.[4]

War and terrorism

In the absence of a common, cogent definition, the internationalist doctrine that prevails in Western nations considers that an act of terrorism—and a terrorist organization—is characterized by the indiscriminate use of violence against a civil population with the aim of spreading panic and pressurizing a government or an international political authority. Ideological or political motivations are always seen to underlie terrorism, and this sets it apart from criminal acts motivated by private concerns, such as the pursuit of profit or personal revenge. But this interpretation—which has been reformulated by Antonio Cassese[5]—begs all sorts of questions,

---

4. See High-Level Panel on Threats, Challenges and Change, *A More Secure World: Our Shared Responsibility*, at www.un.org/secureworld.

5. See A. Cassese, *Lineamenti di diritto internazionale penale*, Bologna: Il Mulino, 2005, p. 167.

as emerged dramatically at the Euro-Mediterranean summit held in Barcelona on 27 November 2005. Many commentators, and not only in the sphere of Islam, reject it primarily because it fails to take into account the condition of populations who have suffered military defeat and are oppressed by violent occupation, such as the Palestinians. These authors maintain that 'freedom fighters' or partisans who are fighting for the liberation of their country—like the South Africans who opposed apartheid or the Palestinians who for decades have been resisting the occupation of their territory by the state of Israel—cannot be considered terrorists, whatever military actions they engage in. In such cases, the killing of civilians, even though forbidden under international law as a war crime—in particular by the 1949 Geneva Conventions—should not be regarded as terrorism. This position was strenuously reiterated in the international conventions held in 1998 and 1999 by the Arab League and the Organization of the Islamic Conference.

This is not, we should emphasize, a merely formal question, since labelling an organization as terrorist—as in the lists arbitrarily drawn up by the State Department of the United States and the European Union—carries highly significant consequences. Some pieces of national legislation have brought in specific anti-terrorism laws: in Italy and Britain, for example, the governments of Berlusconi and Blair have introduced very severe measures, not to mention the USA Patriot Act and its accompanying spread of illegal espionage in the United States, justified by the executive as contributing to the fight against terrorism. The 'terrorist' label also has consequences in terms of international law. It has become standard practice to consider a large-scale terrorist attack—chiefly the events of 11 September 2001—as a military attack on the nation involved. And some Western authors maintain that, in the light of Article 51 of the UN Charter, this justifies the international use of force against states considered in some way responsible for the attack. The military attack launched by the United States against Afghanistan in October 2001—in patent contravention of current international law—was motivated, and in practice justified by the United Nations, as an act of legitimate self-defence against the threat of terrorism.

There is another serious reservation concerning the notion of global terrorism that has taken hold in the Western world in recent years, without actually becoming a customary norm in international law or the object of a multilateral treaty. This is the idea, in part based on a glaring shortcoming in the international legal order, that no conduct falling under the aegis of state sovereignty is to be considered as terrorism. Terrorists are exclusively members of organizations that operate privately and under cover, never military personnel or their commanders serving in national armies. Nations and their armed forces are never to be considered the equivalent of terrorist criminal organizations. Any action they may undertake—even the most violent, destructive and exorbitant in terms of harm to the lives and possessions of innocent civilians—is not to be regarded as terrorist activity.

Even a war of aggression that, like the recent war waged by the United States and Britain in Iraq, produces thousands of victims in the civilian population (such as the wholesale slaughter of civilians perpetrated in Fallujah in November 2004, with the use of napalm and white phosphorus) can in no way be likened to terrorism. This is legitimate military conduct, since the destruction of human lives is nothing other than a 'side effect' of a war that can ensure its own legitimation thanks to the overwhelming political and military advantage of the major powers that wage it with success. The universalist international institutions that came into being in the first half of last century—principally the United Nations—do not have any power whatsoever to de-legitimize wars of aggression conducted triumphantly by the major powers. Only the wars of the vanquished are illegitimate.

By the same token, Palestine under military occupation is accused of being the breeding-ground of Islamic terrorism, and in particular of suicide bombers. It is conveniently forgotten that the first acts of terrorism in Palestine were carried out by Jewish organizations like the Stern Gang, led by Yitzhak Shamir, and the Irgun Zwai Leumi, under the command of Menachem Begin, which was responsible for the infamous massacre at Deir Yassin. It is the attacks on the Israeli population by militants of Hamas and other radical organizations that are labelled and universally stigmatized as terrorist attacks. At the same time the devastating operations of the Israeli army, which continues to occupy Palestinian territory in violation of numerous Security Council resolutions, are at most identified as violations of the laws of war (or 'humanitarian law'). And this is the case even when they indiscriminately strike the civilian population, as in the so-called 'targeted killings' which, in addition to being illegal per se, invariably cause the death or mutilation of many innocent people.

This violation of international law goes entirely unpunished: the International Criminal Court has no competence over countries that have not ratified the 1998 Treaty of Rome, and these include both the United States and Israel. But, in more general terms, the Court lacks the necessary material resources, since it is not financed or backed by the United States, as are the international ad hoc tribunals, in particular that in the Hague for the former Yugoslavia. And whenever questions are raised about the conduct of the major powers, the members of the Court seem to lack the courage to launch an investigation and proceed to an indictment. As Antonio Cassese has pointed out, in the first three years of its existence the Court had still to celebrate a single trial.[6]

As we have already seen, the slaughter of hundreds of thousands of innocent people in the atomic bombings of Hiroshima and Nagasaki, ordered by President Truman (with the war already won) to leave the Soviet Union in no doubt as to US hegemony on the Pacific seaboard, has never been labelled an act of terrorism. And the same goes for the bombing raids carried out in the closing stages of the Second World War by the Allied governments against the German civilian population. Here the cost in human lives was in excess of 300,000, and 800,000 people were left wounded, with whole cities—Dresden, Hamburg, Berlin—razed to the ground (in Dresden at least 100,000 civilians were killed in a single night). These massacres, which rank alongside the Nazi concentration camps as among the cruellest and most bloodthirsty episodes in the history of humankind, have never been labelled 'terrorist' actions, and have gone unpunished. Indeed, they have even been morally justified, in particular by the apologist for 'just war' Michael Walzer, in the name of his grotesque theory of the 'supreme emergency'.[7] Meanwhile the Boeing B-29 *Enola Gay*, which dropped the atomic bomb on Hiroshima on 6

---

6. See A. Cassese, *Il processo a Saddam e i nobili fini della giustizia*, *La Repubblica*, 19 October 2005, p. 23.

7. See Walzer, *Just and Unjust Wars*, pp. 132ff.

August 1945, killing 230,000 civilians, has recently been restored and given pride of place in the US Air Force museum in Washington.[8]

In spite of all this, it now seems undeniable that, while the strategies of terrorism in its various forms are increasingly coming to resemble 'global civil war'—to use Carl Schmitt's expression[9]—'global war' has in its turn taken on the features of terrorism, if we agree to define terrorism, according to Western practice, as the indiscriminate use of violence against the civilian population of a country with the aim of spreading panic and pressurizing the political authorities. Yet both the aim of spreading panic and the objective of political coercion may be considered psychological or ideological elements that have no relevance in arriving at a normative definition of terrorism. What should count is that these are military operations in which systematic use is made of weapons of mass destruction that strike the civilian populations indiscriminately. The time-honoured distinction between combatants and non-combatants no longer applies, while the criterion of maintaining due proportion between 'legitimate' military objectives and the destruction of human lives, goods, the natural environment, and so on, eludes any possible calculation.

It appears, then, that the whole doctrine of the *bellum justum*—with its ancient ethical and theological roots—has been superseded, as has the distinction between *jus ad bellum* and *jus in bello*, which still tacitly underlay the 1949 Geneva Conventions. Military operations that cause the slaughter of innocent civilians (the 'terrorist bombings'—as even Michael Walzer has referred to them[10]—of the German cities; the holocausts of Hiroshima and Nagasaki; the Gulf War of 1991; and the wars for Kosovo, in Afghanistan and in Iraq) ought to be considered 'terrorist', and hence be prohibited under

---

8.   See V. Zucconi, 'Un museo per 'Enola Gay l'aereo che cancellò Hiroshima', *La Repubblica*, 19 August 2003, p. 18. 'Enola Gay', as many know, was the name of the mother of the B-29 pilot who dropped the atomic bomb on Hiroshima, which the pilot himself had inscribed in block capitals on the plane's fuselage.

9.   See C. Schmitt, *The Nomos of the Earth in the International Law of the Jus Publicum Europaeum*, New York: Telos Press, 2006, p. 271. Schmitt uses 'global civil war' (*globaler Weltbürgerkrieg*) to refer to a global war that is no longer subject to Westphalian international law, and is thus extremely destructive and sanguinary.

10.   See M. Walzer, *Just and Unjust Wars Wars*.

international law, whatever their initial justification or alleged *justa causa*. And this should be the case even when such terrorist wars have been 'legitimized' by a UN Security Council resolution, as happened for the Gulf War in 1991.

From this point of view the 'preventive war' of the United States and Britain against Iraq, with liberal use of weapons of mass destruction, civilian massacres, military occupation of the country, and depredation of its energy resources, is paradigmatic of the illegal and terroristic nature of the 'preventive global war' being waged on 'global terrorism'.

Terrorism as the last resort

In Western political culture the idea has taken hold that 'global terrorism' expresses the will of non-Western nations—and of the Islamic world in particular—to annihilate Western civilization and its fundamental values, meaning liberty, democracy, the rule of law and the market economy. Moreover, it is claimed that terrorism expresses a profoundly irrational will to obtain this result in the most ruthless, destructive and violent way possible, without any respect for human life. The figure of the kamikaze terrorist, associated in particular with Palestine, is taken as a paradigm of terrorists' irrationality, fanaticism and nihilism, because a suicide bomber obviously sets no store by his or her own life. At the heart of Palestinian and Islamic terrorism—the mainspring for all other terrorist manifestations—there is alleged to be a theological hate for the West, disseminated by the fundamentalist Qur'anic schools. From this perspective no other 'cause' can lie at the roots of the phenomenon, and it is even regarded as reprehensible to look for political, economic or social reasons for terrorism.

These are quite clearly untenable theses which carry serious risks. Terrorism is in fact a much less irrational phenomenon than it is made out to be. First of all, in the forms that came to predominate during the 1990s, terrorism received a decisive impulse from the 'global trauma' that the 1991 Gulf War produced in the non-Western world—above all in the Islamic world, which suffered a crushing blow to its civilization, faith and sacred places. The war launched by George H.W. Bush was one of the greatest military expeditions ever seen, and caused no less than 150,000 deaths, among them Palestinians, Jordanians, Sudanese and Egyptians, as well as Iraqis.[11] It was a war, as Fatema Mernissi has argued vehemently, that showed the overwhelming, invincible power of the United States and the extreme fragility of the Arab-Islamic world and its millennial civilization.[12] What is more, it enabled the US army to set up permanent garrisons in Saudi Arabia and other Arab-Muslim states in the Gulf, starting with Kuwait, and put paid once and for all to the expectations of a new dawn for the Palestinian people, condemning them to irreversible ethnocide.

The standard Western platitude according to which the West is under attack from Islamic terrorism—in particular in the wake of 9/11—reinforces the idea that the use of military force by the United States and Britain is merely a defensive response, necessary to ensure the survival of the West and its values in the face of a new barbarism.[13] But this is pure neo-colonial rhetoric, as was abundantly demonstrated during the visit of the president of the Italian Senate to the United States in 2005, with his talk of the necessary struggle of Western civilization against the 'cannibalism' besetting it.[14] In reality, the terrorism that developed within the Arab-Islamic world—including suicide bombing—is a strategic response to the

---

11.   On the topic of the strategic premises and impact of the Gulf War, see D. Zolo, *Cosmopolis: Prospects for World Government*, Cambridge: Polity Press, 1997, esp. Chapter 2, pp. 19–52.

12.   See F. Mernissi, *Islam and Democracy: Fear of the Modern World*, Cambridge, MA: Perseus, 1992.

13.   On this topic see G. Preterossi, *L'Occidente contro se stesso*, Rome/Bari: Laterza, 2004.

14.   In the lecture entitled 'Liberals, Cannibals and Christians', which he gave on 22 September 2005 at the University of Georgetown in the United States, Marcello Pera proclaimed among other things that

The Islamic terrorists have declared a 'holy war'—jihad—on America and on the West as a whole. Their purpose involves, on one hand, overthrowing the Islamic and Arab regimes which intend to maintain good relations with the West, and on the other, once this operation is completed, striking directly at the heart of Western civilization and throttling it by encirclement.

He ended by likening the Islamic integrists to cannibals: either the Western liberals and Christians manage to convert the integrists to their principles, or they risk being devoured.

hegemony of the Western world. It constitutes a revolt against the overwhelming power of the latter's weapons of mass destruction and the extensive military control it exercises in the territories that have historically been the cradle of Islam. At heart, it represents a protest against the increasing disparity in power and wealth that sets the 'club' of the most industrialized nations apart from the vast majority of weak and poor countries, including most of the countries in which Islam prevails.

Robert Pape has argued that the decisive variable in the genesis of terrorism, and in particular of suicide terrorism, is not religious fundamentalism, nor indeed poverty or under-development. In the great majority of cases, it is an organized response to what is seen as a condition of military occupation of the terrorists' own countries.[15] Besides being a territorial conquest, this form of military occupation involves the invasive presence and ideological pressure of a foreign power intent on effecting a radical transformation in the social, economic and political structures of the occupied country. As we saw in Chapter 4, the United States has elaborated a project of 'democratization' for the Arab-Islamic countries under the name of 'Broader Middle East', in the context of a more comprehensive strategy of global preventive war against terrorism. According to Pape, the Islamic terrorist organizations pursue a 'secular and strategic' goal, essentially aiming to liberate the world of Islam from the foreigner's invasive presence. Referring to the occupation of Iraq, he argues that, with each day that passes, the prolonged and massive presence of Western armies in Muslim countries increases the probability of a second, no less dramatic 9/11.

Pape backs up his thesis with a significant volume of empirical data, related in particular to suicide terrorism. Since 1980, of 315 attacks in all, no less than 301 have been the result of collectively organized terrorist campaigns, and more than half have been conducted by non-religious organizations (seventy-six can be

15. See R. Pape, *Dying to Win: The Strategic Logic of Suicide Terrorism*, New York: Random House, 2005. For the considerations that follow I am indebted to Pietro Montanari's commentary on Pape's book: see P. Montanari, *Morire per vincere: La strategia del terrorismo suicida*, on the *Jura Gentium Journal* website at www.juragentium.unifi.it.

attributed to the Tamil Tigers). In Pape's opinion, this demonstrates the political and predominantly secular nature of the terrorist struggle, which receives further confirmation in the declarations of the leaders of the terrorist groups themselves, including religious leaders. The rational character of the recourse to suicide terrorism can be seen in the fact that it involves a lesser loss of human lives than conventional guerrilla warfare, and is significantly more effective. It is the 'last resource' available to weak agents operating in conditions of total asymmetry concerning the forces deployed: it is in fact 'a realistic option', as al-Shaqaqi, general secretary of the Islamic Jihad, defined it in 1995.[16]

How can terrorism be defeated?

Alan Dershowitz, one of the most prominent 'liberal' lawyers in the United States, maintains that there is no point enquiring into the 'profound reasons' underlying terrorism.[17] Indeed, such an enquiry might itself be hazardous. The worst mistake that the adversaries of terrorism can commit is to pause and give thought to its 'causes'. In the face of terrorism, one has to adopt precisely the opposite strategy: never to try to understand and eliminate its alleged causes, but merely to meet it with a stark intransigence that admits of no dialogue or negotiations. The message to be sent to terrorists must make no acknowledgement of their claims or goals: even if their claims were excellent and their goals legitimate, these would still have to be denied and rejected as irrelevant. Failure to do this would mean inciting all those who believe themselves to be victims of injustice, oppression or exploitation to use terrorism to advance their cause.

There is only one strategy to stop the terrorists: prevent them from deriving any advantage from their actions, and make it clear to them in advance that their bloody actions will reap no benefits. However, in order to break the chain of cause and effect that nurtures international terrorism, it is necessary to intervene with much more energetic measures than those the West has adopted

---

16. See Pape, *Dying to Win*, pp. 32, 70–1.
17. See Dershowitz, *Why Terrorism Works*.

to date. Severe punishments have to be inflicted on the terrorists, 'incapacitating' their militants by arresting or killing them, and introducing preventive and punitive measures including torture, assassination, infiltration with spies, corruption, blackmail, collective reprisals, and the destruction of the homes of suicide bombers' relatives. To illustrate the strategy of incapacitation, Dershowitz uses the graphic metaphor of a zoo—quite possibly prompted by the cages at Guantánamo. In a zoo, wild animals are kept behind bars: no attempt is made to modify the animals' natural propensities; it is simply a matter of putting up an insuperable barrier between us and them.[18]

Over the last thirty years, Dershowitz maintains, the international community has systematically rewarded terrorists. This is true of the United Nations, but also of some European governments, including France, Germany and Italy. The tragedy of 9/11 would not have happened without the tolerance shown by such authorities, who can be charged with objective complicity for permitting such tolerance to be interpreted as encouragement. If this tendency is reversed, there can be no doubt that the terrorists, and the Islamic groups in particular, will be rapidly eliminated.

In putting forward these arguments, Dershowitz refers not only to al-Qaeda but also, and above all, to the Palestine Liberation Organization and the Palestinian National Authority. He believes that it is impossible to explain the events of 9/11 without considering the development and success of Palestinian terrorism. By analyzing the whole course of the Palestinian reaction to Israel's military occupation of its territories from the perspective of terrorism, Dershowitz is able to propound a radical denial of the right of the Palestinian people to their own land and future.[19] Above all, this enables him to invest them with a crushing burden of guilt, as the originators of the suicide terrorism that led to the massacres of Manhattan and the Pentagon.[20]

---

18. See ibid., p. 17.

19. On this topic see E. Said, *The Question of Palestine*, New York: Vintage Books Edition, 1992.

20. The central chapter of *Why Terrorism Works* is devoted to proving that the concessions that the European allies and the United Nations have made to the Palestinian people since 1968 rendered 9/11 inevitable. Dershowitz even regards

There is no doubt that the question of how to face up to and defeat international terrorism is one of the gravest issues confronting us today. In this respect, Dershowitz is perfectly right. No one would dispute that terrorism is not to be encouraged in any way whatsoever. And it is equally vital to come up with concrete measures to defeat it, depriving it of its ideal justifications and popular support. But it is precisely for this reason that Dershowitz's whole approach, including his arguments and his proposals, must be firmly rejected. In order to defeat terrorism we have to start from a realistic analysis of the reasons behind it, rather than denying them out of hand. Terrorism is successful because there are people in the Western world ready to adopt stances like those of the 'liberal' Dershowitz, and governments that base the fight against terrorism precisely on the principles he endorses. Whether in the microcosm of Palestine or worldwide, terrorism functions because the answers to it that have been tried to date—the repression, involving ethnocide, of the second Palestinian Intifada, the wars of aggression in Afghanistan and Iraq, the strategy of 'preventive' global war—are exactly the ones that Dershowitz is advocating as something new and decisive. In reality they are no less bloody than the terrorist attacks, and every bit as morally reprihensible. What is more, rather than being motivated by the desperate will of a people to resist oppression, they betray the ruthless will of a great power (or of an ally like Israel, endowed with state-of-the-art military equipment and nuclear weapons) to impose on the world the diktat of power.

In taking such an approach, such apologists merely provide a theoretical and rational justification for an anti-terrorist strategy that has been in action for years: that of Ariel Sharon in the Middle East and George W. Bush on the global scale. It is an aggressive strategy which in Palestine has prevented both the United Nations and European diplomacy from attempting a political mediation between the contending parties, involving the use of troops to create no-go zones and ensure peace-keeping. And it has also been a failure

---

international recognition of the Palestine Liberation Organization as an example of yielding to terrorism. In his opinion a unanimous condemnation of the Arab stance and outright refusal to recognize the PLO would have placed the Arab–Israeli conflict in a different perspective, and strangled terrorism at birth.

in Afghanistan and Iraq, where the 'preventive' war of aggression has sucked its participants into a vortex of hate, fear, destruction and death that risks engulfing the world in a never-ending terrorist war. In theory the alternative is exceedingly simple, even though in practice it will be difficult, if not impossible, to carry out in the current situation. The world has to be freed from the economic, political and military dominion of the United States and its closest European allies. For the primary, if not exclusive, source of international terrorism is the excessive power of the new, highly civilized 'cannibals', who are white, Christian, and Western.

7

FROM NUREMBERG TO BAGHDAD

A new start for international criminal justice

Following the protracted parenthesis of the Cold War, the experience of international criminal justice, inaugurated in 1945 and 1946 with the Nuremberg and Tokyo Tribunals, was revived in 1993 by the Security Council of the United Nations. On the instigation of the United States, the International Criminal Tribunal for the former Yugoslavia was created in the Hague, followed in 1994 by that for Rwanda, based at Arusha in Tanzania. In the summer of 1998, after laborious preparations, the representatives of 120 nations gathered in Rome to approve the Statute of the International Criminal Court. It was inaugurated in the Hague five years later, following the ratification of its statute. Unlike the four ad hoc international Tribunals that preceded it, this Court is endowed with a universal and permanent jurisdiction, which nonetheless remains complementary to national jurisdictions.

Alongside the creation of the two Tribunals and the Court, the 1990s saw a proliferation of cases of 'mixed' jurisdiction—in Cambodia, Sierra Leone, Kosovo, East Timor—in which international and national judges presided jointly and the domestic criminal system was complemented by international criminal law.[1] Then, in December

---

1. In Sierra Leone the normal activity of penal jurisdiction was flanked by a 'Commission for truth and reconciliation'. The mixed systems adopted in Cambodia (for the punishment of crimes connected with the Khmer Rouge), Kosovo and East Timor were all rigorously judicial. In the latter case the structure of the Tribunal was substantially based on the Indonesian national system, but it was obliged to apply international criminal law. On these topics see A. Lollini, 'Le processus de

2003, at the behest of the United States, the Iraqi Special Tribunal was set up in Baghdad: although this was a national court, it had many affinities with the ad hoc international criminal Tribunals, not least because it was instituted by occupying forces to pass judgement on the vanquished. Its legitimacy, as we shall see, is fiercely contested on account of the ongoing presence of occupation troops on Iraqi territory and the lack of legal powers and political autonomy that characterizes the Governing Council, which is formally responsible for its statute.[2]

In the opinion of many authors—notably Jürgen Habermas, Ulrich Beck and Michael Ignatieff—the rapid and formidable development of international criminal justice is a highly positive phenomenon. The international legal system, it is argued, is adapting quickly to a global scenario in which state sovereignty is in decline, new subjects are emerging, and the Grotian principle of the exclusion of individuals as subjects of international law is being superseded. In addition, in the wake of the Cold War, international criminal justice is emerging as a timely response to the spread of ethnic conflicts, virulent nationalism and religious fundamentalism, all of which are seeing widespread and serious violations of human rights. In the future no one must believe they can get away with fomenting conflicts or conducting nationalistic campaigns culminating in genocide without facing the sanctions of a criminal court, and being pursued by an international police force. In this sense the penal instrument is seen as exercising an effective preventive function even with respect to the 'new wars'.

The international criminal courts are alleged to be substantially more effective than their national counterparts in punishing war crimes and crimes against humanity. Domestic courts are basically unwilling to deal with crimes that have no significant territorial or

---

judiciarisation de la résolution des conflits: les alternatives', in E. Fronza and S. Manacorda, eds, *La justice pénale internationale dans les décisions des tribunaux ad hoc*, Milan: Dalloz-Giuffrè, 2003. Both when ad hoc international courts have been set up and in cases of mixed jurisdiction—in Sierra Leone, for example—procedures for conflict resolution have also been tried, on the initiative of and backed by national governments, which are alternative or complementary to the penal process.

2.   See the statute of the Iraqi Special Tribunal in the survey 'War, Law and Global Order', *Jura Gentium* journal, at www.juragentium. unifi.it.

national links with the state in which they function. Technically, international courts are more competent to establish and interpret international law, judge crimes from an impartial standpoint, and guarantee uniform legal standards. What is more, the fact that international trials attract much greater coverage in the mass media is taken to mean that they can better express the will of the international community to punish those guilty of serious international crimes and the function of public censure that lies behind the sentences.

The 'precedent' of Nuremberg

In spite of the profuse optimism of those we might call the 'legal globalists', the institutional and normative status of international criminal justice remains uncertain and controversial on various counts. These include the autonomy and impartiality of the courts (and of the prosecutors in particular), respect for the accused's rights of habeas corpus, and the quality of the punishments handed down, together with their motivation and effectiveness as a deterrent.

As is well known, criticisms and reservations concerning both the normative foundation and the efficacy of international criminal jurisdiction have been voiced by many authors, in particular with respect to the Nuremberg trials. Prominent among the critics have been Hannah Arendt, Bert Röling, Hedley Bull and Hans Kelsen.[3] Arendt declared the motivations advanced by the victorious nations in justifying the legal powers they attributed to the Nuremberg Tribunal to be extremely weak. The alleged precedent of the indictment of Kaiser Wilhelm II of Hohenzollern actually involved the violation of treaties and not the crime of aggression, although this was the chief imputation in the Nuremberg proceedings. Moreover,

---

3. See H. Arendt, *Eichmann in Jerusalem: A Report on the Banality of Evil*, New York: Viking Press, 1963; B.V.A. Röling, 'The Nuremberg and the Tokyo Trials in Retrospect', in C. Bassiouni and U.P. Nanda, eds, *A Treatise on International Criminal Law*, Springfield: Charles C. Thomas, 1973; H. Bull, *The Anarchical Society*, London: Macmillan, 1977, p. 89; H. Kelsen, *Peace through Law*, Chapel Hill: The University of North Carolina Press, 1944, pp. 88ff; H. Kelsen, 'Will the Judgment in the Nuremberg Trial Constitute a Precedent in International Law?' *International Law Quarterly* 1 (2), 1947, p. 115.

the Kellogg-Briand Pact, which in 1928 condemned wars of aggression as an instrument of national policy, established no criterion for defining wars of aggression, and nor did it contemplate sanctions against states, let alone individuals.[4]

The Dutch jurist Bert Röling, who sat on the Tokyo Tribunal, ends his acute analysis of the Nuremberg and Tokyo trials by stating in no uncertain terms that the objective of the two trials had not been the exercise of justice: they had been deliberately used by the victors for propaganda purposes and to conceal their own misdeeds.[5] For his part, Hedley Bull, in *The Anarchical Society*, denounced the selective and 'exemplary' nature of international criminal justice. In his opinion these attributes violated the principle of the formal equality of individuals before the law, and invested the jurisdiction of the International Tribunals with an archaic and sinister sacrificial function. The penal sanctions—in many cases, the death sentence—had been applied only to a few subjects, who were generically held to be those most responsible at the political level, or most heavily involved in criminal activities.[6]

In spite of coming out strongly in favour of the institution of an international criminal court at the end of the Second World War in his famous pacifist manifesto *Peace through Law*, Hans Kelsen emerged as one of the Nuremberg Tribunal's harshest critics.[7] In an essay bearing the significant title 'Will the Judgment in the Nuremberg Trial Constitute a Precedent in International Law?' Kelsen argued that the trial and sentence of Nuremberg could not be allowed to stand as a legal precedent. If the principles applied at Nuremberg were to persist, then at the end of every war the

---

4. See Arendt, *Eichmann in Jerusalem*.

5. See Röling, 'The Nuremberg and the Tokyo Trials'.

6. H. Bull, *Anarchical Society*, p. 89.

7. In 1944 Kelsen outlined a 'permanent league for the maintenance of peace' which grafted one important innovation onto the old model of the League of Nations: a key role was attributed to judicial functions, not to the executive and legislative functions. Individual citizens guilty of war crimes were to be indicted by an international court, and their states were to make them available to the court. In spite of this position, in *Peace through Law* Kelsen was highly critical of the Allied powers for their intention, reiterated several times in the years 1942 and 1943, to set up an international criminal tribunal comprising judges belonging to the victorious nations. See Kelsen, *Peace through Law*, pp. 88ff.

victorious nations could put the governments of the vanquished on trial for committing 'crimes' unilaterally and retroactively defined as such by the victors themselves.[8] The imputation of penal responsibility to individual subjects on the grounds of the criminal nature of wars of aggression had ignored the fact that the international law in force, including the Kellogg-Briand Pact, only contemplated the collective responsibility of states, so that sanctions could not apply to individuals. The only legal basis for the trial celebrated at Nuremberg was the agreement reached in London in August 1945— but this was a partisan deal between countries who had won the war and intended to punish the crimes they themselves attributed to the defeated.

In Kelsen's opinion, the punishment of war criminals should be an act of justice and not the continuation of hostilities in forms which are ostensibly legal but in reality based on the desire for revenge. The victorious states should have consented to any citizens of their own who were believed to be guilty of war crimes standing trial before an international court. And this would have had to be an impartial body with a wide-ranging jurisdiction, not a tribunal set up by a military occupying force with highly selective competence.[9] Moreover, Kelsen denounced the scandalous infringement of the imperative *nulla culpa sine iudicio* ('no penalty without a law'), which was invalidated not only by the court's composition and the procedures adopted, but also by the general presumption of the guilt of those accused. Such a presumption anticipated the court's findings, and turned the proceedings into mere show trials.

The 'Nuremberg model'

On the basis of these lucid and authoritative criticisms, we can outline the structural and functional limitations of the first experience of international criminal justice. This involves examining not only the topics of the autonomy of the court and the rights of the

---

8. See Kelsen, *Will the Judgment in the Nuremberg Trial Constitute a Precedent in International Law?*, p. 115.

9. See Kelsen, *Peace through Law*, pp. 110–15. Kelsen was in no doubt that the Allied powers too—in particular the Soviet Union—had violated international of law.

accused, but also the crucial question of the quality of the justice enacted and the motivation of the punishments. The outcome will be the portrait of a victors' justice which I propose to label the 'Nuremberg model'. We will see that this model, for all Kelsen's eloquence, has imposed itself in the subsequent development of international criminal justice not only as a precedent but as an authentic paradigm: from Nuremberg to Tokyo, to the Hague, and to Baghdad.

Synthesizing radically, we can identify three constituent elements of the Nuremberg model:

1. The first is the failure of the court to be autonomous and impartial, requisites which were also seriously lacking both in Nuremberg and in Tokyo. What distinguishes the legal approach from political activity in general—and all the more so from military activity—is the attempt to create a neutral institutional 'space' that is independent of the direct confrontation of the parties having a stake in the conflict. The legal approach attempts to deconstruct the conflict and contain its aggressive pressures so as to limit its destructive effects. Naturally, the pursuit of a perfect legal impartiality belongs in the realm of utopia, and one can recognize, with Pier Paolo Portinaro, that a contamination of justice and politics is inevitable in any organ of international jurisdiction.[10] But if the sphere of independence is wholly compromised, we are faced with the dramatic oxymoron of 'political justice'. If the imperative *nulla culpa sine iudicio* is invalidated by an attribution of guilt already determined by the court's political sponsors and anticipating its findings, then justice has been made subordinate to politics, serving merely to supply symbolic trappings and to inflate the immunity and arbitrariness of power.[11] In *Politische Justiz*,

---

10. See P.P. Portinaro, 'Introduzione' in A. Demandt, ed., *Processare il nemico: Da Socrate a Norimberga*, Turin, Einaudi, 1996, pp. xii–xxi.

11. As Pier Paolo Portinaro has said,

In everyday speech, politics and justice are usually viewed as opposites, and there is surely good reason for this. Politics is basically factiousness, division, struggle

Otto Kirchheimer argued that if the functional differentiation between justice and politics is abolished, the penal trial ends by performing merely para- or extra-legal functions: a theatrical ritualization of the political struggle in which the enemy is personalized and stigmatized, and the measures to be taken (including physical elimination) are given a procedural legitimation, as in an expiatory sacrifice.[12] These factors are all clearly present in the Nuremberg model.

2. The second element is the violation of the rights of habeas corpus, and more generally of the subjective rights of the accused. As we have seen, the most forceful and widespread criticism concerns the violation of the principle of non-retroactivity of criminal law, in relation to both the crime of aggression and crimes against humanity. There was clear precedent only for war crimes, in the first two Hague Conventions, agreed in 1899, and in the third of 1907, although these documents never contemplated the incrimination of individuals. Together with the violation of the principle of non-retroactivity, we can also note the retroactive character of the Tribunal's jurisdiction, for it claimed competence over conduct that preceded its institution, infringing the principle of rule of law which precludes the constitution of special tribunals.

The violation of habeas corpus involved first and foremost infringement of the principle of equality before the law, since the accused were selected according to arbitrary criteria such as their status in the political, financial or military hierarchies of the Nazi regime, and whether they had

---

and strategic manoeuvring aiming at success, while justice is the pursuit of impartiality, neutrality, equidistance from the contending parties, acting in order to achieve agreement in a normative framework ('Introduzione' in A. Demandt, ed., *Processare il nemico*, pp. xii–xiii).

See also P.P. Portinaro, *Crimini politici e giustizia internazionale: Ricerca storica e questioni teoriche*, Turin: Working Papers, Dipartimento di Studi Politici dell'Università di Torino, 2005, pp. 75–8.

12.   See O. Kirchheimer, *Politische Justiz*, Frankfurt: Europäische Verlaganstalt, 1981.

occupied 'a high position in the state' or 'decisive positions' in the preparation of international crimes. No less inimical to the fundamental rights of the accused was the fact that, in the absence of pre-existing general norms, it was the judges and prosecutors of the Tribunal themselves who established the procedural rules and the nature of the punishments. These figures in turn were bound by the directives issued by the victorious nations, who kept a firm grip on the conduct of the trial.[13] Lastly, the rights of the defence were subject to the discretionary powers of the judges, including the inadmissibility of evidence regarding the unilateral nature of the court, appointed by victors who had been responsible for the same, or indeed more serious, crimes as those imputed to the losers. The Tribunal's statute ruled out any consideration of such criminal behaviour as the saturation bombing of German and Japanese cities by the Anglo-American forces, or the dropping of the atomic bombs on Hiroshima and Nagasaki.

3. The third element is the quality of the punishments handed down by the Tribunal and, more generally, its underlying philosophy of punishment. There can be no doubt that the penal conception of the Tribunal judges was based on expiation and retribution: the proof for this is their extensive recourse to the death sentence, with the impossibility of appeal and the immediacy of execution. The court tended to calculate the nature of the sanction according to the gravity it attributed to the crime in question, without any consideration of such 'subjective elements' as whether or not it had been committed voluntarily, with any awareness of the consequences, and whether there were personal motives at stake—or of the wider social and cultural

---

13. See H. Ahlbrecht, *Geschichte der völkerrechtlichen Strafgerichtsbarkeit in 20. Jahrhundert*, Baden-Baden: Nomos, 1999, pp. 73–4; L. Douglas, *The Memory of Judgment: Making Law and History in the Trials of the Holocaust*, New Haven: Yale University Press, 2001, pp. 39–64; W. Maser, *Nürnberg: Tribunal der Sieger*, Düsseldorf: Econ, 1977.

context. The retributive option was in fact an elemental
and unreflected course of action, denoting a failure even
to attempt to elaborate a theory of punishment, whether in
the Tribunal's statute or in its final pronouncement.

Prosecutors and judges do not seem to have given the slightest thought
to the issue of the purpose of punishment or its effects on the personality and future of those convicted. The sanction—whether the death
sentence, life imprisonment or a specified prison sentence—had a
purely afflictive value. It was merely a matter of persecuting the guilty
party so as to cause suffering, mortification and humiliation to the
point of physical and moral annihilation. Indeed, even the efficacy
of punishment as a deterrent appears to have been subordinated
to its 'exemplary' quality. The sentences handed down were clearly
designed much less to prevent any future perpetration of crimes
than to celebrate the might of the victors—themselves responsible for
grave international crimes—just as, in pre-modern times, the 'splen-
dour' of the condemned man's torment was a collective celebration
of the majesty of king or emperor.[14]

If this is a plausible reconstruction of the Nuremberg model as
the incarnation of victors' justice, then we are faced once again with
Hans Kelsen's radical query: Can the Nuremberg trials be taken as
a model to be imitated? Or, on the contrary, were they a negative
precedent, an original sin of international justice? Is the autonomy
of criminal courts vis-à-vis the powers that set up, assist and finance
them to be regarded as a figment of the imagination of ingenuous
jurists unversed in *Realpolitik*? Do the fundamental rights of individuals have to capitulate before the prerogatives of a victors' justice
that cannot go into niceties—even when the victors maintain they
have used force for humanitarian ends—because it is operating in the
context of potestative strategies on a planetary scale? And last, but by
no means least, what purpose should be attributed to international
criminal sanctions? Must they, like any other form of revenge, have
a strictly retributive function? Must they impose expiation for the
criminal's failings and foster his redemption? Or must they rather be

14. See M. Foucault, *Surveiller et punir: Naissance de la prison*, Paris:
Gallimard, 1975.

commensurate with the real extent of the convict's threat to society? Can a single individual be held penally responsible for a collective event of such complexity as a war of aggression? Must the punishment go to offset the specific damage done, or should it instead fulfil the function of general prevention of international criminal activity and thus, in the last instance, of war?

These questions are anything but academic, for definition of the quality of sanctions is crucial in determining the rationale and purpose of criminal jurisdiction.[15] Has the new beginning of international criminal justice seen in the 1990s come up with convincing answers to these questions? Or will the 'Nuremberg syndrome', as Antonio Cassese has called it, prove to have infected both the International Criminal Tribunal for the former Yugoslavia—of which Cassese was the first president—and the Iraqi Special Tribunal, which was created to try the former dictator Saddam Hussein?[16]

The 'Nuremberg model' at the Hague

I shall pass over the Arusha Tribunal for Rwanda, because it really had little significance either in the country itself or at the international level. At the beginning of 2000, six years after the Tribunal

---

15. See E. Fronza and J. Tricot, 'Fonction symbolique et droit pénal international: une analyse du discours des tribunaux pénaux internationaux', in E. Fronza and S. Manacorda, eds, *La justice pénale internationale*, p. 299. See also S. Manacorda, 'Les peines dans la pratique du Tribunal pénal international pour l'ex-Yugoslavie: l'affaiblissement des principes et la quête de contrepoids', in ibid.; J.C. Nemitz, 'Sentencing in the jurisprudence of the International Criminal Tribunals for the Former Yugoslavia and Rwanda', in H. Fisher, C. Kress and S.R. Lüder, eds, *International and National Prosecution of Crimes under International Law: Currents Developments*, Berlin: Duncker & Humblot, 2001.

16. See A. Cassese, 'Il processo a Saddam e i nobili fini della giustizia', *La Repubblica*, 19 October 2005, p. 23:

When it came to ascertaining whether NATO personnel had committed war crimes in Serbia in 1999, the Chief Prosecutor in the Hague chose not to open an investigation ... Thus the 'Nuremberg syndrome' is haunting the tribunal, undermining its activity ... This syndrome exploded on the grand scale in the case of Iraq. The Tribunal for Saddam represents a blatant step in the wrong direction. It is an exclusively national organ: set up in practice by the leading occupying power, on 10 December 2003, it is made up exclusively of Iraqi judges, carefully chosen by the occupier. It is also a special tribunal, constituted virtually *ad personam*...

was set up, there were something like 120,000 inmates languishing in desperate conditions in Rwandan prisons, while thirty-eight detainees stood accused of genocide. The International Tribunal had tried five of the accused, while in all likelihood tens of thousands of people had been responsible either directly or indirectly for a tragedy that had engulfed the whole population, causing the deaths of something approaching a million people. International justice proved quite incapable of intervening effectively in the social context of Rwanda, while more significant results do seem to have been achieved through traditional forms of justice such as the *Gacaca*, which bears some affinities with the non-judicial model of pacification applied in South Africa's Truth and Reconciliation Commission.[17]

I shall also abstain from treating here the International Criminal Court, whose activity, more than three years after its institution, seems quite insubstantial: to date not a single trial has been held. Not only does the Court lack adequate financial resources and international political backing, but it is being effectively sabotaged by the United States, which has not ratified its statute and does not intend to permit a sole US citizen to be brought before it. The United States does not appear to conceive of any international justice other than that of the victors—on condition, of course, that it is one of them.

I am going to concentrate here on the experience of the ad hoc Tribunal for the former Yugoslavia, set up in 1993 by the UN Security Council. In the next section I shall look at the Iraqi Special Tribunal which the United States, as the occupying power, imposed on that nation. Although it is a national tribunal, it has much in common with the international criminal tribunals set up by the occupying powers in Germany: the judges are Iraqi, but they work under the orders of the occupiers, just as the judges at Nuremberg did, according to a statute drawn up by US jurists.[18]

---

17. On the experience of the *Gacaca*, see A. Lollini, 'L'istituzione delle giurisdizioni Gacaca: giustizia post-genocidio e processo costituente in Ruanda', *Rivista di Diritto pubblico comparato ed europeo* 2, 2004.

18. Antonio Cassese has said that

the trial that has opened in Baghdad merely reflects the will of the Americans to do justice as they please, keeping complete control over the process ... I am afraid that the trial cannot possibly be fair on a number of counts. First of all for the make up of the Tribunal: the judges are all Iraqi and chosen by a political organ. According

The Tribunal for the former Yugoslavia, as I have argued and amply documented elsewhere,[19] has on numerous occasions shown its direct dependence on the directions of the United States, which brought it into being and continues to support and finance it. Moreover, from the closing years of the war in Bosnia, the Prosecutor's Office of the Tribunal and the NATO forces deployed on the territory of the former Yugoslavia began to work in close collaboration. The Ifor and Sfor contingents fulfilled the standard functions of a police force, carrying out investigations, pursuing incriminated persons and arresting them. This anomalous collaboration came to resemble nothing short of institutional synergy when the US judge Gabrielle Kirk McDonald became president of the Hague Tribunal and the Canadian Louise Arbour was appointed chief prosecutor . In frequent exchanges with journalists, the latter made no secret of her wholehearted adherence to the political aims of the Western powers and her hostility to the Yugoslav government and its president, Slobodan Milošević.[20]

In the early months of 1996 the chief prosecutor had a meeting with the secretary-general of NATO and the Supreme Allied Command in Europe to 'establish contacts and begin discussing modalities of cooperation and assistance' between NATO and the Prosecutor's Office. On 9 May that year a memorandum was signed between the Prosecutor's Office and the Supreme NATO Headquarters in Europe. This set out the practical details of the assistance that NATO was to provide to the Prosecutor's Office, including consignment of those wanted by the Tribunal on their arrest by the contingents operating in the former Yugoslavia. This

---

to its statute, the Council of Ministers chooses the judges on the recommendation of a magistrates' council. Thus the judges have been chosen on the basis of political criteria which are neither transparent nor impartial. Secondly, the tribunal includes no international judges. It would have been advisable to include at least some judges from other Arab countries, since their presence would have ensured a greater degree of impartiality (see also 'Ma non è un processo equo', interview by Guido Ruotolo, *La Stampa*, 20 October 2005, p. 3).

19. See D. Zolo, *Invoking Humanity: War, Law and Global Order*, London/New York: Continuum, 2002, where I dedicate a large part of Chapter 4 (pp. 106–20) to documenting the subordination of the Chief Prosecutor's Office to NATO directives.

20. See L. Arbour, 'Così porterò alla sbarra tutti i boia di Milošević', interview by N. Lombardozzi, *La Repubblica*, 7 May 1999, p. 11.

first meeting was followed by others, including one with the NATO commander General Wesley Clark.[21]

A few years later a subsequent chief prosecutor, Carla del Ponte, reciprocated by ignoring—just as Arbour had done—violations of international law committed by NATO personnel in the seventy-eight days of uninterrupted bombing conducted during the war for Kosovo. Three official denunciations were presented to the Tribunal—by a delegation from the Russian parliament, by the Belgrade government, and by a group of authoritative Canadian jurists led by Michael Mandel—but the chief prosecutor simply dismissed them as being manifestly unfounded, showing no scruples about placing international justice at the service of those powers on which the Tribunal was both politically and financially dependent. Thus Arbour and del Ponte acted in perfect accord with the precedent of Nuremberg, adopting the same attitude as the prosecution counsel in that trial, namely Robert Jackson, Hartley Shawcross, François de Menthon, and the infamous Soviet general Roman Rudenko.[22] This time round there was the aggravating circumstance that the Hague Tribunal had been set up by the United Nations, not by a military alliance.

As to respect for the fundamental rights of the accused, we cannot fail to observe that many of the limitations identified in the statute of Nuremberg and in the conduct of the prosecutors and judges have been replicated in the Hague. This is true first of all for the retroactivity of the jurisdiction: instituted in 1993, the Tribunal for the former Yugoslavia is accorded precedence over the domestic courts of all the states that have come into being following the disintegration of the Yugoslav Socialist Federal Republic—Slovenia, Croatia, Serbia, Bosnia-Herzegovina, Macedonia, Montenegro—and exercises retroactive jurisdictional competence in all these countries as from January 1991. Thus, while it has avoided patent violation of

---

21. See C. Black, 'The International Criminal Tribunal: Instrument of Justice?' Proceedings of the Conference on *Justice and War*, 25 October 1999, Paris—special issue (31/32) of *Dialogue* 2000, p. 109; J. Laughland, *Le tribunal penal international*, Paris: François-Xavier de Guibert, 2003.

22. See A.-M. de Zayas, 'Der Nürnberger Prozess', in A. Demandt, ed., *Macht und Recht: Grosse Prozesse in der Geschichte*, München: Beck'sche Verlagsbuchhandlung, 1990. Roman Rudenko had achieved great notoriety as a prosecutor during Stalin's purges in the 1930s.

the principle of non-retroactivity of penal law, the Tribunal's statute has violated the no less significant prohobition of retroactivity of penal jurisdiction, enshrined in the legal principle that forbids the constitution of special tribunals.

The Tribunal's violation of the principle of equality proves to be as serious as that seen in Nuremberg and Tokyo. The accused were selected on the basis of criteria that were not legally defined; and preference tended to be given to notorious figures who would add lustre to the Tribunal and ensure the attention of the mass media, as was the case in 1999 with the sensational incrimination of the head of state Slobodan Milošević while the war for Kosovo was still in progress.[23] As some commentators have pointed out, in the absence of pre-existing general and procedural norms, the rights of the accused were also infringed (as at Nuremberg) because the judges took it upon themselves to dictate the proceedings, restricting the rights of the defence and creating a situation of widespread uncertainty as to penal law.[24] On occasion, the Tribunal even went so far as to issue

---

23.   Following the massacre of Raçak, the Chief Prosecutor Louise Arbour showed up in person at the Yugoslav border, with Christiane Amanpour at her side—a CNN reporter well known not only for her professional activity but also as the wife of James Rubin, an influential State Department spokesman. Paolo Soldini adds that

> many will recall the images of Arbour being restrained by the Serbs as she tried to enter Kosovo. Few know that the scene was set up by the CNN on the initiative of Amanpour, with the company providing its equipment and cameras. And it is thanks to her friendship with the Chief Prosecutor that the CNN correspondent was the first to give news of the incrimination of Milošević (see P. Soldini, 'La guerra dello scoop sul fronte del Kosovo', *L'Unità*, 8 August 1999, p. 15).

24.   For a critique of the procedural decisions of the Hague Tribunal, see P. Burns, 'An International Criminal Tribunal: The Difficult Union of Principles and Politics', in S. Clark and M. Sann, eds, *The Prosecutions of International Crimes: A Critical Study of the International Tribunal for the Former Yugoslavia*, New Brunswick: Transaction Publishers, 1996, pp. 125–64; M. Pellet, 'Le Tribunal criminel international pour l'ex-Yugoslavie: poudre aux yeux ou avancée décisive?', *Revue General de Droit General Public* 7, 1994. On the normative role of international criminal judges, see A. Lollini, 'L'expansion 'interne et externe' du rôle du juge dans le processus de création du droit international pénal', in M. Delmas-Marty, E. Fronza and É. Lambert-Abdelgawad, eds, *Les sources du droit international pénal*, Paris: Société de Législation Comparée, 2004. On the process of the formation of

decisions *in causa propria* ('in which it was a party'), as in the case of the trial of Duško Tadić. When challenged by the defence counsel, the Hague Tribunal went ahead and established its competence to adjudicate on its own competence, reaching—as was only to be expected—a favourable decision. As has been pointed out, by means of a circular argument the Tribunal claimed the competence to pronounce on the legality of decisions made by the international organ which had set it up, namely the Security Council.[25]

Finally, the necessity of reassessing the 'quality of justice' administered until now by the ad hoc international criminal Tribunals is an issue which, albeit with considerable delay, has become apparent to at least some of the officials and jurists involved in the experience. Here, too, it largely comes down to whether the model of criminal justice implemented at Nuremberg and Tokyo should be taken as a precedent to follow or as a paradigm to be contrasted and avoided. In terms of the discussion of the 'quality of the punishment' applied by the criminal Tribunal for the former Yugoslavia, we can identify three topics that enable us to assess it on the basis of the sentences issued by the Tribunal in the first instance and on appeal:[26]

'general principles' of international criminal law, see M. Virgilio, 'Verso i principi generali del diritto criminale internazionale', in G. Illuminati, L. Stortoni and M. Virgilio, eds, *Crimini internazionali fra diritto e giustizia*, Turin, Giappichelli, 2000 pp. 41–67; F. Raimondo, 'General principles of law as a source of international criminal law: An appraisal of the ICTY and ICTR jurisprudence', communication to the seminar *Le fonti del diritto internazionale penale: l'esperienza dei Tribunali penali internazionali*, at the Istituto di Applicazione Forense 'E. Redenti', Università di Bologna, 12 March 2004.

25. See J.E. Alvarez, 'Nuremberg Revisited: The Tadic Case', *European Journal of International Law* 7 (2), 1996, pp. 245–64; C. Greenwood, 'International Humanitarian Law and the Tadic Case', in ibid., pp. 265–83; B. Conforti, *Diritto internazionale*, Napoli: Editoriale Scientifica, 1997, pp. 401–2.

26. See R. Henham, 'The Philosophical Foundations of International Sentencing', *Journal of International Criminal Justice* 1 (1), 2003, pp. 64–85. Following a scrupulous analysis of the motivations of the sentences of the ad hoc international criminal courts, Henham roundly denounced the 'obfuscation and confusion' of the motives attributed by judges to the sanctions they hand down. On the delicate problems connected with the interpretation of international criminal norms see E. Fronza, 'I crimini di diritto internazionale nell'interpretation della giurisprudenza internazionale: il caso Akayesu', in Illuminati, Stortoni and Virgilio, eds, *Crimini internazionali fra diritto e*

the imperative to impose penal sanctions on those responsible for serious international crimes, the exemplary nature of the punishments, and their retributive function.

1. *Impunity*. One of the formulae most commonly used in motivating international criminal justice is the declaration of an intent to put an end to impunity. It is argued that the most serious war crimes and crimes against humanity tend to go unpunished on account of the complicity, ineptitude or indifference of domestic jurisdictions. And it is maintained that in the regions traumatized by conflict, the punishment of those responsible for criminal actions is a fundamental prerequisite for initiating the transition towards a new political regime, and hence towards peace.

   'To put an end to impunity' is also something of a leitmotif in the documents of the Hague Tribunal.[27] But it can be observed that, to date, the Hague Tribunal—as was also the case for the Nuremberg and Tokyo trials and is today for Rwanda—has exercised penal punishment only over a very limited number of subjects, generically identified on the basis of the most disparate criteria of opportunity. The chief prosecutors have relied on intuitive and highly discretionary evaluations that have even taken into account factors such as shortcomings in logistical structures, the insufficiency of the investigative forces, and shortage of funding. In the first six years of the Tribunal's activity, no more than ninety people were charged, while about twenty were arrested and around the same number put on trial. It is clear that, in similar circumstances, very little has changed with regard to the issue of impunity. In particular, those responsible for crimes against peace—which is to say, one of the most serious infringements of international law— have gone unpunished, since those responsible for these

giustizia, pp. 69–97.

27. See E. Fronza and J. Tricot, 'Fonction symbolique et droit pénal international', pp. 300–3.

crimes are completely immune from the jurisdiction of ad hoc courts, or indeed of any other.

2. *Exemplarity.* The exemplarity of sanctions has been extolled as an important characteristic of international criminal justice, which does not hesitate to call to account even the most prominent political figures, including heads of state such as Slobodan Milošević. It is taken to be one of the proofs of the superior impartiality and moral austerity of this legal organ, and moreover to guarantee the pedagogical efficacy of its sentences. Cherif Bassiouni, for example, has argued that the task of international criminal jurisdictions is to 'apply an exemplary and retributive justice' in order to 'reinforce social values and individual rectitude, educate present and future generations, and discourage and deter the committing of other crimes'.[28] And the Hague Tribunal, like the Nuremberg Tribunal before it—except for the exclusion of the death sentence—has imposed sanctions that have been exemplary for their afflictive severity (in many cases sentences of life imprisonment, or of up to fifty years in prison), for the solemn formality of the rites, and also for the high-profile and spectacular nature of their reporting by the mass media.

Obviously, when confronted by this sort of strategy and penological rhetoric, one might observe that exemplarity is a characteristic of sentences in pre-modern penal systems, when, rather than the equality of subjects before the law, what counted was the paternalistic and pedagogical criterion of the (public) execution of the sentence as potestative narration, reinforcing the popular perception of hierarchy.[29] And one could refer to the literature which in the second half of last century represented the penal trial as a ritual of degradation for the defendant—a collective

---

28. See C. Bassiouni, 'Etude historique: 1919–1998', *Nouvelles Etudes Pénales* 2, 1999.

29. See M. Foucault, *Surveiller et punir*.

ceremony of symbolic stigmatization serving to confirm the moral and religious prejudices shared by a social majority.[30] The more degrading and stigmatizing a trial, the more 'exemplary' it is, holding up to public opprobrium an individual who has profaned collective values and merits a 'fate worse than death'.

One could also recall what René Girard had to say about the function of scapegoat that the sacrifice of the political leader (or a 'domestic alien') performs in primitive cultures.[31] In situations of grave conflict and social instability the penal rite gives a symbolic focus to the group sense of guilt, and discharges it onto the figure of the victim, whose sacrifice serves to restore peace and regain the favour of the gods. Thus the exemplarity of the penal sentence reveals elements of ancestral irrationality, attaching a sacrificial and persecutory function to the sanction.

As for the pedagogical and dissuasive efficacy of the exemplarity of an international criminal sentence, we can recall, as a significant antecedent, that Japanese public opinion perceived the Tokyo trial as a legal parody serving merely to satisfy the desire of the United States for revenge following the attack on Pearl Harbor. It is not perhaps widely known that, from 1978, the seven Japanese citizens sentenced to death by the Tokyo Tribunal were accorded the honours reserved for martyrs of the homeland in the temple of Yasukum.[32] And something similar happened in Serbia, where the televising of proceedings in the trial of Slobodan Milošević seems to have produced the opposite effect to what was desired.

More generally, we can ask whether handing down 'exemplary' sentences to a very small number of individuals actually fulfils any useful dissuasive function with respect

---

30. See H. Garfinkel, *Studies in Ethnomethodology*, Englewood Cliffs, NJ: Prentice-Hall, 1967; J. Heritage, *Garfinkel and Ethno-methodology*, Cambridge: Polity Press, 1984.

31. See R. Girard, *Le bouc émissaire*, Paris: Editions Grasset & Fasquelle, 1982.

32. See A.-M. de Zayas, 'Der Nürnberger Prozess'.

to civil conflicts and war. It has been shown that the international criminal proceedings celebrated since the Second World War have had practically no efficacy as a deterrent. The second half of the century saw no diminution in the level of deportations, atrocities, war crimes, crimes against humanity or genocide. And numerous wars of aggression, waged above all by the nations which instigated the trials in Nuremberg and Tokyo, have claimed hundreds of thousands of victims. Nor does the punitive activity carried out in Bosnia by the Hague Tribunal between 1993 and 1998 appear to have had any deterrent effect, in view of the fact that atrocities of great gravity occurred, at the hands of all the belligerents—including NATO—in the 1999 war for Kosovo. In reality, there seems to be no evidence that the legal imposition of 'exemplary' sanctions on individuals has any impact on the macro-structural dimensions of war—meaning the profound reasons underlying conflict and armed violence.

3. *Retributiveness.* It has been demonstrated that the sentences issued to date by the ad hoc international Tribunals have taken as their paradigm the retributive and stigmatizing function of the punishment administered.[33] If this is the case, it provides one more factor that goes to make international criminal justice a phenomenon of 'revengeful' political justice, once again in terms of the Nuremberg model.

The retributive model of punishment is one of the most ancient; it harks back to the biblical tradition, and was elaborated in its most representative form by medieval Catholic theology. This type of punitive and afflictive justice regards examples of deviant behaviour as violations of an objective order and infringements on the universal harmony of the cosmos. Punishment and expiation serve to repristinate the ontological equilibrium upset by immoral or illegal behaviour. The suffering imposed on the deviant

---

33. R. Henham, 'The Philosophical Foundations of International Sentencing', pp. 66–9.

thus has both a penitentiary value—with effects of redemption and purification—and a reparatory value. From this derives the retributive idea whereby human justice must impose on the guilty party a suffering proportional to the gravity of guilt—a gravity that is objective because it is gauged according to absolute parameters of an ethical and theological nature.

Starting in the second half of the eighteenth century, modern penology has gradually moved away from this afflictive and penitentiary archetype (at least in principle), and embraced a secularized idea of the penal sanction based on the utilitarian paradigm of protecting society and re-socializing of the culprit. The penal sanction serves to neutralize the dangerousness of deviant subjects, and readmit them to the group once they have been 're-educated' and rendered harmless. The suffering inflicted is no longer seen as expiation, purification and redemption: coinciding with the restriction of liberty, it has a correctional and dissuasive function. The memory of the suffering endured is intended to dissuade the offender from repeating criminal behaviour, while the social spectacle of inflicting suffering on deviant subjects is designed to induce the majority of citizens to respect the collective rules with which the group has freely endowed itself. Thus the key criterion in the application of the sanction is neither 'retributive' nor 'vindictive': the punishment is commensurate with the 'social dangerousness' of the offender, and takes into account the evolution of his personality, arranging for a series of 'alternative measures' to imprisonment, so as to ensure flexibility in the application of punishment.

On the contrary, the retributive character of punishment excludes the purpose of social reintegration, runs counter to the idea of alternative measures to imprisonment, rejects the very notion of flexibility of the sanction, and does not contemplate any measures for aiding the convict to reacquire social skills. It renders absolute the prison house's role as a place of custody and affliction, and decontextualizes it as an instrument of exclusion and isolation for the culprit, involving irreversible, exemplary stigmatization. These are precisely the aspects of imprisonment that come in for most criticism from the exponents of contemporary penology and penitentiary sociology, ranging from Michel Foucault to David Garland and Loïc Wacquant, and in Italy Dario Melossi and Emilio Santoro.[34] Prison becomes simply a place of suffering—if not downright physical and mental torture—and violation of the most elementary individual rights. It is an instrument for annihilating anyone deemed to be an enemy of society.

In the experience of first the Nuremberg trial, and then the Tribunal for the former Yugoslavia, we have seen the development in Western legal culture of a simplified vision of the relationship between the exercise of judicial power at the international level, the phenomenon of war, the safeguarding of human rights, and the processes of pacification. This has reflected a penal optimism that has applied in the international arena elementary models of retributive justice, quantitatively deduced from national experience, in spite of the many queries concerning these models raised by Western penology and criminology during the twentieth century.[35] Yves Cartuyvels may well be right to speak of penal and penitentiary fetishism, and to reject the tendency to view the penal response to war crimes and to the violation of human rights as the key to peace and international justice.[36]

---

34. See M. Foucault, *Surveiller et punir*; D. Garland, *Punishment and Modern Society: A Study in Social Theory*, Chicago: University of Chicago Press, 1990; D. Garland, *The Culture of Control: Crime and Social Order in Contemporary Society*, Oxford: Clarendon, 2001; Loïc Wacquant, *Les prisons de la misère*, Paris: Editions Raisons d'Agir, 1999; D. Melossi, *The State of Social Control*, Cambridge: Polity Press, 1990; D. Melossi, *Stato, controllo sociale, devianza*, Milan: Mondadori, 2002; E. Santoro, 'Criminal Policy', in R. Bellamy and A. Manson, eds, *Political Concepts*, Manchester/New York: Manchester University Press, 2003.

35. On this topic see the recent contribution by E. Santoro, *Carcere e società liberale*, Turin: Giappichelli, 2004, second edn; D. Zolo, 'Filosofia della pena e istituzioni penitenziarie', *Iride* 14 (32), 2001, pp. 47–58.

36. See Y. Cartuyvels, 'Le droit pénal et l'État: des frontières 'naturelles' en question', in M. Henzelin and R. Roth, eds, *Le droit pénal à l'épreuve de l'internationalisation*, Paris: LGDJ, 2002, p. 27.

The 'Nuremberg model' in Baghdad

On 10 December 2003, the provisional Iraqi government, set up by the Coalition Provisional Authority at the behest of the US 'proconsul', Paul Bremer, formalized the statute of the Iraqi Special Tribunal.[37] This legal assembly, charged with judging Saddam Hussein and numerous exponents of the deposed Ba'ath regime, began its duties on 19 October 2005. It was a national tribunal made up exclusively of Iraqi magistrates, presided over until 15 January 2006 by the Kurd Rizkar Mohammed Amin.[38]

Its architects had obviously had to rule out the International Criminal Court of The Hague, since the Iraqi authorities had not ratified the Statute of Rome. In any case, the Court of The Hague is specifically forbidden from exercising retroactive jurisdiction, unlike all the other international criminal courts.[39] Nor did the chief occupying power, the United States, consider getting the UN Security Council to set up a new ad hoc international criminal tribunal, on the model of those for the former Yugoslavia and Rwanda. The power of the Security Council to create special international tribunals on the grounds of its 'implicit powers' is notoriously controversial.[40] The occupiers also discarded the idea of setting up,

---

37.   See the survey 'War, Law and Global Order', in *Jura Gentium* journal website, at www.juragentium.unifi.it.

38.   Rizkar Mohammed Amin, accused of being too soft in his conduct of the trial, and of giving too much of a hearing to the remonstrances of Saddam Hussein and his seven fellow defendants, resigned, ostensibly for personal reasons. He was replaced by another Kurdish judge, Rauf Rashid Abdel Rahman, who proved considerably less indulgent towards the defendants. The trial had already undergone a serious setback with the killing of the two lawyers of the defence counsel, and Saddam Hussein's reiterated claims that he had been tortured by his US gaolers.

39.   Article 11 of the statute recognizes its competence *ratione temporis* only for crimes committed after it came into effect, in July 2003.

40.   See G. Arangio-Ruiz, 'The Establishment of the International Criminal Tribunal for the Former Territory of Yugoslavia and the Doctrine of the Implied Powers of the United Nations', in F. Lattanzi and E. Sciso, eds, *Dai Tribunali Penali Internazionali ad hoc ad una Corte Permanente*, Napoli: Editoriale Scientifica, 1995; A. Bernardini, 'Il Tribunale penale internazionale per la ex Jugoslavia', *I diritti dell'uomo* 21, 1993, pp. 15–25; P. Palchetti, 'Il potere del Consiglio di Sicurezza di istituire il Tribunale Penale Internazionale', *Rivista di diritto internazionale* 79 (2), 1996, pp. 143ff.

in cooperation with the United Nations, a mixed court made up of national and international judges, on the model implemented in Sierra Leone and East Timor.[41] Nor again did the idea find favour of assigning the investigations and prosecution to the occupying powers, as had also been proposed.[42] The general opinion was that Saddam Hussein had to receive the death sentence, and for it to be carried out—the only doubt being whether by hanging or shooting. The former head of state had to perish on the gallows if he were a common criminal, and be shot if he had been allowed to stand trial, as he himself demanded, as commander-in-chief of the armed forces of his country.[43]

An autonomous and impartial tribunal?

It is widely believed in the West that the condemnation of the former Iraqi dictator and his collaborators by the special Tribunal—as happened with the Nazi leaders in Nuremberg—constitutes an important success for international law and justice. And it is also presented as a decisive step towards the pacification and democratic reconstruction of a country that the Anglo-American armies have liberated from a despotic and sanguinary regime. Obviously this is the point of view of those who side with the Western powers who, in 2003, in blatant violation of the UN Charter and general international law, attacked and invaded Iraq.

Taking a less partisan standpoint, one can recognize that the former Iraqi dictator and his chief collaborators deserved to be put on trial by legitimate representatives of the Iraqi people. And it can also be conceded that, in the country's present situation, there were

---

41.   See for example the letter sent on 22 December 2003 by Michael Posner, director of the Lawyers Committee for Human Rights, based in New York, to Abdel Aziz al-Hakim, president of the Iraqi Governing Council, available at www.lchr.org. See also F. McKay, 'Give Hussein Due Process', *Miami Herald*, 17 December 2003 (the author directs the Justice Program for the Lawyers Committee for Human Rights).

42.   This hypothesis was advanced n particular by Antonio Cassese in the interview granted to U. de Giovannangeli, 'Processo in Iraq, ma giudici internazionali', *L'Unità*, 21 December 2003, p. 14.

43.   See the interview given by Salem Chalabi to a correspondent of *Corriere della sera*, 19 December 2003, p. 13.

no plausible alternatives to a special Tribunal in order to make a break with the preceding despotic regime and inaugurate a new political direction. This thesis can be sustained in spite of the grave limits that any special Tribunal presents, starting from the compression of the rights of the defence and the substantial violation of the principle of *nulla culpa sine judicio* ('no fault without a law'), which requires a rigorous presumption of innocence for the accused. It should be added that, in the trial that took place, this principle already appeared to have been seriously violated, if only in the treatment being shown to the principal defendant, Saddam Hussein. The former president was held captive in a secret locality not by Iraqi authorities, but by the US forces that captured him, and illegally subjected to harsh interrogations and possibly tortured, which he himself did not tire of denouncing with the utmost vehemence.

Apart from the normative anomalies and distortions that we shall come on to, there are good grounds for casting doubt on the international legality, political legitimacy and independence of the Iraqi Special Tribunal, since it was set up in the context of a military occupation and at the will of an occupying power that controlled the whole scenario. From a political standpoint, the power exercised by the civilian and military personnel of the United States and the other contingents present on Iraqi territory is wholly illegitimate. It is a power that was won by force of arms—at the cost of thousands of Iraqi lives—in a war of aggression that violated both the UN Charter and customary international law. And from a strictly legal viewpoint—of *jus in bello*—it certainly cannot be maintained that the 1949 Geneva Conventions attribute to an occupying power the authority to set up special tribunals to judge the leaders of a deposed regime. Indeed one can argue, as I have done elsewhere, that, being international criminals, the occupiers have no rights whatsoever with regard to the occupied, but only obligations.[44]

There is little to be gained by invoking Resolution 1511 of the Security Council which, in the interpretation of some Western commentators, 'remedied' the original illegitimacy of the war of aggression and consequent military occupation.[45] In reality that

---

44. See Chapter 1 of this volume.
45. This can be consulted on the UN website: www.un.org.

document could not have cancelled out the infringement of international law for which the United States and its allies had made themselves responsible. Moreover, Resolution 1511 imposed on the occupiers, as a condition for the legitimacy of the power they exercised in Iraq, a precise timetable for securing approval of a constitution, organizing democratic elections and, obviously, effecting the withdrawal of the occupying forces.

At the formal level, as I have indicated, the political source for the statute of the Tribunal was the Iraqi Governing Council, set up by the Coalition Provisional Authority and thus, in practice, by the US military governor Paul Bremer. No one imagines that the Governing Council, which had no legislative authority and possessed no autonomous sources of funding, was the real power that willed, backed and financed this special Tribunal. It was in fact an occupying power, the United States, that pressed for the institution of a special Tribunal to bring to trial the deposed regime with a rigorous application of the Nuremberg model: try the enemy after his military defeat, in order to annihilate him in moral terms and put him to death.

Moreover, even though it is stated repeatedly in the statute that the members of this Tribunal should be persons of 'high moral character, impartiality and integrity', in fact they offered no guarantee of autonomy with respect to the occupying powers or impartiality towards the accused. This negative presumption is reinforced by the fact that it was the provisional government which designated the judges and prosecutors, at least in part. In any case, according to the statute the Council of Ministers was to choose the judges on the basis of political criteria that could be neither transparent nor impartial. As Hanny Megally and Paul van Zyl have shown, it is hardly surprising that the provisional government, under the supervision of Paul Bremer, lost no time in defining in detail the investigative and procedural strategy to be adopted by the Tribunal, providing an appendix listing those held in prison who were to be tried first.[46]

Moreover, in yet another replication of the Nuremberg model,

---

46. See H. Megally and P. van Zyl, 'US justice with an Iraqi face?', *International Herald Tribune*, 4 December 2003, p. 8.

Article 14 of the Tribunal's statute provides that the court can pronounce on an aggression undertaken by the Ba'ath regime against an Arab country, such as Kuwait, but denies it competence to judge crimes of aggression committed against non-Arab countries. This singular provision was introduced by the US architects of the statute to ensure that the Tribunal did not investigate the war of aggression that Iraq conducted between 1980 and 1988 against Iran, a country that observes the Muslim religion but is not Arab. The reason for this is very simple: the United States gave economic, military and diplomatic backing to that aggression, which caused no less than 800,000 casualties. In addition the United States was an accomplice to Saddam Hussein in failing to denounce some extremely serious crimes committed by Iraqi troops. The attacks carried out against Iran with the use of chemical weapons, and the atrocities in the Anfal campaign against the Kurds, were certainly no less serious than those currently imputed to Saddam Hussein. Thus we see that, just as in Nuremberg, it was a matter of preventing the defence being able to use the *tu quoque* argument, which would have been both legally and politically embarrassing for the Tribunal's sponsors. It was, in fact, a trial that celebrated 'victors' justice' in the most brazen fashion.[47]

The tribunal violates the principles of rule of law

The statute of the Tribunal approved by the provisional government went well beyond the legal abnormality intrinsic to any special tribunal. Although it displayed the normative hallmarks of Western legal culture, the statute violated some fundamental principles of the rule of law normally respected among Western nations, and

---

47. Antonio Cassese has said:

The trial must not only focus on the former dictator, who is the vanquished party: its final pronouncement must address all the crimes committed, whoever was responsible. From this point of view, the whole trial of Saddam is gravely compromised by Article 14 of the statute, which provides that the Tribunal can pronounce on an aggression against an Arab country, like Kuwait, but not against Iran, which is not an Arab country even if it is Muslim. Why two weights and two measures? Because the aggression against Iran, as we know full well, was sponsored by the West ('Ma non è un processo equo', interview by Guido Ruotolo, p. 3).

which were adopted in the statute of the International Criminal Court of The Hague.

The Tribunal could exercise its jurisdiction retroactively, judging conduct that had taken place before its institution, and hence in the absence of its jurisdiction (established as covering the period July 1968–May 2003). While this can be considered an anomaly typical of any special tribunal, the Iraqi Tribunal went further: it actually violated the principle *nullum crimen, nulla poena sine lege*. According to this principle no national tribunal—and such was, or pretended to be, the Iraqi Special Tribunal—can apply to citizens under its jurisdiction punishments which were not contemplated by the legal system in force when the conduct in question (subsequently considered illegitimate) was enacted. Alongside Iraqi criminal legislation (Article 14), the Iraqi Special Tribunal introduced a large number of types of crime (Articles 11, 12 and 13, relating to the crimes of genocide, crimes against humanity and war crimes) transposed from the statutes of the three international criminal courts then operating. Some of these types, as is explicitly recognised in Article 24, had not been contemplated by Iraqi criminal legislation, and were introduced precisely because it was felt that Iraqi positive law was lacking in norms that would make it possible to incriminate and condemn the former dictator and his collaborators.

In view of these lacunae, Article 24 of the statute authorized the Tribunal judges, whenever a crime contemplated by Articles 11, 12 or 13 had no counterpart in the Iraqi criminal system, to determine the nature of the punishment on their own authority (taking into account the gravity of the crime, the individual characteristics of the accused, and international jurisprudence).[48] It is clear that this not only infringed the principle of non-retroactivity of criminal law (incidentally, by an organ—the provisional government—devoid of any legislative power); it also granted to the Tribunal judges such broad discretionary powers as to invest them with the right to

---

48.   Article 24, e), reads:

The penalty for any crimes under Articles 11 to 13 which do not have a counterpart under Iraqi law shall be determined by the Trial Chambers taking into account such factors as the gravity of the crime, the individual circumstances of the convicted person and relevant international precedents.

establish norms that were in practice unquestionable and, as such, illegitimate and despotic. Surely this was the basis for carrying out summary justice on members of the deposed regime, amounting to all intents and purposes to a political purge.

When all is said and done, it is the value of the certainty of criminal law that was compromised. As Albert Venn Dicey has explained, this certainty is not only the cornerstone of the rule of law, but one of the axioms of the Western liberal-democratic tradition:[49] precisely that tradition in the name of which the occupying forces claim to have undertaken the war against Iraq. It is clear that these distortions depend to a large degree on the will of the United States to reject international criminal jurisdiction and any collaboration on the part of the United Nations, and at the same time to attribute to a national Iraqi Tribunal, operating under its close control, the competence *ratione materiae* ('according to subject') of an international criminal court.

An exemplary retribution

The true purpose of the Nuremberg trial (and indeed that of Tokyo) was not to 'do justice'. Doing justice means trying to interrupt the political sequence of division, hate and bloodshed so as to deconstruct the conflict and exorcize it with the use of legal means. Justice, in this sense, is opposed to the factiousness of politics and the violence of war, because it is the pursuit of a sphere of impartiality—the recourse to legal principles capable of resolving and neutralizing the conflict. If the metaphor of politics is the sword, that of justice is the scales. This is precisely why the institution of special Tribunals at the end of a war—whether international or civil—can be, even though it will not necessarily be, the first step towards pacification of the

---

49. See A.V. Dicey, *Introduction to the Study of the Law of the Constitution* [1885], London: Macmillan, 1982, pp. cxxxvii–cxxxviii. Dicey summarizes the rule of law as follows:

In England no man can be made to suffer punishment or to pay damages for any conduct not definitely forbidden by the law; every man's legal rights or liabilities are almost invariably determined by the ordinary Courts of the realm, and each man's individual rights are far less the result of our constitution than the basis on which our constitution is founded (ibid., p. lv).

collective memory and the inhibition of generalized vendetta, much like an amnesty.

The Nuremberg trials brought about a radical change in the idea of international justice, cancelling out its distinction between politics and war. It was a settling of accounts and of old scores, and represents the revenge of the victors over the vanquished. It was a parody of justice, with a lethal symbolic significance. To be defeated and killed in war is a normal matter, and may even be honourable. But to be put to death after being arraigned by the enemy represents an irremediable defeat—the ultimate degradation of a person's dignity and identity.[50]

The United States staged a trial of Saddam Hussein that reproduced and radicalized the rationale of stigmatization and retributive revenge that predominated at Nuremberg. The legal anomy and the void of legitimate power caused by a war of aggression were such that the trial of the former Iraqi dictator came down to a propagandistic and theatrical ritualization of justice, with the principal objectives of concealing the misdeeds of the victors, of making the adversary appear inhuman, and of legitimizing his hostile treatment, as an 'enemy of humankind', to the point of sheer inhumanity. The ritual shedding of the blood of Saddam Hussein made a contribution not to the pacification and democratization of Iraq, but to the cause of hate and terror.

---

50.   See P.P. Portinaro, 'Introduzione' to Demandt, ed., *Processare il nemico*, pp. xxi–xxiv.

BIBLIOGRAPHY

1. The Criminalization of War

Ahlbrecht, H., *Geschichte der völkerrechtlichen Strafgerichtsbarkeit in 20: Jahrhundert*, Baden-Baden: Nomos, 1999.

Amati, E., 'La repressione dei crimini di guerra tra diritto internazionale e diritto interno', in G. Illuminati, L. Stortoni and M. Virgilio, eds, *Crimini internazionali fra diritto e giustizia*, Turin: Giappichelli, 2000.

Arangio-Ruiz, G., *The Establishment of the International Criminal Tribunal for the Former Territory of Yugoslavia and the Doctrine of the Implied Powers of the United Nations*, in F. Lattanzi and E. Sciso, eds, *Dai Tribunali Penali Internazionali ad hoc ad una Corte permanente*, Napoli: Editoriale Scientifica, 1995.

Arendt, H., *Eichmann in Jerusalem: A Report on the Banality of Evil*, New York: Viking Press, 1963.

Ascensio, H., E. Decaux, and A. Pellet, eds, *Droit international pénal*, Paris: Pedine, 2000.

Baldissara, L. and P. Pezzino, *Giudicare e punire: I processi per crimini di guerra tra diritto e politica*, Napoli: L'ancora del Mediterraneo, 2005.

Bassiouni, M.C., ed., *International Criminal Law*, New York: Transnational Publishers, 1998–1999.

Bassiouni, M.C., and O. Manikas, *The Law of the International Criminal Tribunal for the Former Yugoslavia*, Irvington and Hudson: Transnational Publishers, 1996.

Bernardini, A., 'Il Tribunale penale internazionale per la ex Jugoslavia', *I diritti dell'uomo* 21, 1993.

Black, C., 'The International Criminal Tribunal: Instrument of Justice?', proceedings of the Paris, Conference on *Justice and War*, 25 October 1999, special issue of *Dialogue* 31–32, 2000.

Bull, H., *The Anarchical Society*, London: Macmillan, 1977.

Cassese, A., 'On the Current Trends towards Criminal Prosecution and Punishment of Breaches of International Humanitarian Law', *European Journal of International Law* 9 (1), 1998

———, *Lineamenti di diritto internazionale penale*, Bologna: il Mulino, 2005.

———, 'Il processo a Saddam e i nobili fini della giustizia', *La Repubblica*, 19 October 2005.

Clark, R., and M. Sann, *The Prosecution of International Crimes: A Critical Study of the International Tribunal for the Former Yugoslavia*, New Brunswick: Transaction Publishers, 1996.

Davidson, E., *The Nuremberg Fallacy: Wars and War Crimes Since World War II*, New York: Macmillan, 1973.

Demandt, A., ed., *Macht und Recht: Große Prozesse in der Geschichte*, München: Oscar Beck, 1990.

De Stefani, P., *Profili di diritto penale internazionale nella prospettiva dei diritti umani*, Padova: Centro di studi e di formazione sui diritti della persona e dei popoli, 2000.

Fronza, E., and S. Manacorda, eds, *La justice pénale internationale dans les décisions des tribunaux ad hoc*, Milano: Dalloz-Giuffrè, 2003.

Fronza, E., and J. Tricot, *Fonction symbolique et droit pénal international: une analyse du discours des tribunaux pénaux internationaux*, in E. Fronza and S. Manacorda, eds, *La justice pénale internationale dans les décisions des tribunaux ad hoc*, Milano: Dalloz-Giuffré, 2003.

Ginsburg, C., and V.N. Kudriatsev, eds, *The Nuremberg Trial and International Law*, Dordrecht: Kluwer, 1990.

Hazan, P., *La Justice face à la guerre: de Nuremberg à La Haye*, Paris: Stock, 2000.

Henham, R., 'The Philosophical Foundations of International Sentencing', *Journal of International Criminal Justice* 1 (1), 2003.

Illuminati, G., L. Stortoni and M. Virgilio, eds, *Crimini internazionali fra diritto e giustizia*, Turin: Giappichelli, 2000.

Kelsen, H., 'Will the Judgment in the Nuremberg Trial Constitute a Precedent in International Law?', *International Law Quarterly* 1 (2), 1947.

Kirchheimer, O., *Politische Justiz*, Frankfurt: Europäische Verlaganstalt, 1981.

Klabbers, J., 'Just Revenge? The Deterrence Argument in Inter-national Criminal Law', *Finnish Yearbook of International Law* 12, 2001.

Köchler, H., *Global Justice or Global Revenge?* Wien-New York: Springer Verlag, 2003.

Koop, V., *Das Recht der Sieger: Absurde alliierte Befehle im Nachkriegsdeutschland*, Berlin: Be.bra Verlag, 2004.

Lattanzi, F., and E. Sciso, eds, *Dai Tribunali Penali Internazionali ad hoc ad una Corte permanente*, Naples: Editoriale Scientifica, 1995.

Laughland, J., *Le tribunal pénal international*, Paris: François-Xavier de Guibert, 2003.

Lollini, A., 'Le processus de judiciarisation de la résolution des conflits: les alternatives', in E. Fronza and S. Manacorda, eds, *La justice pénale internationale dans les décisions des tribunaux ad hoc*, Milano: Dalloz-Giuffrè, 2003.

Manacorda, S., 'Les peines dans la pratique du Tribunal pénal international pour l'ex-Yugoslavie: l'affablissement des principes et la quête de contrepoids', in E. Fronza and S. Manacorda, eds, *La justice pénale internationale dans les décisions des tribunaux ad hoc*, Milano: Dalloz-Giuffrè, 2003.

Mandel, M., 'Politics and Human Rights in the International Criminal Tribunal for the Former Yugoslavia: Our Case Against NATO and the Lessons to Be Learned from It', *Fordham International Law Journal* 25, 2001.

Maser, W., *Nürnberg: Tribunal der Sieger*, Düsseldorf: Econ, 1977.

Minear, R.H., *Victors' Justice: The Tokyo War Crimes Trial*, Princeton: Princeton University Press, 1971.

Mori, P., *L'istituzionalizzazione della giurisdizione penale internazionale*, Turin: Giappichelli, 2001.

Nemitz, J.C., 'Sentencing in the jurisprudence of the International Criminal Tribunals for the Former Yugoslavia and Rwanda', in H. Fisher, C. Kress and S.R. Lüder, eds, *International and National Prosecution of Crimes Under International Law: Currents Developments*, Berlin: Duncker & Humblot, 2001.

Quaritsch, H., 'Nachwort', in C. Schmitt, *Das internationalrechtliche Verbrechen des Angriffskrieges und der Grundsatz 'Nullum crimen, nulla poena sine lege'*, Berlin: Duncker & Humblot, 1994.

Röling, B.V.A., 'The Nuremberg and the Tokyo Trials in Retrospect', in C. Bassiouni and U.P. Nanda, eds, *A Treatise on International Criminal Law*, Springfield: Charles C. Thomas, 1973.

Röling, B.V.A., and A. Cassese, *The Tokyo Trial and Beyond*, Cambridge: Polity Press, 1993.

Schabas, W.A., *An Introduction to the International Criminal Court*, Cambridge: Cambridge University Press, 2001.

Schmitt, C., *Antworten in Nürnberg*, ed. H. Quaritsch, Berlin: Dunker & Humblot, 2000.

Sewall, S.B., and C. Kaysen, eds, *The United States and the International Criminal Court*, Oxford: American Academy of Arts and Sciences, 2000.

Shraga, D., and R. Zacklin, 'The International Criminal Tribunal for Rwanda', *European Journal for International Law* 7 (4), 1996.

Taylor, T., *The Anatomy of the Nuremberg Trials*, New York: Alfred A. Knopf, 1992.

———, *Nuremberg and Vietnam: An American Tragedy*, Chicago: Quadrangle Books, 1970.

Varaut, J.-M., *Le procès de Nuremberg*, Paris: Perrin, 1992.

Vassalli, G., *La giustizia penale internazionale*, Milano: Giuffrè, 2001.

Virgilio, M., 'Verso i principi generali del diritto criminale internazionale', in G. Illuminati, L. Stortoni and M. Virgilio, eds, *Crimini internazionali fra diritto e giustizia*, Turin: Giappichelli, 2000.

Viticci, M.C., *Il Tribunale ad hoc per la ex-Jugoslavia*, Milan: Giuffrè, 1998.

Zappalà, S., *La giustizia penale internazionale,* Bologna: il Mulino, 2005.

Zolo, D., 'The Lords of Peace: From the Holy Alliance to the New International Criminal Tribunals', in B. Holden, ed., *Global Democracy*, London: Routledge, 2000.

———, 'The Iraqi Special Tribunal', *Journal of International Criminal Justice* 2, 2004.

———, 'Peace through Criminal Law?' *Journal of International Criminal Justice* 2, 2004.

2. Humanitarian War

Carpenter, A., 'The International Criminal Court and the Crime of Aggression', *Nordic Journal of International Law* 64 (223), 1995.

Dinstein, Y., 'The Distinction between War Crimes and Crimes against Peace', *International Yearbook of Human Rights* 24 (1), 1994.

Ferencz, B.B., 'Defining Aggression: Where it Stands and Where it's Going', *American Journal of International Law* 66 (3), 1972.

———, 'A Proposed Definition of Aggression: By Compromise and Consensus', *International and Comparative Law Quartely*, 22 (3), 1973.

———, 'The Draft Code of Offences Against the Peace and Security of Mankind', *American Journal of International Law* 75 (3), 1981.

Gaja, G., 'The Long Journey towards Repressing Aggression', in A. Cassese, P. Gaeta and J.R.W.D. Jones, eds, *The Rome Statute of the International Criminal Court: A Commentary*, Oxford: Oxford University Press, 2002.

Glaser, S., 'Quelques remarques sur la definition de l'aggression en droit international pénal', in *Festschrift für Th. Ritler*, Aalen: Verlag Scientia, 1957.

Gross, L., 'The Criminality of Aggressive War', *American Political Science Review* 41 (2), 1947.

Hogan-Doran, J., and B. van Gimkel, 'Aggression as a Crime under International Law and the Prosecution of Individuals by the Proposed International Criminal Court', *Netherlands International Law Review* 43 (321), 1996.

Jessup, P.C., 'The Crime of Aggression and the Future of International Law', *Political Science Quarterly* 62 (1), 1947.

Kochavi, A.J., *Prelude to Nuremberg: Allied War Crimes Policy and the Question of Punishment*, Chapel Hill: University of North Carolina Press, 1998.

Minear, R., *Victors' Justice: The Tokyo War Crimes Trial*, Princeton: Princeton University Press, 1971.

Politi, M., and G. Nesi, eds, *The International Criminal Court and the Crime of Aggression*, Aldershot: Ashgate, 2004.

Portinaro, P.P., *Crimini politici e giustizia internazionale: Ricerca storica e questioni teoriche*, Turin: Working Papers of the Dipartimento di Studi Politici dell'Università di Torino, 2005.

Röling, B., and C. Rüter, eds, *The Tokyo Judgment*, Amsterdam: Amsterdam University Press, 1977.

Schabas, W.A., 'Origins of the Criminalization of Aggression: How Crimes Against Peace Became the Supreme International Crime', in M. Politi and G. Nesi, eds, *The International Criminal Court and the Crime of Aggression*, Aldershot: Ashgate, 2004.

Stone, J., *Aggression and World Order: A Critique of United Nations Theories of Aggression*, London: Stevens & Sons, 1958.

Triffterer, O., ed., *Commentary on the Rome Statute of the International Criminal Court*, Baden-Baden: Nomos Verlags-gesellschaft, 1999.

Willis, J.W., *Prologue to Nuremberg: The Policy and Diplomacy of Punishing War Criminals of the First World War*, Westport, CT: Greenwood, 1982.

Wright, Q., 'The Concept of Aggression in International Law', *American Journal of International Law* 29, 1935.

———, 'The Test of Aggression in the Italo-Ethiopian War', *American Journal of International Law* 30 (1), 1936.

———, 'The Law of the Nuremberg Trial', *American Journal of International Law* 41, 1947.

3. The Universality of Rights and Humanitarian War

Abiew, F.K., *The Evolution of the Doctrine and Practice of Humanitarian Intervention*, The Hague: Kluwer, 1999.

Beck, U., 'Der militärische Pazifismus: Über den postnationalen Krieg', *Suddeutsche Zeitung*, 19 April 1999.

Beck, U., N. Bobbio, et al., *L'ultima crociata? Ragioni e torti di una guerra giusta*, ed. G. Bosetti, Roma: Libri di Reset, 1999.

Bobbio, N., 'Perché questa guerra ricorda una crociata', in U. Beck, N. Bobbio, et al., *L'ultima crociata? Ragioni e torti di una guerra giusta*, Roma: Libri di Reset, 1999.

Cabona, M., ed., *Ditelo a Sparta: Serbia ed Europa contro l'aggressione della Nato*, Genova: Graphos, 1999.

Cagiati, A., 'La nuova Alleanza Atlantica', *Rivista di studi politici internazionali* 66 (3), 1999.

Cassese, A., 'Ex iniuria ius oritur: Are We Moving towards International Legitimation of Forcible Humanitarian Countermeasures in the World Community?', *European Journal of International Law* 10 (1), 1999.

————, 'A Follow-Up: Forcible Humanitarian Countermeasures and *Opinio Necessitatis*', *European Journal of International Law* 10 (4), 1999.

Chinkin, C.M., 'Kosovo: A 'Good' or 'Bad' War?', *American Journal of International Law* 93 (4), 1999.

Chomsky, N., *The New Military Humanism: Lessons from Kosovo*, London: Pluto Press, 1999.

Debray, R., *Croire, voir, faire*, Paris: Editions Odile Jacob, 1999.

De Sena, P., 'Uso della forza a fini umanitari. Intervento in Jugoslavia e diritto internazionale', *Ragion pratica* 7 (13), 1999.

Di Francesco, T., ed., *La Nato nei Balcani*, Rome: Editori Riuniti, 1999.

Falk, R.A., 'Reflections on the War: Postmodern Warfare Leads to Severe Abuses of the Community that is Supposed to Be Rescued', *Nation*, 11 June 1999.

————, 'Kosovo, World Order, and the Future of International Law', *American Journal of International Law* 93 (4), 1999).

Galtung, J., 'Faschismus ist überall', *Suddeutsche Zeitung*, 7 June 1999.

Gardam, J., ed., *Humanitarian Law*, Brookfield: Ashgate, 1999.

Gill, B., 'Limited Engagement', *Foreign Affairs* 78 (4), 1999.

Glennon, M.J., 'The New Interventionism', *Foreign Affairs* 78 (3), 1999.

Glenny, M., *The Balkans, 1804-1999: Nationalism, War and the Great Powers*, London: Granta Books, 1999.

Greppi, E., and G. Venturini, eds, *Codice di diritto internazionale umanitario*, Turin: Giappichelli, 2003.

Grmek, M., M. Gjidara and N. Simac, *Le nettoyage ethnique*, Paris: Fayard, 1993.

Grove, E., ed., *Global Security: North American, European and Japanese Interdependence in the 1990s*, London: Brassey's, 1991.

Haass, R.N., 'What to do with American Primacy', *Foreign Affairs* 78 (5), 1999.

Habermas, J., 'Bestialität und Humanität: Ein Krieg an der Grenze zwischen Recht und Moral', *Die Zeit* 18, 1999.

Handke, P., 'Der Krieg ist das Gebiet des Zufalls', *Süddeutsche Zeitung*, 5/6 June 1999.

Harding, J., 'Europe's War', *London Review of Books* 21 (9), 1999.

Harriss, J., ed., *The Politics of Humanitarian Intervention*, London/ New York: Pinter, 1995.

Hondrich, K.O., 'Was ist dies für ein Krieg? ' *Die Zeit* 22 , 1999.

Huntington, S.P., 'The Lonely Superpower', *Foreign Affairs* 78 (2), 1999.

Lattanzi, F., *Assistenza umanitaria e interventi di umanità*, Torino: Giappichelli, 1997.

Lind, M., 'Civil War by Other Means', *Foreign Affairs* 78 (5), 1999.

Luttwak, E.N., 'Give War a Chance', *Foreign Affairs* 78 (4), 1999.

Mandelbaum, M., 'A Perfect Failure', *Foreign Affairs* 78 (5), 1999.

Mortellaro, I., *I signori della guerra: La Nato verso il XXI secolo*, Rome: Manifestolibri, 1999.

Pinelli, C., 'Sul fondamento degli interventi armati a fini umanitari', in G. Cotturri, ed., *Guerra—individuo*, Milan: Angeli, 1999.

Pizzorno, A., 'Caro Habermas, l'autoinvestitura della Nato non basta', in U. Beck, N. Bobbio, et al., *L'ultima crociata? Ragioni e torti di una guerra giusta*, Rome: Libri di Reset, 1999.

Roux, M., *Le Kosovo : Dix clefs pour comprendre*, Paris: La Découverte, 1999.

Simma, B., 'NATO, the UN and the Use of Force: Legal Aspects', *European Journal of International Law* 10 (1), 1999.

Spinedi, M., 'Uso della forza da parte della Nato in Jugoslavia e diritto internazionale', *Quaderni Forum* 12 (3), 1999.

Villani, U., 'La guerra del Kosovo: una guerra umanitaria o un crimine internazionale?' *Volontari e terzo mondo* 1–2, 1999.

Zolo, D., 'La filosofia della guerra umanitaria da Kant ad Habermas', *Iride* 12 (27), 1999.

———, *Invoking Humanity: War, Law and Global Order*, London/New York: Continuum, 2002.

4. Preventive Global War

Annan, K., *In Larger Freedom: Towards Development, Security and Human Rights for All*, at www.un.org/largerfreedom.

Cannizzaro, E., 'La dottrina della guerra preventiva e la disciplina internazionale sull'uso della forza', *Rivista di diritto internazionale* 2, 2003.

Dipert, R.R., *Preemptive War and the Epistemological Dimension of Morality of War*, at atlas.usafa.af.mil/jscope/JSCOPE05/Dipert05html.

Falk, R.A., 'Why International Law Matters', in *Jura Gentium* journal, www.juragentium.unifi.it.

Ferencz, B.B., 'Getting Aggressive about Preventing Aggression', *Brown Journal of World Affairs* 6 (87), 1999.

High-Level Panel on Threats, Challenges and Change, *A More Secure World: Our Shared Responsibility*, at www.un.org.

Vander, F., *Kant, Schmitt e la guerra preventiva: Diritto e politica nell'epoca del conflitto globale*, Rome: Manifestolibri, 2004.

Walzer, M., *Just and Unjust Wars*, New York: Basic Books, 1992.

———, *Arguing about War*, New Haven: Yale University Press, 2004.

White House, *National Security Strategy of the United States of America*, 17 September 2002, in *Jura Gentium* journal, at dex1.unifi.it/juragentium.

Wright, Q., 'The Prevention of Aggression', *American Journal of International Law* 50 (3), 1956.

5. Empire and War

Calore, A., ed., *'Guerra giusta'? Le metamorfosi di un concetto antico*, Milan: Giuffrè, 2003.

Canto-Sperber, M., *Le bien, la guerre et la terreur: Pour une morale internationale*, Paris: Plon, 2005.

Cardini, F., *Quell'antica festa crudele*, Milan: Oscar Mondadori, 1997.

Elshtain, J.B., ed., *Just War Theory*, Oxford: Basil Blackwell, 1992.

Fiorani Piacentini, V., *Il pensiero militare nel mondo musulmano*, Milan: Franco Angeli, 1996.

Haggenmacher, P., *Grotius et la doctrine de la guerre juste*, Paris: Presses Universitaires de France, 1983.

Holmes, R.L., *On War and Morality*, Princeton: Princeton University Press, 1989.

Johnson, J.T., *Can Modern War Be Just?* New Haven: Yale University Press, 1984.

———, *The Quest for Peace: Three Moral Traditions in Western Cultural History*, Princeton: Princeton University Press, 1987.

———, *Holy War Idea. Western and Islamic Traditions*, University Park, PA: Pennsylvania State University, 2001.

Johnson, J.T. and G. Weigel, *Just War and the Gulf War*, Washington: Ethics and Public Policy Center, 1991.

Jones, D.V., *Code of Peace: Ethics and Security in the World of the Warlord States*, Chicago/London: University of Chicago Press, 1989.

Kegley C.W. Jr., and K.L. Schwab, eds, *After the Cold War: Questioning the Morality of Nuclear Deterrence*, Boulder/San Francisco/Oxford: Westview Press, 1991.

Nye J.S., Jr., *Nuclear Ethics*, New York: Free Press, 1986.

O'Brien, W.V., *The Conduct of Just and Limited War*, New York: Praeger, 1981.

Partner, P., *God of Battles: Holy Wars of Christianity and Islam*, Princeton, NJ: Princeton University Press, 1998.

Peters, R.F., *The Jihad in Classical and Modern Islam*, Princeton: Markus Wiener Publishers, 1996.

Potter, R.B., *War and Moral Discourse*, Richmond, VA: John Knox Press, 1973.

Ramsey, P., *War and the Christian Conscience: How Shall Modern War Be Conducted Justly?*, Durham, NC: Duke University Press, 1961.

Russell, F.H., *The Just War in the Middle Ages*, Cambridge: Cambridge University Press, 1975.

Zolo, D., 'La riproposizione moderna del ' bellum justum': Kelsen, Walzer e Bobbio', in A. Calore, ed., *'Guerra giusta'? Le metamorfosi di un concetto antico*, Milan: Giuffrè, 2003.

6. *The Reasons behind Terrorism*

Allegretti, U., M. Dinucci and D. Gallo, *La strategia dell'impero*, Firenze: Edizioni Cultura della Pace, 1992.

Baran, P.A., and P.M. Sweezy, *Monopoly Capital: An Essay on the American Economic and Social Order*, New York: Monthly Review Press, 1966.

Betts, R.F., *The False Dawn: European Imperialism in the Nineteenth Century*, Minneapolis: University of Minnesota Press, 1975.

Campi, A., 'Grande spazio contro universalismo', in A. Campi, *Schmitt, Freund, Miglio*, Firenze: Akropolis, 1996.

Cohen, B.J., *The Question of Imperialism: The Political Economy of Dominance and Dependence*, New York: Basic Books, 1973.

De Benoist, A., *L'Impero interiore: Mito, autorità, potere nell'Europa moderna e contemporanea*, Firenze: Ponte alle Grazie, 1996.

De Francisci, P., *Arcana Imperii*, Rome: Bulzoni, 1970.

Di Rienzo, E., 'L'impero-nazione di Napoleone Bonaparte', *Filosofia politica* 16 (1), 2002.

Doyle, M.W., *Empires*, Ithaca, NY: Cornell University Press, 1986.

Eisenstadt, S.N., *The Political Systems of Empires*, London/New York: Free Press, 1963.

Gunder Frank, A.G., *Capitalism and Underdevelopment in Latin America: Historical Studies of Chile and Brazil*, New York: Monthly Press Review, 1967.

Hardt, M., and A. Negri, *Empire*, Cambridge, MA: Harvard University Press, 2000.

Ignatieff, M., 'The Burden', *New York Times Magazine*, 5 January 2003.

Kemp, T., *Theories of Imperialism*, London: Dobson, 1967.

Martinelli, A., *La teoria dell'imperialismo*, Turin: Loescher, 1974.

Mommsen, W.J., *Das Zeitalter des Imperialismus*, Frankfurt: Fischer Bücherei, 1969.

———, *Imperialismustheorien*, Göttingen: Vandenkoek-Ruprecht, 1977.

Monteleone, R., *Teorie sull'imperialismo*, Rome: Editori Riuniti, 1974.

Musi, A., 'L'impero spagnolo', *Filosofia politica* 16 (1), 2002.

Negri, A., *Guide: Cinque lezioni su Impero e dintorni*, Milano: Raffaello Cortina, 2003.

Negri, A., and D. Zolo, 'L'Impero e la moltitudine: Dialogo sul nuovo ordine della globalizzazione', *Reset* 73 (2002).

Owen, R., and B. Sutcliff, *Studies in the Theory of Imperialism*, London: Longman, 1972.

Parsi, V.E., 'L'impero come fato? Gli Stati Uniti e l'ordine globale', *Filosofia politica* 16 (1), 2002.

Poma, G., 'L'impero romano: ideologia e prassi', *Filosofia politica* 16 (1), 2002.

Portinaro, P.P., *La crisi dello Jus Publicum Europaeum*, Milan: Edizioni di Comunità, 1982.

Schmitt, C., *Völkerrechtliche Formen des modernen Imperialismus*, Auslandsstudien 8, 1933, also in C. Schmitt, *Positionen und Begriffe im Kampf mit Weimer, Genf, Versailles 1923–1939*, Hamburg: Hanseatische Verlagsanstalt, 1940.

———, 'Völkerrechtliche Grossraumordnung mit Interventionsverbot für raumfremde Mächte. Ein Beitrag zum Reichsbegriff im Völkerrecht', *Schriften des Instituts für Politik und Internationales Recht an der Universität Kiel* 7, 1939, also in C. Schmitt, *Staat, Grossraum, Nomos*, ed. G. Maschke, Berlin: Duncker & Humblot, 1995.

Snyder, J., *Myths of Empire: Domestic Politics and International Ambition*, Ithaca, NY: Cornell University Press, 1991.

7. From Nuremberg to Baghdad

Anderson, P., 'Arms and Rights: Rawls, Habermas and Bobbio in an Age of War', *New Left Review* 31 (2005).

Badie, B., *La fin des territoires : Essai sur le désordre international et l'utilité sociale du respect*, Paris: Fayard, 1995.

Bertrand, M., *La fin de l'ordre militaire*, Paris: Presses de Sciences Po, 1996.

Bimbi, L., ed., *Not in My Name: Guerra e diritto*, Rome: Editori Riuniti, 2003.

Bobbio, N., *Il problema della guerra e le vie della pace*, Bologna: Il Mulino, 1984.

Bresheeth, H., and N. Yuval-Davis, eds, *The Gulf War and the New World Order*, London: Zed Books, 1991.

Brzezinski, Z., *The Grand Chessboard*, New York: Basic Books, 1997.

Cagiati, A., 'La nuova Alleanza Atlantica', *Rivista di studi politici internazionali* 66 (3), 1999.

Cassese, A., 'Terrorism Is Also Disrupting Some Crucial Legal Categories of International Law', *European Journal of International Law* 12 (5), 2001.

———, *International Law*, Oxford: Oxford University Press, 2005.

Clark, G. and L.B. Sohn, *World Peace through World Law*, Cambridge, MA: Harvard University Press, 1960.

Dal Lago, A., *Polizia globale: Guerra e conflitti dopo l'11 settembre*, Verona: Ombre corte, 2003.

De Benoist, A., 'Ripensare la guerra', *Trasgressioni* 14 (1), 1999.

Delmas, P., *Le bel avenir de la guerre*, Paris: Gallimard, 1995.

de la Maisonneuve, E., *La violence qui vient*, Paris: Arléa, 1997.

Dershowitz, A.M., *Why Terrorism Works: Understanding the Threat, Responding to the Challenge*, New Haven: Yale University Press, 2002.

D'Orsi, A., ed., *Guerre globali: Capire i conflitti del XXI secolo*, Rome: Carocci, 2003.

Falk, R.A., *The Great Terror War*, New York: Olive Branch Press, 2003.

Falk, R.A. and S.S. Kim, eds, *The War System: An Interdisciplinary*

Approach, Boulder: Westview Press, 1980.

Galli, C., *Guerra globale*, Rome/Bari: Laterza, 2002.

Gilpin, R., *War and Change in World Politics*, Cambridge: Cambridge University Press, 1981.

Grove E., ed., *Global Security: North American, European and Japanese Interdependence in the 1990s*, London: Brassey's, 1991.

Haass, R.N., *The Reluctant Sheriff: The United States after the Cold War*, New York: Council of Foreign Relations, 1997.

Habermas, J., 'Kants Idee des ewigen Friedens—aus dem historischen Abstand von 200 Jahren', *Kritische Justiz* 28, 1995.

Hirst, P., *War and Power in the 21st Century*, Cambridge: Polity Press, 2001.

Holsti, K.J., *War, the State, and the State of War*, Cambridge: Cambridge University Press, 1996.

Huntington, S.P., *The Clash of Civilizations and the Remaking of the World Order*, New York: Simon & Schuster, 1996.

———, 'The Lonely Superpower', *Foreign Affairs* 78 (2), 1999.

Ignatieff, M., *The Lesser Evil: Political Ethics in an Age of Terror*, Princeton: Princeton University Press, 2004.

Kaldor, M., *New and Old Wars: Organized Violence in a Global Era*, Cambridge: Polity Press, 1999.

Larrabee, F.S., R.D. Asmus and R.L. Kluger, 'Building a New NATO', *Foreign Affairs* 72 (5), 1993.

Luttwak, E.N., 'A Post-Heroic Military Policy', *Foreign Affairs* 75 (4), 1996.

Matthews, K., *The Gulf Conflict and International Relations*, London: Routledge, 1993.

Nabulsi, K., *Traditions of War: Occupation, Resistance, and the Law*, Oxford: Oxford University Press, 1999.

Pape, R., *Dying to Win: The Strategic Logic of Suicide Terrorism*, New York: Random House, 2005.

Picone, P., ed., *Interventi delle Nazioni Unite e diritto internazionale*, Padova: Cedam, 1995.

Preterossi, G., *L'Occidente contro se stesso*, Rome/Bari: Laterza, 2004.

Robinson, W.I., *Promoting Polyarchy: Globalization, US Intervention and Hegemony*, Cambridge: Cambridge University Press, 1996.

Schmitt, C., *The Nomos of the Earth in the International Law of the Jus Publicum Europaeum*, New York: Telos Press Publishing, 2006.

Singer, M. and Wildavsky, A., *The Real World Order: Zones of Peace, Zones of Turmoil*, Chatham, NJ: Chatham House Publishers, 1993.

Thompson, W.R., *On Global War*, Colombia: University of South Carolina Press, 1988.

Toffler, A., and H. Toffler, *War and Anti-War: Survival at the Dawn of the XXI Century*, New York: Little, Brown & Co., 1993.

Verdross, A. and B. Simma, B., *Universelles Völkerrecht*, Berlin: Duncker und Humblot, 1976.

Weiss, T.G., ed., *Collective Security in a Changing World*, Boulder/London: Lynne Rienner, 1993.

Wolton, D., *War Game: L'information et la guerre*, Paris: Flammarion, 1991.

Zolo, D., *Cosmopolis: Prospects for World Government*, Cambridge: Polity Press, 1997.

———, 'Hans Kelsen: International Peace through International Law', *European Journal of International Law* 9 (2), 1998.

———, '*I signori della pace: Una critica del globalismo giuridico*, Rome: Carocci, 1998.

———, 'Jürgen Habermas' Cosmopolitan Philosophy', *Ratio Juris* 12 (4), 1999.

INDEX